265 beer hop varieties f...

THE HOPS LIST
FIRST EDITION
2016

Compiled By
JULIAN HEALEY

This book is a self-published work.

Copyright © 2016 Julian Healey

www.hopslist.com

About the Author

Julian Healey

Julian is not a brewing professional. He's not a hop farmer and he's certainly not an agricultural scientist. He's just a 32-year-old guy that really likes brewing his own beer.

Professionally, he's a freelance digital marketing consultant and writer that has spent over a decade working in the digital media industry and half a decade in the Australian magazine industry. When he's not consulting or writing, he's talking up a retail line of bake-them-yourself croissants – a Melbourne-based food business he helps runs with his friend Charlotte.

"I didn't start brewing until I was 25.

"I ploughed through web forums for days before I bought my first kit. I have great memories of the homebrewandbeer.com.au community and the super helpful guys on there who'd done it all before me. Credit to them, they listened to all my particularly dumb questions and provided all the right answers.

"My paranoia of failure in the lead up to that first batch was intense and laughably so unwarranted in retrospect. The result was great and I've been a fan of brewing ever since."

Homebrew has a pretty bad reputation in Australia, but Julian thinks things are changing.

Preface

Two years ago at Christmas I sat down with my laptop on my parents couch and searched the web for books on wine grapes – a topic we'd been discussing at dinner. After a short time, I was taken back by the diversity of styles and varieties available to the modern winemaker. There were so many more than I knew about. Naturally, I wondered, did brewers have a similar resource? It turns out they didn't.

With this book I wanted to create something that both novice and professional brewers could reference when creating their recipes. Instead of fumbling about with the twenty most common varieties thinking "this for bitterness and that for aroma" I really wanted brewers to be able to think specific flavors and aromas when choosing something. Hops that incite notes of grapefruit, banana, mint, pine, strawberry, blossom, molasses, peach – they're all out there.

It turned out that there was even more to these 265 different hops than just their impact on the palate. The relationships between hops and their lineages and origins are intensely interesting and go a long way to explaining why particular hops bitter, taste and smell the way they do.

Further to that, you'll learn a few things about hop development in this book. Something that astounded me in particular was the development timeframes of many of the world's most cherished varieties. While some hops come about quickly and purely by accident, the vast majority don't. Varieties can spend upward of 15-20 years in development before they ever catch sight of a fermenter.

Research for the book was done primarily online using a number of sources. These ranged from online stores and forums to grower data sheets and industry publications dating back more than 100 years. Books specific to hops from scientific minds like R.A. Neve were also invaluable in compiling this resource. I'd like to thank all of the sources referenced in this book for taking the time to publish their words and data for the world to see.

I'd also like to thank the various homebrewers around the web for contributing their comments, Julian Greene for helping me research and write many of the early descriptors for hopslist.com and my family and friends for their support over the past two years.

When I started this endeavor, I'll admit, I wasn't even really an IPA fan. That has changed. Hops are one of the most critical components to a unforgettable brew and when it comes to the flavors and aromas in our beer, at no point in history have we ever had this much choice.

Julian Healey

Using this Resource

There are potentially four components to each entry in this book.

The first, the descriptor, is a brief summary of each hop that usually includes its origin, lineage, notes about its commercial use along with interesting facts, tasting notes and utilization. Not all of this information is available for every variety, so you'll find some entries are more detailed than others.

Tasting notes in particular are the amalgamation of available tasting notes from multiple sources. Interpretations of flavor and aroma are highly subjective. I have not personally tasted each and every variety in this guide, though I have sampled a great many. Hopefully I'll conquer the list one day, but for now, please recognize tasting notes for what they are – a collective opinion.

The second and third components are poignant comments by notable professional brewers and home brewing community. With the later, I've tried to include a spectrum of opinions and experiences. You'll notice that these comments don't always align with the official descriptors, or each other. While some believe it is, I don't believe brewing is an exact science and outcomes are subjective.

The fourth is a summary and data chart that includes information relevant to both brewers and growers. A few points to note; purpose encompasses typical application and should not be considered the only way to use a given hop. Acid and oil percentage ranges are a combination of multiple sources and when available, include multiple years of crop data. They are an indication of what is possible, not what is typical and indicate the widest recorded range with the average falling somewhere in between.

Substitute and beer styles should be viewed only as a guide. Don't let these suggestions stop you from experimenting. Some substitutes may be more suitable than others, depending on your taste and interpretation. Testing each hop for real is truly the only way to properly master a given hops utilization so get out there are get brewing!

It is my intention to add to *The Hops List*. As such, if you're aware of data or research on a particular variety that is missing from this resource, please contact me at julian@hopslist.com

Admiral

Admiral is an excellent mid-season hop variety derived from grandparent Challenger and likely parent, Northdown. Its exact lineage is unclear. Hailing from Wye College, England it was released to the brewing world in 1998 as a potential high-alpha replacement or complimentary addition to Target hops.

It features higher acid content than either of its elders, possesses aggressive but smooth bittering qualities and boasts an orange-citrus and herbal resonance making it perfect for more bitter Pale Ales and ESBs. Chapel Down employs Admiral almost exclusively in its Curious Porter due to its outstanding bittering abilities.

Homebrewer's Comments

Admiral is a good bittering hop. It's usually pretty high in AAs, too, so make sure you measure well. It's bred from Challenger and Northdown, if memory serves, so it has some classic English bittering heritage. The flavor is very subdued if you throw them in at 60+ minutes. I've never used them in a late addition, so I can't comment on that. *(GuldTuborg via homebrewtalk.com)*

Also Known As	
Characteristics	Aggressive but smooth bittering with an orange-citrus and herbal resonance, typical English-style aroma
Purpose	Bittering
Alpha Acid Composition	13%-16.2%
Beta Acid Composition	4.8%-6.1%
Cohumulone Composition	37%-45%
Country	UK
Cone Size	Small to medium
Cone Density	Compact
Seasonal Maturity	Mid
Yield Amount	1300-1900 kg/hectare (1160-1700 lbs/acre)
Growth Rate	Very high

Resistant to	Resistant to verticillium wilt and downy mildew
Susceptible to	Susceptible to powdery mildew
Storability	Retains 85% alpha acid after 6 months storage at 20ºC (68ºF)
Ease of Harvest	Easy to moderate
Total Oil	1-1.7 mL/100g
Myrcene Oil	39%-48%
Humulene Oil	23%-26%
Caryophyllene Oil	6%-7%
Farnesene Oil	1.8%-2.2%
Substitutes	Chinook, Northdown, Challenger, Centennial, Cascade (US), Amarillo®, Target, Northdown, Challenger
Style Guide	Extra Special Bitter, American India Pale Ale, Belgian India Pale Ale, Imperial India Pale Ale, India Pale Ale, Pale Ale, Bitter

References

http://beerlegends.com/admiral-hops
https://www.hopunion.com/uk-admiral/
http://www.charlesfaram.co.uk/hop-varieties/admiral/
https://craftbrewer.com.au/shop/details.asp?PID=3222

Agnus

Agnus is the first high-alpha bittering hop to come out of the Czech Republic. It's name is derived from Czech hop breeder Frantisek Beranek, who's surname translated into Latin is Agnum – or Lamb in English. Registered in 2000 and released the following year, Agnus is a bittering hop with strong spicy and herbal notes and has been compared by some to Nugget and Magnum.

Its lineage includes a complex array of coveted varieties including Bor, Fuggle, Saaz, Sladek and Northern Brewer. Though primarily a bittering hop, it is useful as a flavor addition and it's abundant oil content may even make it suitable for dry hopping.

Also Known As	
Characteristics	Strong spicy and herbal notes
Purpose	Bittering & Aroma
Alpha Acid Composition	9%-14%
Beta Acid Composition	4%-6.5%
Cohumulone Composition	30%-40%
Country	Czech Republic
Cone Size	
Cone Density	
Seasonal Maturity	
Yield Amount	
Growth Rate	
Resistant to	
Susceptible to	
Storability	Fair to poor
Ease of Harvest	
Total Oil	2.0-3.0 mL/100g
Myrcene Oil	40%-55%
Humulene Oil	15%-20%
Caryophyllene Oil	8%-10%
Farnesene Oil	< 1%
Substitutes	
Style Guide	Czech Pilsner, German Lager, Pale Ale

References

http://czhops.cz/index.php/en/hop-growing

http://www.charlesfaram.co.uk/hop-varieties/agnus/

https://www.ulprospector.com/en/na/Food/Detail/10746/327106/Agnus

http://www.brewstore.co.uk/agnus-czech-hops-100-grams

https://books.google.com.au/books?id=Hs2QAwAAQBAJ&pg=PA139&lpg=PA139&dq=agnus+hops&source=bl&ots=BgIS1rCf0J&sig=Nap4D9XJVaL1P6BEQONsHRdzsTI&hl=en&sa=X&ved=0ahUKEwihvqmr_cXJAhVTHI4KHUA2Avs4ChDoAQg6MAY#v=onepage&q=agnus%20hops&f=false

http://www.johnihaas.com/wp-content/uploads/2015/01/Agnus.pdf

Ahil

Ahil hops are somewhat hard to come by with its cultivation in Slovenia having been severely reduced. There has also been some confusion over its true classification. It was introduced as a Superstyrian hop in 1972 care of hop breeder, Dr Tone Wagner at the Hop Research Institute in Zatec. In actuality though, it is not a Superstyrian, it's a hybrid, a cross between Brewer's Gold and a wild male and was only intended to be Superstyrian-like in style.

Originally used primarily as an aroma hop, Ahil production has dwindled in Slovenia due to the popularity of the older, more established and authentic Styrian, Savinski Golding. It was initially produced in an attempt to create a hop with both high alpha and an intense aroma profile.

Also Known As	
Characteristics	
Purpose	Aroma
Alpha Acid Composition	10%-12%
Beta Acid Composition	4%-5%
Cohumulone Composition	25%
Country	Slovenia
Cone Size	Small to medium
Cone Density	
Seasonal Maturity	
Yield Amount	1540 kg/hectare (1370 lbs/acre)
Growth Rate	
Resistant to	
Susceptible to	
Storability	Retains 46% alpha acid after 6 months storage at 20ºC (68ºF)
Ease of Harvest	
Total Oil	1.8-2.2 mL/100g
Myrcene Oil	61.1%

Humulene Oil	7.6%
Caryophyllene Oil	4.3%
Farnesene Oil	10.4%
Substitutes	
Style Guide	Belgian Ale

References

http://www.ars.usda.gov/SP2UserFiles/person/2450/hopchem/21050.html

http://www.ars.usda.gov/SP2UserFiles/person/2450/hopcultivars/21050.html

Ahtanum™

Yakima Valley bred Ahtanum™ is sweet and peppery with a piney-citrus aspect. Warmly aromatic and moderately bittering, Ahtanum™ is a hop of distinction. It is often likened to Cascade though without going that far, it makes more sense to say that Cascade may be an acceptable substitute. In comparison, Ahtanum™ is less bitter, its alpha acids are lower and its grapefruit essence is significantly more pronounced. It really is more akin to Willamette, with its notes of lemon and grapefruit. Ahtanum's distinct citrus character led to it being used as the singular hop in Dogfish Head's Blood Orange Heffeweisen and Stone Brewing's Pale Ale.

Homebrewer's Comments

> Less grapefruit than Cascade but otherwise very similar. I started using it as a replacement for Cascade in my House IPA and stuck with it because it gives a mellower, more balanced flavor that more people can get on board with. *(PtreeCreekBrew via homebrewtalk.com)*

Also Known As	
Characteristics	Distinct citrus chracter with notes of grapefruit
Purpose	Aroma
Alpha Acid Composition	4%-6.3%
Beta Acid Composition	5%-6.5%
Cohumulone Composition	30%-35%

Country	US
Cone Size	Small
Cone Density	Compact
Seasonal Maturity	Mid
Yield Amount	1775-1950 kg/hectare (1585-1740 lbs/acre)
Growth Rate	Moderate
Resistant to	Resistant to downy mildew and Peronospora
Susceptible to	
Storability	Retains 50%-55% alpha acid after 6 months storage at 20ºC (68ºF)
Ease of Harvest	
Total Oil	0.8-1.2 mL/100g
Myrcene Oil	50%-55%
Humulene Oil	16%-20%
Caryophyllene Oil	9%-12%
Farnesene Oil	0%-1%
Substitutes	Cascade, Amarillo®, Simcoe®, Centennial, Willamette
Style Guide	India Pale Ale, Pale Ale, Heffeweisen, American Ales, Lagers, Californian Common, Bitters

References
http://beerlegends.com/ahtanum-hops
http://www.brew365.com/hops_ahtanum.php

Alliance

Alliance is a daughter of Whitbread Golding and was developed at Wye College alongside Progress in the early 1960's. It is not known to be grown commercially anywhere at this time. It enjoyed a high yield in England but this was much more inconsistent in US plots. Originally bred to replace Fuggle, but after it resulted in only a marginal improvement the variety was deemed a failure.

Also Known As	
Characteristics	
Purpose	Bittering & Aroma
Alpha Acid Composition	4.6%-7.5%
Beta Acid Composition	1.6%-5.1%
Cohumulone Composition	29%
Country	UK
Cone Size	
Cone Density	
Seasonal Maturity	Early
Yield Amount	1050 kg/hectare (940 lbs/arce)
Growth Rate	
Resistant to	Moderately resistant to verticillium wilt
Susceptible to	
Storability	Retains 78% alpha acid after 6 months storage at 20ºC (68ºF)
Ease of Harvest	
Total Oil	0.47-1.35 mL/100g
Myrcene Oil	36.7%
Humulene Oil	33%
Caryophyllene Oil	11.3%
Farnesene Oil	1.9%
Substitutes	
Style Guide	

References
http://freshops.com/usda-named-hop-variety-descriptions/#usda_id_66050

Amallia

Native to New Mexico, Amallia is a neomexicanus varietal with a deeply earthy aroma and pronounced flavors of orange citrus. Bold and unique, it is considered well suited to brown or dark ales for both bittering and aroma. This variety was being trialed in Michigan by Michigan State University researchers in 2014.

Also Known As	
Characteristics	Deep earthy aroma
Purpose	Bittering & Aroma
Alpha Acid Composition	5.5%-9%
Beta Acid Composition	4.2%-8.3%
Cohumulone Composition	
Country	US
Cone Size	
Cone Density	
Seasonal Maturity	Early
Yield Amount	
Growth Rate	
Resistant to	
Susceptible to	
Storability	
Ease of Harvest	
Total Oil	
Myrcene Oil	
Humulene Oil	
Caryophyllene Oil	
Farnesene Oil	
Substitutes	
Style Guide	Brown Ale, Dark Ale

References
http://www.rnventerprises.com/files/Variety_Descriptions_20134.pdf
http://www.homebrewing.org/New-Mexican-Amallia-Hop-Rhizomes-_p_3512.html
http://www.beechcrestfarm.com/docs/Hops%20Variety%20Information%20Sheet.pdf
http://www.ipm.msu.edu/uploads/files/IPMA/Hops_Descriptions_List_2014.pdf

Amarillo®

Ubiquitous Amarillo® hops are used in several commercial beers where its ultra-high myrcene content creates a delicious orange citrus flavor. It is also highly acidic, making it perfect for ESB's and Pale Ales. A varietal of Virgil Gamache Farms, Inc., Amarillo® was discovered to be a mutation from another variety.

Brewmaster's Comments

Amarillo is relatively new to me. It has a great, smooth citrus flare. Lemon, lime, a little orange, great for a lite body brew. It can be tri-purpose, flavor and aroma definitely and even for bittering. *(Nick Nock, Head Brewer at SweetWater Brewing Company)*

Amarillo is what I'd call a "very hoppy hop", meaning that it doesn't smell like dank weed or garlic or flowers or oranges – Amarillo smells like hops. And that's a great aroma! Best in dry hopping. *(Garrett Oliver, Brewmaster at Brooklyn Brewery)*

If I had to pick just one hop it would be Amarillo, even though they are so hard to get. They can be an incredibly complex hop, when harvested at the correct time, for making beers with fruit notes or character. I've seen the variation from early picked - bright floral citrus hops - to late picked dank hops coming through. People are surprised at how much the citrus, specifically orange notes, come out along with some papaya and melon. Those particular flavors accent fruits like pears and pit fruits, helping to bring them forward. And well, they make a pretty good IPA also. *(Tim Hawn, Head of Production at BrewDog)*

Homebrewer's Comments

Amarillo has been in just about every pale ale I've made since I first tasted it. Dry hop or boiled as a late addition, it's awesome. *(SteveM via homebrewtalk.com)*

Also Known As	Amarillo Gold
Characteristics	Orange citrus flavor
Purpose	Aroma
Alpha Acid Composition	8%-11%
Beta Acid Composition	6%-7%
Cohumulone Composition	21%-24%
Country	US
Cone Size	Small
Cone Density	Compact
Seasonal Maturity	Mid
Yield Amount	1200-1600 kg/hectare (1075-1420 lbs/acre)
Growth Rate	Moderate to high
Resistant to	
Susceptible to	
Storability	Retains 96% alpha acid after 6 months storage at 20ºC (68ºF)
Ease of Harvest	Moderate
Total Oil	1.5-1.9 mL/100g
Myrcene Oil	68%-70%
Humulene Oil	9%-11%
Caryophyllene Oil	2%-4%
Farnesene Oil	2%-4%
Substitutes	Cascade, Centennial, Summit™, Ahtanum™, Chinook, Saaz
Style Guide	American Pale Ale, India Pale Ale, American Wheat, Bitter, Wheat Beer, Red Ale, ESB

References
http://beerlegends.com/amarillo-hops

Amethyst

Amethyst is an aroma hop from the Czech Republic and is a derivative of

Saaz. It features a notably low alpha acid percentage and notes of earthy, citrus and spice. Amethyst's aroma profile is suited well to full-bodied lagers and pale ales.

Also Known As	
Characteristics	Notably earthy, citrusy and spicy
Purpose	Aroma
Alpha Acid Composition	2%-6%
Beta Acid Composition	7%-8%
Cohumulone Composition	20%-28%
Country	Czech Republic
Cone Size	
Cone Density	
Seasonal Maturity	
Yield Amount	
Growth Rate	
Resistant to	
Susceptible to	
Storability	
Ease of Harvest	
Total Oil	0.4-1 mL/100g
Myrcene Oil	42%
Humulene Oil	19%
Caryophyllene Oil	6%
Farnesene Oil	
Substitutes	
Style Guide	Pale Ale, Lager

References
http://www.brewersselect.co.uk/ingredients/products/amethyst
http://www.charlesfaram.co.uk/hop-varieties/amethyst/
https://www.morebeer.com/articles/homebrew_beer_hops

Apollo

Super-alpha hop Apollo was first bred in 2000 by Hopsteiner and released to the public in 2006. it is descended from Zeus and two other unnamed USDA varieties. It tends to be quite expensive, though quantities used tend to be smaller due to its ultra-high concentration of alpha-acids.

To it's credit, Apollo's abundance of alpha acids also come with a sharp, clean bittering profile with other highly desirable factors being great storage stability and disease tolerance. It is usually employed alongside aroma hops in order to achieve balance but when used as a late addition or dry hop itself, some grapefruit notes become evident.

You'll find Apollo in Brown Bison Ale, Pirate Pale Ale, Pin-Head Pilsner and Belgo Pale Ale to name a few and often alongside varieties Glacier and Palisade®. It is principally grown in the US.

Homebrewer's Comments

> I use these a lot, they're a great hop! They are awesome for bittering, super clean and not harsh at all. They have a very dank pungent aroma with some citrus too. I've only used them for aroma in conjunction with other hops though and I've heard they can overpower if you're not careful. (Bramstoker17 via homebrewtalk.com)

Also Known As	
Characteristics	Sharp, clean bittering, grapefruit notes
Purpose	Bittering
Alpha Acid Composition	15%-20%
Beta Acid Composition	5.5%-8%
Cohumulone Composition	23%-28%
Country	US
Cone Size	Small to medium
Cone Density	Compact
Seasonal Maturity	Mid to late
Yield Amount	2900-3350 kg/hectare (2600-3000 lbs/acre)

Growth Rate	Moderate
Resistant to	Resistant to downy mildew
Susceptible to	Susceptible to powdery mildew
Storability	Retains 80%-90% alpha acid after 6 months storage at 20°C (68°F)
Ease of Harvest	Fair
Total Oil	1.5-2.5 mL/100g
Myrcene Oil	30%-50%
Humulene Oil	20%-35%
Caryophyllene Oil	14%-20%
Farnesene Oil	1%
Substitutes	Nugget, Columbus, Zeus, Magnum, Millennium
Style Guide	India Pale Ale, Imperial India Pale Ale, Experimental Beers

References

http://beerlegends.com/apollo-hops

http://hopsteiner.com/wp-content/uploads/2014/03/73_03_Apollo_e.pdf

http://hopsteiner.com/wp-content/uploads/vpdf/Apollo.pdf

http://www.usahops.org/graphics/File/HGA%20BCI%20Reports/Variety%20Manual%207-24-12.pdf

http://www.usahops.org/index.cfm?fuseaction=hop_info&pageID=9

Apolon

Apolon hops are hard to come by with cultivation dwindling since its Super Styrian status was brought into question. Originally introduced as a Super Styrian in the 1970's, it has since been reclassified as a Slovenian hybrid and is a cross between Brewer's Gold and a Yugoslavian wild male.

Apolon can be used as both an aroma and a bittering hop and is considered excellent for both though traditionally it was intended solely for bittering. It is not restricted and is commercially viable but despite this, it is still not often employed by commercial brewers.

Ahil and Atlas are both siblings of Apolon.

Also Known As	
Characteristics	
Purpose	Bittering & Aroma
Alpha Acid Composition	10%-12%
Beta Acid Composition	4%
Cohumulone Composition	2.25%
Country	Slovenia
Cone Size	
Cone Density	
Seasonal Maturity	Late
Yield Amount	1000 kg/hectare (890 lbs/acre)
Growth Rate	High to very high
Resistant to	Moderately resistant to downy mildew
Susceptible to	
Storability	Retains 57% alpha acid after 6 months storage at 20ºC (68ºF)
Ease of Harvest	
Total Oil	1.3-1.6 mL/100g
Myrcene Oil	63%
Humulene Oil	26%
Caryophyllene Oil	4%
Farnesene Oil	11.3%
Substitutes	
Style Guide	Bitter, India Pale Ale

References

http://www.hausofhomebrew.com/hop-chart.html

https://translate.google.com.au/translate?hl=en&sl=nl&u=https://nl.wikipedia.org/wiki/Apolon&prev=search

http://cropandsoil.oregonstate.edu/hopcultivars/21051.html

Aquila

Aquila was developed in the U.S. and was established in three-acre commercial trials throughout the Northwest in 1988. It was officially released in 1994 but due to its overly high cohumulone content, its use was been considered limited and it is no longer available commercially. North American brewing giant Anheuser Busch lost interest in the variety in 1996, ultimately spelling a death knell for Aquila's commercial record.

Also Known As	
Characteristics	
Purpose	Aroma
Alpha Acid Composition	6.7%-8.9%
Beta Acid Composition	4.1%-4.9%
Cohumulone Composition	46%
Country	US
Cone Size	
Cone Density	
Seasonal Maturity	Mid to late
Yield Amount	2380 kg/hectare (2120 lbs/acre)
Growth Rate	Very high
Resistant to	Moderately resistant to downy mildew, resistant to verticillium wilt
Susceptible to	
Storability	Retains 40% alpha acid after 6 months storage at 20ºC (68ºF)
Ease of Harvest	
Total Oil	1.45 mL/100g
Myrcene Oil	62%
Humulene Oil	2%
Caryophyllene Oil	5%
Farnesene Oil	2.2%
Substitutes	Cluster, Galena

References
http://www.beersmith.com/hops/aquila.htm
http://www.ars.usda.gov/SP2UserFiles/person/2450/hopcultivars/21222.html

Aramis

Aramis is an aroma hop from the Alsace region in France. Crossed in 2002, Aramis is a product of Strisselspalt and Whitbread Golding and was in fact the very first variety to come from the Comptoir Agricole breeding program. It inherited Strisselspalt's excellent aromas while providing a more plentiful and stable bittering quality.

It is sweet and spicy, citrusy and herby. The measure of its aroma and alpha characteristics make it appropriate for any and all kettle stages. Commercially it has been used in New Belgium Hop Kitchen's French Aramis, a dry, refreshing India Pale Ale.

Homebrewer's Comments

Green, sticky, oily to the touch and the aroma! I opened the pack and ..... Bang!! Didn't even need to smell them. The aroma came looking for me! Like Cascade and Nelson Sauvin all over again, only bigger. *(saracen via brewuk.co.uk)*

I see this "tea" aroma commented on. Not sure where this comes from since it seems like one person said it and everyone else cut and pasted it. Stone made a Green Tea beer, and that's maybe part of it. The producer makes a nice spider chart with the aroma qualities and "tea" is not one of them. I don't get a tea aroma at all. I have actually used it. It has a floral, spice, slightly woodsy, earthy thing. No tea. It a non offensive, easy to incorporate hop for a variety of purposes. *(Roger via brew-dudes.com)*

Also Known As	
Characteristics	Sweet with notes of spice, citrus and herbs
Purpose	Aroma

Alpha Acid Composition	7.9%-8.3%
Beta Acid Composition	3.8%-4.5%
Cohumulone Composition	42%
Country	France
Cone Size	
Cone Density	
Seasonal Maturity	
Yield Amount	
Growth Rate	
Resistant to	
Susceptible to	
Storability	
Ease of Harvest	
Total Oil	1.2-1.6 mL/100g
Myrcene Oil	40%
Humulene Oil	21%
Caryophyllene Oil	7.4%
Farnesene Oil	2%-4%
Substitutes	Willamette, Challenger, Ahtanum™, Strisselspalter, Centennial, Chinook, Hallertau, Tettnang
Style Guide	Pilsner, Lager, Wheat, Saison, India Pale Ale, Pale Ale, Porter

References
http://www.hops-comptoir.com/6-hop-aramis-alsace
https://www.hopunion.com/french-aramis/

Atlas

Released in the 1970's, Atlas enjoys both good bittering and aroma qualities with intense notes of lime, blossom and pine. Like its siblings Aurora, Ahil and Apolon, Atlas has been cut back in commercial production over industry confusion stemming from its incorrect classification as a Super Styrian. It's a Slovenian breed but is in actuality a seedling of Brewer's Gold. Developed by Dr Tone Wagner at the Hop Research Institute in Zalec, Atlas has also accomplished USDA accession.

Also Known As	Styrian Atlas
Characteristics	Intense notes of lime, blossom and pine
Purpose	Aroma
Alpha Acid Composition	9%-11%
Beta Acid Composition	4%
Cohumulone Composition	36%
Country	Slovenia
Cone Size	
Cone Density	
Seasonal Maturity	Late
Yield Amount	730 kg/hectare (650 lbs/acre)
Growth Rate	Moderate to high
Resistant to	
Susceptible to	Prunus, Hop Mosaic and Necrotic Ringspot
Storability	Retains 50% alpha acid after 6 months storage at 20ºC (68ºF)
Ease of Harvest	
Total Oil	1.3-1.6 mL/100g
Myrcene Oil	59%
Humulene Oil	9%
Caryophyllene Oil	4%
Farnesene Oil	13.3%
Substitutes	
Style Guide	American Pale Ale, Belgian Ale

References
http://www.ars.usda.gov/SP2UserFiles/person/2450/hopchem/21052.html
http://www.ars.usda.gov/SP2UserFiles/person/2450/hopcultivars/21052.html

Aurora

Diploid hybrid Aurora is the one Super Styrian still enjoying global commercial availability. In fact, it is quite a celebrated hop and one of two distinct varieties prominently produced in Slovenia. Developed as a seedling of Northern Brewer, Aurora's aroma derives from its lovely balance of essential oils.

With nearly twice the alpha acid content as Styrian Golding, another primary Slovenian hop, Aurora is spicy, herbal and moderately bittering. Descriptions and reviews of most beers employing Aurora hops describe them as pleasantly hoppy and velvety smooth.

You will find Aurora in Hopvine Brewing Company's Aurora, in Funwerk's Aurora and as one of Mayflower's single hop ales, Styrian Aurora, among others.

Homebrewer's Comments

> I've used Aurora hops for bittering and combined it with Cascade for the aroma. A very nice combination. It was more fruity than citrus. I highly recommend it. (*ReggaeDave via homebrewtalk.com*)

Also Known As	Super Styrian
Characteristics	Spicy
Purpose	Bittering & Aroma
Alpha Acid Composition	7%-12%
Beta Acid Composition	2.7%-5%
Cohumulone Composition	22%-26%
Country	Slovenia
Cone Size	
Cone Density	
Seasonal Maturity	Mid to late
Yield Amount	1055 kg/hectare (940 lbs/acre)
Growth Rate	High to very high
Resistant to	Moderately resistant to downy mildew

Susceptible to	
Storability	Retains 70%-75% alpha acid after 6 months storage at 20°C (68°F)
Ease of Harvest	
Total Oil	0.9-1.8 mL/100g
Myrcene Oil	51%
Humulene Oil	17%-25%
Caryophyllene Oil	5%-9%
Farnesene Oil	5%-10%
Substitutes	Styrian Golding, Northern Brewer
Style Guide	American Pale Ale, Dark Lager

References

http://beerlegends.com/super-styrian-aurora-hops

https://books.google.com.au/books?id=_H1yBgAAQBAJ&pg=PA205&lpg=PA205&dq=apolon+hops&source=bl&ots=O9XDZHeDjd&sig=ZwZUJXRucRR5SlL78RjSFgtOwPk&hl=en&sa=X&ved=0ahUKEwisq_mbp8LMAhUGF5QKHV8QDR0Q6AEIPDAG#v=onepage&q=apolon%20hops&f=false

https://ychhops.com/varieties/aurora

http://www.hoppris.com/node/12

https://www.craftbrewer.com.au/shop/details.asp?PID=3851

Azacca®

Azacca was the Haitian god of agriculture. The hope variety however is one of a new brood of dwarf bittering hops. Descended directly from Toyomidori, Azacca®'s greater parentage also includes Summit™ and Northern Brewer. It is considered well suited to IPA brewing.

Even with its high alpha acids, it still works well as a dual-use hop, giving off a pleasant mix of tropical fruits kissed with citrus. On the palate this hop is particularly spicy, with mango, pineapple and some piney tangerine qualities. It has been likened in nature to many New Zealand-bred dual-use hops.

Homebrewer's Comments

I've brewed with Azaaca a few times now, both at typical usage and Imperial IPA rates. Single hopped. At lower amounts, they have a pleasant tropical-citrus character that goes almost mango and citrus rind with a little dank. Would be nice in hoppier Belgian styles. In higher amounts it has a very strong, overripe fruit character, sort of like rotting peaches and oranges, but in a good way. They are similar to Galaxy in that they both have an overripe fruit character, but the Azaaca is not nearly as strong. They would be nice paired with more citrus forward hops like Cascade, Centennial or Columbus. *(bierhaus15 via homebrewtalk.com)*

I made a single hop IPA using Azacca. The aroma is quite enjoyable. Tropical fruits and citrus mainly. The flavor majors on mango, ripe pineapple and generic citrus (maybe bending toward tangerine), juicy fruit gum. I liked it. *(yso191 via homebrewersassociation.org)*

Also Known As	Azaaca
Characteristics	Aromas of tropical fruits and citrus. Flavors of spicy mango, pineapple, tangerine and pine.
Purpose	Bittering & Aroma
Alpha Acid Composition	14%-16%
Beta Acid Composition	4%-5.5%
Cohumulone Composition	38%-45%
Country	US
Cone Size	
Cone Density	
Seasonal Maturity	Mid to late
Yield Amount	2465-2690 kg/hectare (2200-2400 lbs/acre)
Growth Rate	
Resistant to	
Susceptible to	

Storability	
Ease of Harvest	
Total Oil	1.6-2.5 mL/100g
Myrcene Oil	46%-55%
Humulene Oil	14%-18%
Caryophyllene Oil	8%-12%
Farnesene Oil	< 1%
Substitutes	
Style Guide	India Pale Ale

References

http://www.bear-flavored.com/2014/02/new-hops-alert-azacca-vic-secret-adha.html
http://www.adha.us/varietals/azacca-adha-483
https://bsgcraftbrewing.com/hops-american-hops-azacca

Backa

Dating back to 1956, Backa is an old, rare variety of aroma hop with an unknown land race pedigree. It has the potential for high yield in its native Backa region of the Slovenian state of the former Yugoslavia but doesn't seem to do all that well elsewhere. It's highly aromatic and is said to have similar qualities to many European "Noble Hops". The USDA lists two strains of Backa (56002) and (21080), but there seems to be some disagreement as to whether or not they are identical.

Also Known As	
Characteristics	
Purpose	Aroma
Alpha Acid Composition	3.1%-6.9%
Beta Acid Composition	4%-7.4%
Cohumulone Composition	25%
Country	Slovenia
Cone Size	
Cone Density	
Seasonal Maturity	

Yield Amount	
Growth Rate	High to very high
Resistant to	
Susceptible to	Moderately susceptible to downy mildew
Storability	Retains 67% alpha acid after 6 months storage at 20°C (68°F)
Ease of Harvest	
Total Oil	0.60 mL/100g
Myrcene Oil	
Humulene Oil	
Caryophyllene Oil	
Farnesene Oil	
Substitutes	
Style Guide	Lager, Pilsner

References
http://www.ars.usda.gov/SP2UserFiles/person/2450/hopcultivars/21080.html
http://www.ars.usda.gov/SP2UserFiles/person/2450/hopcultivars/56002.html

Banner

Banner did not fare well on the commercial market. Bred from a Brewer's Gold seedling in the early 1970's through open pollination, its first test plot was abandoned due to severe mildew problems.

It was finally released along with its half-sister Aquila in 1996 having caught the interest of goliath American brewing company Anheuser Busch. Eventually though, after several years of evaluation, it was eliminated from further testing.

Banner is known to have moderately high alpha acids, a pleasant aroma and a good yield but exhibits poor storability, which along with its mildew susceptibility makes it largely unviable.

Also Known As	
Characteristics	Moderate bittering potential, pleasant aroma
Purpose	Bittering
Alpha Acid Composition	8.4%-13%
Beta Acid Composition	5.3%-8%
Cohumulone Composition	34%
Country	US
Cone Size	
Cone Density	
Seasonal Maturity	Early
Yield Amount	2017 kg/hectare (1800 lbs/acre)
Growth Rate	Moderate to high
Resistant to	
Susceptible to	Susceptible to downy mildew
Storability	Retains 43% alpha acid after 6 months storage at 20ºC (68ºF)
Ease of Harvest	
Total Oil	2.17 mL/100g
Myrcene Oil	66.4%
Humulene Oil	11.8%
Caryophyllene Oil	7.7%
Farnesene Oil	Trace
Substitutes	Aquila, Cluster, Galena
Style Guide	Bitter

References
http://www.ars.usda.gov/SP2UserFiles/person/2450/hopcultivars/21287.html
http://www.brewerslair.com/index.php?p=brewhouse&d=hops&id=&v=&term=6

Bate's Brewer

Bate's Brewer is a very old hop variety that is no longer grown. Used to breed Whitbread Golding, like it's progeny, is not considered to be a true

Golding variety. It was used extensively by Wye College in the early 1900's to breed new varieties.

Also Known As

Characteristics

Purpose

Alpha Acid Composition

Beta Acid Composition

Cohumulone Composition

Country   UK

Cone Size

Cone Density

Seasonal Maturity

Yield Amount

Growth Rate

Resistant to

Susceptible to

Storability

Ease of Harvest

Total Oil

Myrcene Oil

Humulene Oil

Caryophyllene Oil

Farnesene Oil

Substitutes

Style Guide

References

https://beerandbrewing.com/dictionary/igpgp4u2tb/whitbread-golding-variety-hop/

http://onlinelibrary.wiley.com/store/10.1002/j.2050-0416.1924.tb04864.x/asset/j.2050-0416.1924.tb04864.x.pdf;jsessionid=FFB2BE175768053509AEDDAED3FC8171.f01t04?v=1&t=io2lk8gu&s=77ef42b9826e408c01d0060e9a000d7bb5500dc1&systemMessage=Wiley+Online+Library+will+be+unavailable+on+Saturday+14th+May+11%3A00-14%3A00+BST+%2F+06%3A00-09%3A00+EDT+%2F+18%3A00-21%3A00+SGT+for+essential+maintenance.Apologies+for+the+inconvenience

Belma

Belma hops are a recent addition from Hops Direct and Puterbaugh Farms in the Yakima Valley. Belma has been tested as a dual-use hop and found to have an ambrosial mix of orange, melon, strawberry and pineapple with a slight hint of grapefruit. Backing that up, OSU created a Pale Malt with Belma which carried those same aroma and flavor characteristics.

To date, Belma has also seen plenty of activity in the recreational brewing space with many homebrewers documenting its use online in Pale Ales, IPAs, Blonde Ales and more. Virtually all have given it favorable marks. It was released in 2012.

Homebrewer's Comments

What I have found to LOVE about belma is it's head promotion properties and the "kind" of head it produces. In my cream ale (a beer known for a quickly fading head), it promoted a full rocky head that lasted nearly the entire glass. It's unlike any other hop I've used at head promotion. (*stpug via homebrewtalk.com*)

This is one of my favorite newer hops. Aroma and flavor are very much geared towards strawberry peachy blueberry character with strawberry being most prevalent. My current favorite thing to do with it is to pair it with Huell Melon to make like a fruit salad character for my IPAs. Both of these hops [aren't] very assertive though so you need to be pretty liberal. (*m00ps via email*)

Also Known As	
Characteristics	Notes of orange, melon, strawberry, pineapple with a hint of grapefruit
Purpose	Bittering & Aroma
Alpha Acid Composition	9.4%-12.1%
Beta Acid Composition	
Cohumulone Composition	
Country	US
Cone Size	
Cone Density	

Seasonal Maturity	
Yield Amount	
Growth Rate	
Resistant to	
Susceptible to	
Storability	
Ease of Harvest	
Total Oil	
Myrcene Oil	
Humulene Oil	
Caryophyllene Oil	
Farnesene Oil	
Substitutes	
Style Guide	Pale Ale, Blonde, IPA

References
http://www.hopsdirect.com/belma-pellets/
http://hermitagebrewing.com/single-hop-series-belma
http://www.farmhousebrewingsupply.com/belma-1-lb-2015-new-crop/
http://www.brew-dudes.com/belma-hops/4185

Bianca

Bianca (a.k.a. Bianco and Bianca Gold), with its lemon yellow color and red-brown to pink contrasting stem, is bred strictly as an ornamental hop. It must be grown in semi-shaded areas as its light leaves are subject to leaf burn in the sun. While not bred for commercial use, it is said that the cones can be used for flavoring if a Saazer-style aroma and taste is desired. Sunbeam, Bianca's half-sister has similar characteristics.

Also Known As	Bianco, Bianca Gold
Characteristics	
Purpose	Aroma
Alpha Acid Composition	7%-8%
Beta Acid Composition	3.4%

Cohumulone Composition	20%-28%
Country	US
Cone Size	
Cone Density	
Seasonal Maturity	Early
Yield Amount	
Growth Rate	High to very high
Resistant to	Moderately resistant to downy mildew
Susceptible to	
Storability	
Ease of Harvest	
Total Oil	0.6-1.0 mL/100g
Myrcene Oil	30%
Humulene Oil	25%
Caryophyllene Oil	8%
Farnesene Oil	13%
Substitutes	Sunbeam
Style Guide	Lager, Pilsner, Belgian Ale

References

http://www.ars.usda.gov/SP2UserFiles/person/2450/hopchem/21698.html
http://www.ars.usda.gov/SP2UserFiles/person/2450/hopcultivars/21698.html

Bitter Gold

Super-alpha variety Bitter Gold's heritage comes from varieties Bullion, Brewer's Gold, Comet and Fuggle. It features an alpha-acid percentage higher than any of its parents and higher even than Galena or Nugget, to which it is often compared.

Released for production in 1999, Bitter Gold is quite versatile and can be used as a bittering or flavor addition imparting strong flavors reminiscent of stone fruit, watermelon and pear.

Also Known As	
Characteristics	Use for bittering only, has no notable aroma
Purpose	Bittering
Alpha Acid Composition	15.4%-18.8%
Beta Acid Composition	6.1%-8%
Cohumulone Composition	36%-41%
Country	US
Cone Size	
Cone Density	
Seasonal Maturity	
Yield Amount	
Growth Rate	
Resistant to	
Susceptible to	
Storability	Retains 55.6% alpha acid after 6 months storage at 20ºC (68ºF)
Ease of Harvest	
Total Oil	0.81-3.92 mL/100g
Myrcene Oil	68.2%
Humulene Oil	7.5%
Caryophyllene Oil	8.4%
Farnesene Oil	1.2%
Substitutes	Galena, Nugget
Style Guide	Ale, Lager, Pilsner, Bitter, India Pale Ale

References

http://www.usahops.org/index.cfm?fuseaction=press&pressID=57

http://www.homebrewtalk.com/wiki/index.php/List_of_hop_varieties_by_country_of_origin

https://www.hopunion.com/bitter-gold/

Blato

Blato was one of the first hops authorized in Czechoslovakia (now the Czech Republic) for commercial production. It is not usually singled out, but is one of the collective known as Saaz Hops, or Bohemian Early Red. It doesn't yield very well in the U.S., but it is suspected to be much more prolific in its native homeland. Zatec Hop Company in the Czech Republic states that in the analysis of the oils and resins, Blato and its siblings have proven to have the same fine aromatic profile of other Saaz hops one that is genuine and delicate.

Also Known As	
Characteristics	Similar delicate aroma profile to other Saazer hops
Purpose	Aroma
Alpha Acid Composition	4.5%
Beta Acid Composition	3.5%
Cohumulone Composition	21%
Country	Czech Republic
Cone Size	
Cone Density	
Seasonal Maturity	
Yield Amount	670 kg/hectare (600 lbs/acre)
Growth Rate	Low
Resistant to	
Susceptible to	Moderately susceptible to downy mildew
Storability	Retains 65% alpha acid after 6 months storage at 20ºC (68ºF)
Ease of Harvest	
Total Oil	0.65 mL/100g
Myrcene Oil	47%
Humulene Oil	18%
Caryophyllene Oil	5%
Farnesene Oil	11.2%
Substitutes	

References
http://www.ars.usda.gov/SP2UserFiles/person/2450/hopchem/21527.html

Blisk

Dating back to the late 1970's, Blisk was bred in its native Zalec region of Slovenia, along with Bobek and Buket in an attempt to instill both high alpha content and pleasant aroma in one cultivar. It is a cross between Atlas and a Yugoslavian male. Despite its decent yield, Blisk is not being commercially produced.

Also Known As	
Characteristics	
Purpose	Aroma
Alpha Acid Composition	9.7%-14.1%
Beta Acid Composition	3.3%-4.8%
Cohumulone Composition	33%
Country	Slovenia
Cone Size	
Cone Density	
Seasonal Maturity	Mid to late
Yield Amount	1350-3250 kg/hectare (1200-2900 lbs/acre)
Growth Rate	Very high
Resistant to	Resistant to downy mildew
Susceptible to	
Storability	Retains 45% alpha acid after 6 months storage at 20°C (68°F)
Ease of Harvest	
Total Oil	2.01 mL/100g
Myrcene Oil	58%
Humulene Oil	12%

Caryophyllene Oil	3.7%
Farnesene Oil	15.6%
Substitutes	
Style Guide	English Ale, Extra Special Bitter, Lager, Pilsner

References
http://www.ars.usda.gov/SP2UserFiles/person/2450/hopchem/21238.html
http://www.ars.usda.gov/SP2UserFiles/person/2450/hopcultivars/21238.html

Blue Northern Brewer

The Blue Northern Brewer was discovered as a mutant with deep reddish-blue leaves growing in a Belgian hop yard in the early 1970's. It was released as an ornamental variety in 1992. Its use for brewing is plausible but tentative.

Also Known As	
Characteristics	
Purpose	Bittering & Aroma
Alpha Acid Composition	6%-8%
Beta Acid Composition	3%-4%
Cohumulone Composition	24%
Country	Belgium
Cone Size	
Cone Density	
Seasonal Maturity	Early
Yield Amount	90-730 kg/hectare (80-650 lbs/acre)
Growth Rate	
Resistant to	Resistant to downy mildew and moderately resistant to verticillium wilt
Susceptible to	
Storability	Retains 78% alpha acid after 6 months storage at 20ºC (68ºF)

Ease of Harvest	
Total Oil	0.76 mL/100g
Myrcene Oil	27%-40%
Humulene Oil	29%
Caryophyllene Oil	10%
Farnesene Oil	None
Substitutes	Chinook
Style Guide	India Pale Ale

References

http://www.uvm.edu/~pass/perry/hopvars.html

http://www.ars-grin.gov/npgs/pi_books/scans/200pt3/pi200pt3_522.pdf

https://www.ars.usda.gov/SP2UserFiles/person/2450/hopcultivars/21079.html

Boadicea

Released in 2004, Boadicea is a finishing hop bred by Horticulture Research International. Known as the first aphid-resistant variety in the world, it also exhibits excellent resistance to wilt and downy mildew. As a dwarf/hedgerow variety, it grows to a shorter height than traditional varieties and yields just the same, making it an easier prospect to harvest.

Boadicea is said to have the delicate aroma of orchard blossoms, it's also slightly floral and its farnesene presence appears to give it some spicy character. Her alpha content isn't extraordinarily high, but high enough to produce a light-bodied and rounded bitterness when used in that capacity.

Homebrewer's Comments

> Very nice aroma & flavor, typical British, bit resiny, flowery, hay but not grassy, very pleasant. But it's much less intense than Goldings, you need to put much more, like 2 - 3 times to get similar aroma intensity. Bitterness is very clean, elegant and short. *(zgoda via thehomebrewforum.co.uk)*

Also Known As	
Characteristics	Delicate aroma of orchard blossoms and grass. Subtle spicy character.
Purpose	Aroma
Alpha Acid Composition	7%-10%
Beta Acid Composition	3%-4%
Cohumulone Composition	26%
Country	UK
Cone Size	
Cone Density	
Seasonal Maturity	
Yield Amount	
Growth Rate	
Resistant to	Resistant to wilt and downy mildew
Susceptible to	
Storability	
Ease of Harvest	
Total Oil	1.4-2.0 mL/100g
Myrcene Oil	33%
Humulene Oil	20%
Caryophyllene Oil	15%-19%
Farnesene Oil	5%
Substitutes	
Style Guide	Pilsner

References
http://www.britishhops.org.uk/boadicea/
https://www.hopunion.com/uk-boadicea/

Bobek

Diploid hybrid Bobek features a pleasant floral aroma. Bred in its native Zalec region of Slovenia alongside Blisk and Buket, Bobek was an attempt to create both high alpha and good aroma in one cultivar. Bobek is not being commercially produced at this time. Its parents are Northern Brewer and a Slovenian male.

Homebrewer's Comments

> I would use it on its own and it's nicer than Cascade or Centennial. I can't tell the difference between Bobek and Styrian Goldings. If anything, the Bobeks are slightly brighter. It's a hop that's great drunk fresh, but it mellows into something altogether nicer as the weeks go buy. *(mysterio via jimsbeerkit.co.uk)*

Also Known As	Styrian Golding B, Styrian Bobek
Characteristics	Pleasant floral aroma, pine
Purpose	Bittering & Aroma
Alpha Acid Composition	3.5%-9.3%
Beta Acid Composition	4%-6.6%
Cohumulone Composition	26%-31%
Country	Slovenia
Cone Size	Small
Cone Density	
Seasonal Maturity	Medium to late
Yield Amount	900 kg/hectare (800 lbs/acre)
Growth Rate	Moderate
Resistant to	Moderately resistant to downy mildew, resistant to verticillium wilt
Susceptible to	
Storability	Retains 66% alpha acid after 6 months storage at 20ºC (68ºF)
Ease of Harvest	
Total Oil	0.7-4 mL/100g
Myrcene Oil	30%-63%
Humulene Oil	12%-19%
Caryophyllene Oil	4%-6%
Farnesene Oil	3%-7%

| Substitutes | Fuggle, Willamette, Styrian Golding |
| Style Guide | English Ale, Extra Special Bitter, Lager, Pilsner |

References
http://www.globalhops.com/hopvariations.html
https://ychhops.com/varieties/bobek
http://www.hoppris.com/node/13
https://www.morebeer.com/products/styrian-bobek-pellet-hops.html

BOR

Selected by Dr Bob Romanko, BOR 704 was so named for it's planting position, row 7, plant 04, in the Prosser "Bone Yard" in the Yakima Valley. It features an aroma profile that is distinctly European. While BOR exhibits a relatively poor yield, it has been used to breed other seedlings in an effort to pass on its low cohumulone rate that is sometimes as low as 14%. However, its low alpha content has hindered it from gaining any successful foothold in commercial hops production.

There seems to be some confusion over its parentage. Some sources say it's a seedling of Hallertau Mittelfrueh while others say it is of Czech Saaz and Northern Brewer descent. The former is most likely true.

Also Known As	BOR 704
Characteristics	
Purpose	Aroma
Alpha Acid Composition	2%-3%
Beta Acid Composition	3%-4%
Cohumulone Composition	14%-20%
Country	US
Cone Size	
Cone Density	
Seasonal Maturity	Early
Yield Amount	1010-1790 kg/hectare (900-1600 lbs/acre)
Growth Rate	Moderate to high

Resistant to	Resistant to verticillium wilt
Susceptible to	Moderately susceptible to downy mildew
Storability	Retains 67% alpha acid after 6 months storage at 20°C (68°F)
Ease of Harvest	
Total Oil	0.65 mL/100g
Myrcene Oil	21%
Humulene Oil	46%
Caryophyllene Oil	13%
Farnesene Oil	Trace Amounts
Substitutes	
Style Guide	German Pilsner, Pale Ale, Wheat Beer

References

http://www.ars.usda.gov/SP2UserFiles/person/2450/hopcultivars/21285.html

Bouclier

Emerging in 2005, Bouclier is a cross between Alsace-grown Strisselspalt and a wild male from Wye, Kent. It is unclear however if this variety was first developed in the UK or across the Channel in France.

The aroma of the cones is herby and grassy with a sniff of spice. In a brew, Bouclier extracts a citrusy and floral character – great for adding a French kiss to traditional English styles.

Homebrewer's Comments

It's quite delicate and floral, so I reckon [it would suit] a pale ale or even a lager. *(craigheap via R.E.B.E.L Homebrew Club)*

Also Known As	
Characteristics	Aromas of herb, grass and spice alongside a citrus and floral character
Purpose	Bittering & Aroma

Alpha Acid Composition	5.2%-9%
Beta Acid Composition	2.4%-3.3%
Cohumulone Composition	20-25%
Country	
Cone Size	
Cone Density	
Seasonal Maturity	
Yield Amount	
Growth Rate	
Resistant to	
Susceptible to	
Storability	
Ease of Harvest	
Total Oil	1.1-1.6 mL/100g
Myrcene Oil	38%
Humulene Oil	34%
Caryophyllene Oil	
Farnesene Oil	
Substitutes	
Style Guide	English Ales, Pale Ale, Lager, Imperial Stout, Saison, Pils, Blonde

References

http://www.hops-comptoir.com/hop-bouclier-alsace/80-hop-bouclier-pellets-90.html
http://www.hopsdirect.com/bouclier-pellets/
http://www.charlesfaram.co.uk/hop-varieties/bouclier/
http://www.hops-comptoir.com/20-hop-bouclier-alsace

Bramling

Bramling was a popular and prolific hop in England around the turn of the 20th century and it is known to have been widely cultivated by 1865 for use in golden and rye ales primarily. But its increasingly low yield has caused it to fall out of favor. It is grown in British Columbia for Canadian breweries desiring aroma hops. Its origin is unknown. Its profile is of very low alpha acids and moderately low cohumulone. It is said to have a pleasant European aroma profile.

Also Known As	
Characteristics	Pleasant European aroma
Purpose	Aroma
Alpha Acid Composition	5.8%
Beta Acid Composition	3%
Cohumulone Composition	27%
Country	UK
Cone Size	
Cone Density	
Seasonal Maturity	Early
Yield Amount	670-1120 kg/hectare (600-1000 lbs/acre)
Growth Rate	Low
Resistant to	Resistant to verticillium wilt
Susceptible to	Moderately susceptible to downy mildew
Storability	Retains 76% alpha acid after 6 months storage at 20ºC (68ºF)
Ease of Harvest	
Total Oil	0.90 mL/100g
Myrcene Oil	
Humulene Oil	
Caryophyllene Oil	
Farnesene Oil	
Substitutes	Whitbread Golding, Progress, East Kent Golding
Style Guide	Golden Ale, Bitter, Rye Ale, India Pale Ale, Stout, Golden Ale, Imperial Stout, Pale Ale, Holiday Ale

References

http://www.ars.usda.gov/SP2UserFiles/person/2450/hopcultivars/21284.html

Bramling Cross

Bramling Cross is a rather rare breed and is mostly available in the UK. First harvested in 1927 at Wye College its lineage is a cross between Golding and a wild Manitoban (Canadian) hop. It is considered well suited to cask conditioned recipes as well as Christmas and fruit beers.

BrewDog Brewery says it best when they speak of Bramling Cross as being "elegant, refined, assured, (boring) and understated". They suggest people often don't use enough of Bramling Cross to let its true flavors and eccentricities shine.

When used in large quantities the fruity element in Bramling Cross springs to life. This use exhibits complex fruity notes of lemon, blackcurrant and pear, particularly when used as a late addition. Some brewers have also recorded notes of blackberries and plums.

Homebrewer's Comments

Brambling Cross isn't particularly good for aroma. *(johnnyboy1965 via thehomebrewforum.co.uk)*

I love BX as a bittering hop in stouts and porters. *(Hawks via thehomebrewforum.co.uk)*

Also Known As	
Characteristics	Notes of lemon, blackcurrant, blackberries and plums particularly when used as a late addition.
Purpose	Bittering & Aroma
Alpha Acid Composition	5%-7.8%
Beta Acid Composition	2.3%-3.2%
Cohumulone Composition	33%-35%
Country	UK
Cone Size	Medium
Cone Density	Moderate
Seasonal Maturity	Early to mid

Yield Amount	1500-1680 kg/hectare (1340-500 lbs/acre)
Growth Rate	Moderate to high
Resistant to	Resistant to powdery mildew and downy mildew
Susceptible to	Susceptible to verticillium wilt
Storability	Retains 60%-70% alpha acid after 6 months storage at 20°C (68°F)
Ease of Harvest	Difficult
Total Oil	0.7-1.2 mL/100g
Myrcene Oil	35%-40%
Humulene Oil	28%-33%
Caryophyllene Oil	14%-18%
Farnesene Oil	0%-1%
Substitutes	Whitbread Golding, Progress, East Kent Golding
Style Guide	Golden Ale, Strong Ale, Stout, Porter

References

http://beerlegends.com/bramling-cross-hops
https://ychhops.com/varieties/bramling-cross
https://www.brewdog.com/lowdown/blog/ipa-is-dead-on-sale-now
https://www.craftbrewer.com.au/shop/details.asp?PID=753

Bravo

Bravo's high alpha content is largely attributable to its parent variety, Zeus. It's bittering quality is considered smooth and in addition features light floral aromas and subtle flavors of orange and stone fruit making it highly desirable for use in many different ale styles.

Developed as part of the Hopsteiner Breeding Program, Bravo hops were released to the public in 2006 as a high-yielding and vigorous late-season hop with a high alpha profile and balanced oils. Bravo also has a history of being picked up by US West Coast breweries where similar hops have been in low supply.

Brewmaster's Comments

Nugget and Bravo are my favourite for bittering. They provide very solid, repeatable bitterness and light flavour for most ales without adding astringency. *(Ryan Schmiege, Assistant Brewmaster at Deschutes Brewery)*

Homebrewer's Comments

I use Bravo for bittering just about all of my American ales. Cheap, high AA and not at all what I'd call harsh. More along the lines of assertive bitterness. *(Phenry via homebrewtalk.com)*

Bravo I have used in combination with some Organic American Palisades in a Green Tea Blonde and feel that it lent a lot of the fruity notes that I was looking for from it. I also used it as a single hop in an all-organic pale ale that I just did and I also have some dry hopping in it right now. I definitely get the fruit notes in this beer and the apple and pear is really present and it has a nice clean, moderate bitterness. *(keesimps via homebrewtalk.com)*

Also Known As	
Characteristics	Spicy, earthy and lightly floral aroma
Purpose	Bittering
Alpha Acid Composition	14%-17%
Beta Acid Composition	3%-5%
Cohumulone Composition	29%-34%
Country	US
Cone Size	Medium
Cone Density	Moderate to compact
Seasonal Maturity	Late
Yield Amount	2700-3100 kg/hectare (2410-2770 lbs/acre)
Growth Rate	Very high
Resistant to	Resistant to powdery mildew and verticillium wilt
Susceptible to	Susceptible to downy mildew

Storability	Retains 70% alpha acid after 6 months storage at 20°C (68°F)
Ease of Harvest	Difficult
Total Oil	1.6-2.4 mL/100g
Myrcene Oil	25%-50%
Humulene Oil	18%-20%
Caryophyllene Oil	10%-12%
Farnesene Oil	0%-1%
Substitutes	Columbus, Zeus, Apollo, Magnum, Nugget
Style Guide	India Pale Ale, American Pale Ale, Extra Special Bitter

References
http://beerlegends.com/bravo-hops
https://www.hopunion.com/bravo/
http://www.usahops.org/index.cfm?fuseaction=hop_info&pageID=9
https://www.craftbrewer.com.au/shop/details.asp?PID=4817
http://shop.beerbelly.com.au/bravo-hops-pellets-100gm.html

Brewer's Gold

Brewer's Gold hops were selected by Ernest Stanley Salmon at Wye College in England in 1919 and were the result of the open pollination of a wild hop sourced from Morden, Manitoba. Despite its initial popularity, the advent of super-alpha hop varieties in the 1980's rendered Brewer's Gold largely redundant from a commercial perspective.

For brewer's wishing to experiment though, Brewer's Gold is still a good choice for late bittering with desirable notes of spice and blackcurrant. It is also nearly identical to sister selection Bullion.

Brewer's Gold's main claim to fame is arguably it's direct relation to most modern super-alpha hops. It was used to breed notable varieties like Galena, as well as Nugget, Centennial and many others and is still used for breeding today.

Homebrewer's Comments

I like these in lightly hopped ales as a bittering and late addition. They give a bit more of a twang than a cleaner bittering hop, for example, in barley wines and golden ales. In more heavily hopped ales I like them as late additions, where they give some good dark fruit and blackcurrant flavours (try a single hop pale ale).

I've got mixed results when dry-hopping with them as they aren't the most pungent hops out there, but they definitively do have an American character to them.

They would be ok in an IPA as part of a mix of hops, but wouldn't stand out to Simcoe, Citra, Amarillo or other modern more heavily flavoured hops. One of their positives is that they barely have any of that grapefruit / citrus flavour, so you can highlight more floral or dark fruit flavours using them. *(JKaranka via homebrewtalk.com)*

Also Known As	
Characteristics	Notes of spice and blackcurrant
Purpose	Bittering
Alpha Acid Composition	7.1%-11.3%
Beta Acid Composition	3.3%-6.1%
Cohumulone Composition	36%-45%
Country	UK
Cone Size	Small
Cone Density	Compact
Seasonal Maturity	Late
Yield Amount	1681-2690 kg/hectare (1500-2400 lbs/acre)
Growth Rate	Very high
Resistant to	Resistant to verticillium wilt, moderately resistant to downy mildew
Susceptible to	

Storability	Retains 60%-70% alpha acid after 6 months storage at 20ºC (68ºF)
Ease of Harvest	Easy
Total Oil	1.96 mL/100g
Myrcene Oil	66.7%
Humulene Oil	11.6%
Caryophyllene Oil	6.5%
Farnesene Oil	None
Substitutes	Bullion, Cascade, Galena, Northern Brewer (US), Northdown
Style Guide	Ale, American Pale Ale, Bitter, Barley Wine, Imperial Stout

References

http://beerlegends.com/brewers-gold-hops
http://www.ars.usda.gov/SP2UserFiles/person/2450/hopcultivars/19001.html
https://www.hopunion.com/german-brewers-gold/

Brewer's Gold (US)

Sister to Bullion, US-grown Brewer's Gold is a cultivar of the original English variety, Brewer's Gold. Despite having been developed in England, its origin is undoubtedly North American having been initially derived from a wild hop sourced from Canada's Pembina Valley in Manitoba. The American version is naturally similar to the original but contains higher alpha acids on average.

The USDA used heat therapy and other techniques to adapt the variety to local conditions and to improve disease resistance. It was grown predominantly in Oregon and on significant acreage until the advent of super-alpha varieties in the 1980's. It was discontinued from commercial production in 1985 but is still available today, albeit largely for the homebrew market.

Homebrewer's Comments

BGs really aren't intended for late additions but are a great bittering hop for many ales. They have an "old time" subtle flavor of dark fruit/berries that lends a nice character to pale ales, stouts and porters. BGs are also a necessity when brewing one of the old Ballantine XXX or IPA recipes. *(BigEd via homebrewtalk.com)*

Also Known As	Brewer's Gold, v.f.
Characteristics	Notes of spice and blackcurrant
Purpose	Bittering
Alpha Acid Composition	8.1%-13.1%
Beta Acid Composition	3.7%-6.8%
Cohumulone Composition	41%
Country	US
Cone Size	Medium
Cone Density	
Seasonal Maturity	Late
Yield Amount	1681-2690 kg/hectare (1500-2400 lbs/acre)
Growth Rate	
Resistant to	Resistant to verticillium wilt, moderately resistant to downy mildew, virus free
Susceptible to	
Storability	Poor
Ease of Harvest	
Total Oil	1.8 mL/100g
Myrcene Oil	40%
Humulene Oil	35%
Caryophyllene Oil	35%
Farnesene Oil	Trace
Substitutes	Bullion, Cascade, Galena, Northern Brewer, Northdown
Style Guide	India Pale Ale

References

http://www.usahops.org/graphics/File/HGA%20BCI%20Reports/Variety%20Manual%207-24-12.pdf

https://bellsbeer.com/store/products/Brewer's-Gold-(German)-Hops-%252d-1-lb-Pellets.html

http://www.greatlakeshops.com/brewers-gold-us.html

http://gorstvalleyhops.com/commercial-and-craft-brewers/varieties/brewers-gold/

British Columbia Golding

British Columbia Golding is produced, as one might expect, in Canada. Before the hops industry was fully established in the Pacific Northwest, BC Golding was the only North American-grown Golding. Its alphas are low so it's bittering capacity is mild at best while it puts forward an earthy aroma profile and flavors of smooth, rounded spice. BC Golding makes a good, British-style pale and has also been noted for it's successful use in Stouts and Porters.

Also Known As	BC Golding
Characteristics	Exhibits an earthy aroma profile with a flavor profile of smooth, rounded spice.
Purpose	Aroma
Alpha Acid Composition	4%-7%
Beta Acid Composition	
Cohumulone Composition	
Country	Canada
Cone Size	
Cone Density	
Seasonal Maturity	Early
Yield Amount	
Growth Rate	
Resistant to	
Susceptible to	
Storability	
Ease of Harvest	
Total Oil	
Myrcene Oil	
Humulene Oil	

Caryophyllene Oil

Farnesene Oil

Substitutes	East Kent Golding, Golding (US), Fuggle, Willamette
Style Guide	English Pale Ale, Stout, Porter

References

http://www.homebrewtalk.com/wiki/index.php/British_Columbia_Golding

Buket

Buket is a 2nd generation Fuggle and offspring of Northern Brewer. It was first bred in the Zalec region of Slovenia in the mid 1970's alongside Bobek and Blisk. Inspiration for all three of these hops was down to attempts by researchers to create both high alpha and good aroma in one cultivar.

It has not been used to any great extent commercially since its creation.

Also Known As	
Characteristics	
Purpose	Bittering & Aroma
Alpha Acid Composition	11%
Beta Acid Composition	4.9%
Cohumulone Composition	24%
Country	Slovenia
Cone Size	
Cone Density	
Seasonal Maturity	Early
Yield Amount	1190 kg/hectare (1060 lbs/acre)
Growth Rate	Moderate
Resistant to	Moderately resistant to downy mildew, resistant to verticillium wilt
Susceptible to	

Storability	Retains 53% alpha acid after 6 months storage at 20°C (68°F)
Ease of Harvest	
Total Oil	2.15 mL/100g
Myrcene Oil	57%
Humulene Oil	17%
Caryophyllene Oil	5.4%
Farnesene Oil	5.5%
Substitutes	
Style Guide	BEnglish Ale, Extra Special Bitter, Lager, Pilsner

References

http://freshops.com/usda-named-hop-variety-descriptions/#usda_id_21240

http://www.britishhops.org.uk/wp-content/uploads/2014/08/fact-sheet-press-day.-wye-hops.pdf

https://books.google.com.au/books?id=_H1yBgAAQBAJ&pg=PA205&lpg=PA205&dq=buket+hops&source=bl&ots=O9XD-Hazkd&sig=iD1LJDdBt6Bc2llB8SUqL1IrSx8&hl=en&sa=X&ved=0ahUKEwit2-z1_8fMAhWDLaYKHd4-CYMQ6AEINTAF#v=onepage&q=buket%20hops&f=false

Bullion

Sister selection to Brewer's Gold, Bullion was first bred in 1919 at Wye College, England and originates from a wild hop cutting sourced from Manitoba, Canada. It was officially released in 1938.

Bullion features many of the same brewing traits as its sibling with flavors of dark fruit and elements of spice arising from its use as a mid to late addition. Its bitterness is considered by some to be slightly coarse.

Though once popular in professional brewing circles, it, like it's sister, has had it's production capacity slashed in favor of super-alpha varieties with greater bittering potential and greatly increased storage stability. It features high alpha acids and an incredibly high yield but is susceptible to many, if not most, viruses.

Homebrewer's Comments

Bullion makes a good bittering hop for just about any UK ale. Should be OK for bittering in domestic (U.S.) styles too. (*Bryan / BigEd via homebrewtalk.com*)

Also Known As	
Characteristics	Elements of spice and dark fruits
Purpose	Bittering
Alpha Acid Composition	6.7%-12.9%
Beta Acid Composition	3.7%-9.1%
Cohumulone Composition	39%
Country	UK
Cone Size	Medium
Cone Density	Compact
Seasonal Maturity	Early
Yield Amount	2241-2690 kg/hectare (2000-2400 lbs/acre)
Growth Rate	Very high
Resistant to	Resistant to verticillium wilt, moderately resistant to downy mildew
Susceptible to	Infected with most viruses
Storability	Retains 40%-50% alpha acid after 6 months storage at 20ºC (68ºF)
Ease of Harvest	Difficult
Total Oil	1.14-2.70 mL/100g
Myrcene Oil	45%-55%
Humulene Oil	23%-30%
Caryophyllene Oil	9%-11%
Farnesene Oil	None
Substitutes	Columbus, Northern Brewer, Galena, Chinook, Brewer's Gold
Style Guide	Stout, Doppelbock, Barley Wine, Imperial Stout

References

http://www.ars.usda.gov/SP2UserFiles/person/2450/hopcultivars/64100.html
http://www.brewerslair.com/index.php?p=brewhouse&d=hops&id=&v=&term=10
https://www.hopunion.com/bullion/
http://beerlegends.com/bullion-hops

Bullion 10A

Though technically still Bullion, Bullion 10A is a heat-treated and meristem-tip cultured version of the original English variety. Developed by the USDA and released in 1972, it was retired from production in the US in 1985 along with the original Bullion following the introduction of super-alpha varieties.

Also Known As	
Characteristics	Same as Bullion
Purpose	Bittering
Alpha Acid Composition	8%-13.8%
Beta Acid Composition	2.8%-6.9%
Cohumulone Composition	42%
Country	
Cone Size	Small to medium
Cone Density	
Seasonal Maturity	Early
Yield Amount	2240-2800 kg/hectare (2000-2500 lbs/acre)
Growth Rate	Very high
Resistant to	Resistant to verticillium wilt, moderately resistant to downy mildew
Susceptible to	
Storability	Poor
Ease of Harvest	
Total Oil	1.55 mL/100g
Myrcene Oil	63%
Humulene Oil	12%

Caryophyllene Oil	7%
Farnesene Oil	0.2%
Substitutes	Columbus, Northern Brewer, Galena, Chinook, Brewer's Gold
Style Guide	Stout, Doppelbock, Barley Wine, Imperial Stout

References

http://cropandsoil.oregonstate.edu/hopcultivars/21056.html

Buzz Bullets

Buzz Bullets is a proprietary blend created by Yakima Valley Hops. It is said to have a clean bitterness and impart some floral and citrus notes.

Homebrewer's Comments

> Reporting back on my first IPA using Buzz Bullets hops. I bittered with Millennium (1.1 ounces for 60 minutes), 1 ounce of Buzz Bullets for 30 minutes, ½ ounce at flameout, and 1 ½ ounces dry hop. The alphas of this batch of Buzz Bullets is 11.1%. The aroma is somewhat dank but not musty, and definitely not fruity or citrusy. A clean and pleasant bitterness with just a hint of sharp grapefruit-like finish. *(Russ Guill via Brew Nerds / Google+)*

Also Known As	
Characteristics	Floral and citrus notes
Purpose	Bittering & Aroma
Alpha Acid Composition	8%-10%
Beta Acid Composition	
Cohumulone Composition	
Country	US
Cone Size	
Cone Density	
Seasonal Maturity	

Yield Amount

Growth Rate

Resistant to

Susceptible to

Storability

Ease of Harvest

Total Oil

Myrcene Oil

Humulene Oil

Caryophyllene Oil

Farnesene Oil

Substitutes

Style Guide India Pale Ale, Lager, American Ales

References
http://www.yakimavalleyhops.com/BuzzBullets2oz_p/hopsbuzzbullets3-2014crop.htm
https://plus.google.com/+RussGuill/posts/GPGfEP8tMTr

Calicross

New Zealand's Calicross emerged in the 1960's and by-and-large disappeared by the 1980's. Born out of a dire need for disease resistant varieties, Calicross was created as a cross between Fuggle and Late Cluster – the later being the crop decimated in the late 1940's by Black Root Rot.

Developed by New Zealand's then Department of Scientific and Industrial Research, Calicross changed the face of the New Zealand hops industry at the time and its commercial utilization remained strong for nearly 20 years. By 1980 however, its low growth rate made it a target for replacement by more vigorous varieties.

Useful for both aroma and bittering, it exhibits both earthy, fruity flavors and floral aromas closely matching those of Cluster.

Also Known As	
Characteristics	Floral, fruity and earthy flavor and aroma
Purpose	Bittering & Aroma
Alpha Acid Composition	5.8%-7.9%
Beta Acid Composition	4%-7.8%
Cohumulone Composition	36%-44%
Country	New Zealand
Cone Size	
Cone Density	
Seasonal Maturity	Late
Yield Amount	1200-2300 kg/hectare (1070-2050 lbs/acre)
Growth Rate	Moderate to high
Resistant to	
Susceptible to	Susceptible to downy mildew
Storability	Retains 78%-78% alpha acid after 6 months storage at 20°C (68°F)
Ease of Harvest	Difficult
Total Oil	0.42-1.39 mL/100g
Myrcene Oil	54%-68%
Humulene Oil	12%-19%
Caryophyllene Oil	2%-6%
Farnesene Oil	0%-1%
Substitutes	Cluster
Style Guide	English Ale, Porter, Mild Ale, Bitter, Extra Special Bitter, Lambic, Amber Ale, Cask Ale, Stout, Oatmeal Stout, Strong Ale, Nut Brown Ale, Golden Ale, Christmas Ale

References

http://beerlegends.com/calicross-hops

https://ychhops.com/varieties/cluster

http://freshops.com/usda-named-hop-variety-descriptions/#usda_id_66054

http://brooklynbrewshop.com/themash/hop-of-the-month-green-bullet/

Caliente

Caliente means "hot" in Spanish. That is, temperature hot and not spicy hot. It isn't clear exactly why this particular variety was named that but it appears to be reasonably well received by the craft brew market featuring in quite a few commercial brews to date. There is some difference of opinion on it's exact tasting notes but it has been said to impart flavors of citrus, peach, pine and even cherry along with distinct aromas of stone fruit and mandarin. Subtle aromas of peach have also been documented.

Homebrewer's Comments

I brewed a Caliente pale ale a few months back. Not a bad drop. All the usual citrusy C hop goodness with a big dose of mandarin. *(smokomark via aussiehomebrewer.com)*

It would go great with other big sharp/edgey hops like chinook or colombus also methinks. Would probably be an interesting match with citra also. *(Lecterfan via aussiehomebrewer.com)*

Also Known As	
Characteristics	Falvors of citrus, peach and pine, aromas of stone fruit and mandarin
Purpose	Bittering & Aroma
Alpha Acid Composition	15.3%
Beta Acid Composition	4.3%
Cohumulone Composition	35%
Country	US
Cone Size	
Cone Density	
Seasonal Maturity	
Yield Amount	
Growth Rate	
Resistant to	

Susceptible to	
Storability	
Ease of Harvest	
Total Oil	1.9 mL/100g
Myrcene Oil	
Humulene Oil	
Caryophyllene Oil	
Farnesene Oil	
Substitutes	Wheat, Spice Beer, IPA
Style Guide	India Pale Ale, Wheat, Pale Ale

References
http://barleyhaven.com/caliente-pellet-hops.html
http://www.yakimavalleyhops.com/Caliente2oz_p/hopscaliente3-2014crop.htm
http://aussiehomebrewer.com/topic/71553-caliente/
https://www.facebook.com/YakimaHops/posts/474115119282933

California Cluster

Generally considered to be indistinguishable from other Cluster varieties, California Cluster is a true dual use hop. Used prolifically by US brewers in the early-to-mid 1900's, Clusters were widely available and cheap – providing a generic but pleasant bitterness and flavor.

California Cluster's exact lineage is vague. The name itself is also representative of a number of different Cluster varieties. The original California Cluster though is widely noted to be the parent of Calicross and was successfully employed over 50 years ago to produce disease resistant strains, Smooth Cone, Calicross and First Choice.

Hops-Meister hop farm in Clearlake, California claim to have reintroduced two of the "original" variations of California Cluster, trademarked Ivanhoe and Gargoyle. It is unclear exactly which cluster varieties they are however.

Also Known As	
Characteristics	Generic hop bitterness and flavor

Purpose	Bittering
Alpha Acid Composition	5.5%-8.5%
Beta Acid Composition	4.5%-5.5%
Cohumulone Composition	36%-42%
Country	US
Cone Size	
Cone Density	
Seasonal Maturity	
Yield Amount	
Growth Rate	
Resistant to	
Susceptible to	
Storability	
Ease of Harvest	
Total Oil	
Myrcene Oil	
Humulene Oil	
Caryophyllene Oil	
Farnesene Oil	
Substitutes	Eroica, Galena
Style Guide	American Barley Wine, Porter, English Pale Ale, Amber Ale, Honey Ale, Cream Ale

References
http://beerlegends.com/cluster-hops
http://www.hopsmeister.com
http://beerlegends.com/california-cluster-hops
http://inhoppursuit.blogspot.com.au/2010/04/aromas-yes-but-can-willamette-valley.html

Calypso

Calypso is a Yakima Valley bred, dual-purpose diploid hop with Hopsteiner lineage on both sides. Despite its aroma-focused origins, it boasts a high alpha acid percentage. In addition to this, Calypso features crisp, fruity aromas and flavors that exhibit elements of apple, pear and stone fruit brightened with hints of lime citrus. It is marvelously complex with an almost understated earthy, tea-like note.

Brewmaster's Comments

Equinox and Calypso would be right up there with my favourite hops. Both of them are complimentary to so many different spices and make a great beer. None are big pine forward hops, but very complex and have nuances many people fail to pick up or associate them with. Both allow you to make different beers depending upon how you add them and how they are picked. Timing is one of the toughest things, with early and late harvest giving you two different hops. Often, my list is fluid during selection. *(Tim Hawn, Head of Production at BrewDog)*

Homebrewer's Comments

It's a decent hop. I can get some of the apple characteristics that it's described as having, but no pear. The apple is sort of a tart apple. It's got a citrus taste to it, someone described it as Meyer lemon. I would say it's like a tart grapefruit, but different from Centennial and Cascade. I don't think it's great on it's own but that could change depending on the grains used. *(sativen via homebrewtalk.com)*

Also Known As	
Characteristics	Crisp, fruity aroma. Flavour of Apples, pears, stone fruit and lime citrus.
Purpose	Bittering & Aroma
Alpha Acid Composition	12%-14%
Beta Acid Composition	5%-6%
Cohumulone Composition	40%-42%
Country	US
Cone Size	Very large
Cone Density	Compact
Seasonal Maturity	Early
Yield Amount	2800-3370 kg/hectare (2500-3000 lbs/acre)

Growth Rate	
Resistant to	Resistant to powdery mildew and tolerant to downy mildew
Susceptible to	
Storability	Retains 65-70% alpha acid after 6 months storage at 20ºC (68ºF)
Ease of Harvest	
Total Oil	1.6%-2.5%
Myrcene Oil	30–45%
Humulene Oil	20–35%
Caryophyllene Oil	9–15%
Farnesene Oil	<1%
Substitutes	
Style Guide	Ale, Stout, Barley Wine

References

http://hopsteiner.com/pdf/81_01_Calypso_e_letter.pdf

https://www.craftbrewer.com.au/shop/details.asp?PID=4818

http://www.hopsdirect.com/calypusp/

http://www.usahops.org/userfiles/image/1378498284_2013%20Hops%20Variety%20Manual.pdf

Canadian Redvine

Canadian Redvine, with its dense and profuse rhizomes, high vigor, excellent yield and disease resistance makes it seem like an interesting prospect but with such a high cohumulone content and low alphas, it is not widely used. It is said to impart mild flavors of cherry, berries, pine and even citrus.

It is rarely used on its own in a brew. When grown, its ability to be sown late has seen Canadian Redvine used as a quick plant in response to disease disasters. Its exact parentage is unknown.

Homebrewer's Comments

CRV is great for pale ales and IPAs, specifically late flavor and aroma additions. I would not use it as a bittering hop and I would pair it with a few other hops as well, but it is a great heirloom variety hop. I get slight citrus but mostly piney resin. *(OptimusJay via homebrewtalk.com)*

Also Known As	
Characteristics	Mild cherry flavor, grapefruit peel aroma
Purpose	Aroma
Alpha Acid Composition	5%
Beta Acid Composition	5%-6%
Cohumulone Composition	47%
Country	Canada
Cone Size	
Cone Density	
Seasonal Maturity	Late
Yield Amount	2240 kg/hectare (2000 lbs/acre)
Growth Rate	Very high
Resistant to	Moderately resistant to downy mildew
Susceptible to	
Storability	Retains 80% alpha acid after 6 months storage at 20ºC (68ºF)
Ease of Harvest	
Total Oil	11.20 mL/100g
Myrcene Oil	70%
Humulene Oil	2%
Caryophyllene Oil	2%
Farnesene Oil	4%-7%
Substitutes	Newport, Magnum, Galena
Style Guide	Red Ale, Canadian Porter, French Porter

References

http://www.greatlakeshops.com/canadian-red-vine.html
http://www.ars.usda.gov/SP2UserFiles/person/2450/hopcultivars/21679.html

Canterbury Whitebine

Well over 200 years old, Canterbury Whitebine is the cultivar from which the first Goldings were cloned in 1790. Around this time, Whitebine was grown prolifically in Farnham, Canterbury and in Hampshire. Limited information can be found on it except that in its wild state, it gave rise to several different varieties, each suited to be grown in various regions of the UK. Cobbs hops are an example and were selected from a field of Cantebury Whitebine in 1881. Mathon hops have also been stated to share Canterbury Whitebine's "botanical" character. Anecdotaly, it is said to impart a delicate and pleasant flavor.

Also Known As	
Characteristics	Delicate flavor
Purpose	Aroma
Alpha Acid Composition	
Beta Acid Composition	
Cohumulone Composition	
Country	UK
Cone Size	
Cone Density	
Seasonal Maturity	
Yield Amount	
Growth Rate	
Resistant to	
Susceptible to	
Storability	
Ease of Harvest	
Total Oil	
Myrcene Oil	
Humulene Oil	
Caryophyllene Oil	
Farnesene Oil	
Substitutes	East Kent Goldings, Mathon

References

https://bsgcraftbrewing.com/Resources%5CCraftBrewing%5CPDFs%5CAgricultural_Reports_and_Papers/TheBreeding_Varieties.pdf

https://en.m.wikipedia.org/wiki/Styrian_Goldings#Styrian_Golding

http://www.willingham-nurseries.co.uk/books/Hops/english%20hops.pdf

Cascade (Argentina)

Unlike the American Cascade, the Argentine Cascade has a mellow character with notes of lemongrass, pepper and spice. It is not considered interchangeable with the American Cascade, which has a very different profile. It is a fine aroma and finishing hop, excellent for wheat beers, blondes and has been suggested as being especially suited to lightly bittering a cream ale. Argentinian Cascade is often compared to a Hallertau or a Tettnang.

Homebrewer's Comments

> Well, I've been enjoying my Kolsch for a couple weeks now. I think the Argentina Cascades work well. There is a very noticeable lemony aftertaste, but it actually is refreshing in the Kolsch style. Its not the sharp cistrus hit you get with American Cascade. Definitely NOT American Cascade, but a good hop for the right style. (*Brew Engineer via thebrewingnetwork.com*)

Also Known As	
Characteristics	Lemongrass, pepper and spice
Purpose	Aroma
Alpha Acid Composition	3.2%
Beta Acid Composition	4.5%-7%
Cohumulone Composition	33%-40%
Country	Argentina
Cone Size	
Cone Density	
Seasonal Maturity	

Yield Amount	
Growth Rate	
Resistant to	
Susceptible to	
Storability	
Ease of Harvest	
Total Oil	
Myrcene Oil	
Humulene Oil	
Caryophyllene Oil	
Farnesene Oil	
Substitutes	Hallertau, Tettnang, East Kent Golding
Style Guide	Barley Wine, American Pale Ale, Kolsch, Cream Ale, Wheat, Blonde

References

https://bsgcraftbrewing.com/Resources%5CCraftBrewing%5CPDFs%5CAgricultural_Reports_and_Papers/TheBreeding_Varieties.pdf

Cascade (Australia)

Differing from other Cascades in its oil balance, Australian Cascade is predominantly produced in Tasmania. Descended from Fuggle, Serebrianka and wild Native American hops, when grown in Australia, it features all the characteristic citrusy, spicy, floral notes of American Cascade but with an additional delicate essence of grapefruit.

A versatile hop, it can be used in any ale and is used in many Australian lagers. Cascades are extremely popular throughout the world and most widely used in American Pale Ales.

Also Known As	
Characteristics	Same as Cascade (US) but with notes of grapefruit
Purpose	Aroma

Alpha Acid Composition	5%-7%
Beta Acid Composition	5%-7%
Cohumulone Composition	33%-40%
Country	Australia
Cone Size	
Cone Density	
Seasonal Maturity	
Yield Amount	
Growth Rate	
Resistant to	
Susceptible to	
Storability	
Ease of Harvest	
Total Oil	0.8%-1.3%
Myrcene Oil	40%-60%
Humulene Oil	10%-20%
Caryophyllene Oil	3%-9%
Farnesene Oil	5%-9%
Substitutes	Hallertau, Goldings
Style Guide	Barley Wine, American Pale Ale, Australian Lager

References

http://www.hops.com.au/products/cascade

http://www.hops.com.au/media/W1siZiIsIjIwMTMvMDUvMjkvMTdfNDBfNTdfNDkzX0hQQV9DYXNjYWRlX1Byb2R1Y3RfU2hlZXQucGRmIl1d/HPA_Cascade_Product_Sheet.pdf

Cascade (New Zealand)

New Zealand Cascade features largely the same pleasant and distinctive 'Cascade' characteristics enjoyed by its US twin but are higher in alpha acids. Some dispute this comparison however, noting that while its characteristics are similar, New Zealand grown Cascade is more subdued in both flavor and aroma. Original Cascade was developed from English variety Fuggle and the Russian variety, Serebrianka.

Homebrewer's Comments

> I found the NZ version to be more subdued in flavour and
> aroma than the US variety. *(NickB via aussiehomebrewer.com)*

Also Known As	
Characteristics	Similar to US Cascade but more subdued
Purpose	Bittering & Aroma
Alpha Acid Composition	6%-8%
Beta Acid Composition	5%-5.5%
Cohumulone Composition	21%-24%
Country	New Zealand
Cone Size	
Cone Density	
Seasonal Maturity	
Yield Amount	
Growth Rate	
Resistant to	
Susceptible to	
Storability	
Ease of Harvest	
Total Oil	
Myrcene Oil	
Humulene Oil	
Caryophyllene Oil	
Farnesene Oil	
Substitutes	Hallertau, Goldings, Ahtanum™, Centennial
Style Guide	Barley Wine, American Pale Ale, Imperial Stout, Ale, Lager

References
http://www.nzhops.co.nz/varieties/nz_cascade.html

Cascade (US)

Pioneered in the 1950's by Jack Horner and his team at Oregon State University, Cascade has since gone on to become one of the most popular American hops of all time. Released in 1972, Cascade now represents around 10% of all hops grown in the US.

It features an excellent vigor and yield and when brewed exudes a distinct spicy citrus aroma with hints of grapefruit. Well suited to just about any ale and lager, its use is particularly popular in American Pale Ales. Its relatively poor storage stability tends to be a non-issue with its popularity and subsequent large production volumes from major US breweries ensuring harvests don't sit idle for long.

Cascade was originally developed through open pollination of English variety Fuggle and the Russian variety Serebrianka and is named after the Cascade Range, mountains that run from northern California all the way north to British Columbia, Canada.

Brewmaster's Comments

Cascade hops are definitely a favourite variety for us for a few reasons. First, it is the only hop that we use in our Mirror Pond Pale Ale. Cascade hops offer both floral and citrus aromas and exceptionally clean, balanced bittering qualities. They also work in concert with other varieties very well. Use them for any addition, especially late when floral aromas with citrus undertones are desired. *(Ryan Schmiege, Assistant Brewmaster at Deschutes Brewery)*

Cascade, we've been using it for years and now it's the rock star of hops. It brings a refreshing, citrus, pine tree, grapefruit aroma to our beers, open a bottle of Chesterfield Ale and there's no mistaking it. A good tip (for professional brewers) is to contract it from the farmer to ensure you actually will get it! *(John Callahan, Brewmaster at D. G. Yuengling & Son)*

Homebrewer's Comments

Cascade hops have a sort of pungent citrus aroma.. When I was laying out about 4 oz of cascade for a pale ale once, my wife walked into the office and accused me of having some cannabis somewhere in the room until I showed her the hops. That flavor/aroma carries through a bit, especially if you do late additions and even more so when dry-hopping. I happen to enjoy it quite a bit. Personally, I think it will lean toward citrus with clean fermenting yeasts, and seem sort of mango like with the english yeasts I have used 'em with. *(snailsongs via homebrewtalk.com)*

You know, it's not super sexy like mosaic, amarillo or citra. It doesn't pack a huge alpha punch like simcoe. But you know what? It's the greatest American hop in my mind. All these new hops come and go, they are up and they are down, but the cascade remains. It's great, versatile hop and if I were stuck on a desert island and could only brew with one hop for the rest of my life, undoubtedly it would be cascade.. It's just a fantastic all-around hop. It tastes and smells amazing and I've just never found a hop I like better. *(brewhaha_rva via homebrewtalk.com)*

Also Known As	
Characteristics	Floral, with elements of citrus and notes of grapefruit
Purpose	Bittering & Aroma
Alpha Acid Composition	4.5%-8.9%
Beta Acid Composition	3.6%-7.5%
Cohumulone Composition	33%-40%
Country	US
Cone Size	Medium
Cone Density	Compact
Seasonal Maturity	Mid
Yield Amount	2017-2465 kg/hectare (1800-2200 lbs/acre)
Growth Rate	Moderate to high
Resistant to	

Susceptible to	Some resistance to downy mildew and verticillium wilt
Storability	Retains 48%-52% alpha acid after 6 months storage at 20°C (68°F)
Ease of Harvest	Difficult
Total Oil	0.8-1.5 mL/100g
Myrcene Oil	45%-60%
Humulene Oil	8%-16%
Caryophyllene Oil	4%-6%
Farnesene Oil	4%-8%
Substitutes	Centennial, Amarillo®, Columbus, Ahtanum™
Style Guide	Barley Wine, American Pale Ale, Ale, Lager

References

http://beerlegends.com/cascade-us-hops

http://www.inbeertruth.com/2015/07/obituary-jack-horner-father-of-cascade.html

https://en.wikipedia.org/wiki/Cascade_Range

https://www.nass.usda.gov/Statistics_by_State/Regional_Office/Northwest/includes/Publications/Hops/Nat%20Hop%20Rept%202015.pdf

https://www.ars.usda.gov/SP2UserFiles/person/2450/hopcultivars/21092.html

https://ychhops.com/varieties/cascade

Cashmere

Developed by Washington State University and released in 2013, Cashmere is the result of a marriage of Cascade and Northern Brewer. Fortuitously, it features alpha acids higher than that of Cascade.

A good dual-purpose hop, Cashmere showcases flavors lemon, lime and melon, exhibits a smooth bitterness and is mildly aromatic with a subtle herbal bouquet.

Homebrewer's Comments

I got a hold of some last year and used them in a dry hopped

Also Known As	
Characteristics	Smooth bitterness, herbal aroma, flavors of lemon, lime and melon
Purpose	Bittering & Aroma
Alpha Acid Composition	7.7%-9.1%
Beta Acid Composition	3.3%-7.1%
Cohumulone Composition	22%-24%
Country	US
Cone Size	
Cone Density	
Seasonal Maturity	
Yield Amount	
Growth Rate	
Resistant to	
Susceptible to	
Storability	Retains 75% alpha acid after 6 months storage at 20ºC (68ºF)
Ease of Harvest	
Total Oil	1.2-1.4 mL/100g
Myrcene Oil	39%-42%
Humulene Oil	26%-29%
Caryophyllene Oil	11.5%-13%
Farnesene Oil	<1%
Substitutes	
Style Guide	Saison

References

http://www.hopsdirect.com/cashmere-leaf/

http://www.barthhaasgroup.com/images/pdfs/hop-varieties/en/Sortenblatt_Engl_USA_Cashmere.pdf

Cekin

Like its sibling Cicero, Dr Dragica Kralj at the Hop Research Institute in Zalec, Slovenia originally selected Cekin in the 1980's. It is a cross between Aurora and a Yugoslav male. It is not currently grown in large quantities commercially due to a lack of interest from breweries. Its vigor and yield are great in Slovenia but to date it has not proven itself in Corvallis test plots in the US. It is said to have a pleasing, distinctive and continental aroma comparable to Savinjski Golding.

Also Known As	
Characteristics	European aroma, similar to Styrian hops
Purpose	Aroma
Alpha Acid Composition	6%-8%
Beta Acid Composition	2%-3%
Cohumulone Composition	24%
Country	Slovenia
Cone Size	
Cone Density	
Seasonal Maturity	Late
Yield Amount	630 kg/hectare (560 lbs/acre)
Growth Rate	
Resistant to	Moderately resistant to downy mildew
Susceptible to	
Storability	Retains 79% alpha acid after 6 months storage at 20°C (68°F)
Ease of Harvest	
Total Oil	1.07 mL/100g
Myrcene Oil	47.9%
Humulene Oil	16.5%
Caryophyllene Oil	6.2%
Farnesene Oil	7.1%
Substitutes	
Style Guide	

References
http://www.ars.usda.gov/SP2UserFiles/person/2450/hopcultivars/21613.html

Celeia

Celeia is the triploid offspring of a Styrian Golding, an Aurora and a Slovenian wild hop. It features an excellently balanced profile all around and very good storage stability. A versatile hop, it has seen widespread use in Lagers, Pilsners, English-style ales and ESBs. It loves deep clay soil and requires a large planting distance.

Unfortunately, Celeia has not been well received by breweries to date and is not grown in large commercial quantities. It is described as slightly citrus and floral on the nose, pleasantly bitter and in symmetry with its aroma.

Homebrewer's Comments

> I discovered the Celeia hops when Austin Homebrew offered them as a seasonal. They are now sold out and I regret I didn't buy extra while I could. The Belgian style ale I made with Celeia has been a big hit with everyone who has tried it. 1oz Styrian Golding is added at the start of the boil for bittering. 0.5 oz of Celeia is added for the last 15 minutes for flavor. 1 oz of Celeia is added in the last 5 minutes for aroma. The result is a light ale with a very slightly citrus flavor and a pleasing floral aroma. *(Stormrider51 via homebrewtalk.com)*

Also Known As	
Characteristics	Floral and citrus aroma
Purpose	Aroma
Alpha Acid Composition	5%-6%
Beta Acid Composition	3%-4%
Cohumulone Composition	25%
Country	Slovenia
Cone Size	
Cone Density	
Seasonal Maturity	Early

Yield Amount	960 kg/hectare (850 lbs/acre)
Growth Rate	
Resistant to	Moderately resistant to downy mildew
Susceptible to	
Storability	Retains 56% alpha acid after 6 months storage at 20°C (68°F)
Ease of Harvest	
Total Oil	1.31 mL/100g
Myrcene Oil	49.5%
Humulene Oil	17.6%
Caryophyllene Oil	7.2%
Farnesene Oil	5.6%
Substitutes	Saaz, Bobek, Styrian Golding
Style Guide	English Ale, Lager, American Lager, Pilsner, English Ale, Extra Special Bitter

References
http://www.ars.usda.gov/SP2UserFiles/person/2450/hopcultivars/21611.html

Centennial

Centennial owes its existence to a mix of Brewer's Gold, Fuggle, East Kent Golding and Bavarian hops. Developed in 1974 and released in 1990, Centennial was pioneered by Charles (Chuck) Zimmerman and S.T. Kenny at Washington State University.

Centennial is at times referred to as Super Cascade because of its similar citric characteristic. Centennial is a much-celebrated hop in its versatility with its depth of bitterness and forward aroma – two characteristics that balance each other beautifully.

It is well suited to Pale Ales and IPAs with its high alpha content and is floral in both flavor and aroma. Centennial has had its ups and downs in the commercial brewing industry but is currently experiencing a return to popularity, particularly among leading craft breweries.

Brewmaster's Comments

Centennial has been around for a good long bit and I love it as a "go to". It is just natural, like walking from the woods into a beautiful green field with wild flowers. Earthy yet floral. Nicely balanced with the best of both worlds. It even has a citrus kick to it. Centennial can certainly be tri purpose, flavor and aroma definitely and even for bittering. *(Nick Nock, Head Brewer at SweetWater Brewing Company)*

Centennial is still a classic workhorse. Great for IPAs and Pales, always pleasing floral and citrus character. *(Jeremy S Kosmicki, Brewmaster at Founders Brewing Co.)*

Homebrewer's Comments

[My beers featuring Centennial] are always bright, clean and citrusy. I do like to blend them with columbus at the very least though because they can be a little one dimensional on their own. *(majorvices via homebrewersassociation.org)*

Also Known As	Super Cascade
Characteristics	Earthy and floral with an element of citrus
Purpose	Bittering & Aroma
Alpha Acid Composition	9.5%-11.5%
Beta Acid Composition	3.5%-4.5%
Cohumulone Composition	28%-30%
Country	US
Cone Size	Medium
Cone Density	Compact
Seasonal Maturity	Mid
Yield Amount	1500-1750 kg/hectare (1330-1560 lbs/acre)
Growth Rate	Moderate

Resistant to	Resistant to prunus necrotic ring-spot virus, downy mildew and verticillium wilt
Susceptible to	Susceptible to hop mosaic virus
Storability	Retains 60%-65% alpha acid after 6 months storage at 20°C (68°F)
Ease of Harvest	Difficult
Total Oil	1.5-2.5 mL/100g
Myrcene Oil	45%-55%
Humulene Oil	10%-18%
Caryophyllene Oil	5%-8%
Farnesene Oil	0%-1%
Substitutes	Chinook, Galena, Nugget, Zeus, Columbus, Cascade
Style Guide	Extra Special Bitter, Barley Wine, Imperial Stout, India Pale Ale, Pale Ale

References

http://beerlegends.com/centennial-hops
https://ychhops.com/varieties/centennial
http://freshops.com/shop/hop/dual-purpose-hop/centennial-hop/
https://www.craftbrewer.com.au/shop/details.asp?PID=603
http://schmidthops.com/our_hops

Cerera

Cerera, sister to Celeia, has a pleasing continental aroma similar to Saaz. Developed in Slovenia in the 1980's, it hails from Savinja Golding and a Yugoslav male and is classified as a seedless Super Styrian triploid variety. Poor storage stability has made Cerera a poor candidate for widespread commercial production.

It is not considered useful for single hop bittering, as it is high in tannoids. To avoid the astringency that comes with excess tannins, try combining Cerera with other high alpha varieties.

Also Known As	
Characteristics	Saaz-like aroma
Purpose	Bittering & Aroma
Alpha Acid Composition	5%-6%
Beta Acid Composition	4%-4.5%
Cohumulone Composition	25%
Country	Slovenia
Cone Size	
Cone Density	
Seasonal Maturity	Late
Yield Amount	1090 kg/hectare (965 lbs/acre)
Growth Rate	High to very high
Resistant to	Moderately resistant to downy mildew
Susceptible to	
Storability	Retains 49% alpha acid after 6 months storage at 20°C (68°F)
Ease of Harvest	
Total Oil	1.5 mL/100g
Myrcene Oil	58%
Humulene Oil	13.2%
Caryophyllene Oil	6%
Farnesene Oil	3%
Substitutes	
Style Guide	

References

http://freshops.com/usda-named-hop-variety-descriptions/#usda_id_21612

https://books.google.com.au/books?id=fctJLwKUzX4C&pg=PT221&lpg=PT221&dq=cerera+hops&source=bl&ots=DZvZYPZArt&sig=7i4g1G1awsVrArUdjaEdOsV4VRE&hl=en&sa=X&ved=0ahUKEwim2PrXnsjMAhUiLKYKHTvUDcMQ6AEIQDAH#v=onepage&q=cerera%20hops&f=false

Challenger

Released to the public in 1972, Challenger hops were developed at Wye College from varieties Northern Brewer and German Zattler. It accounted for a significant percentage of the hops grown in the UK during the 1980's and 1990's.

Challenger features decent bitterness and a floral aroma and as such are considered fine for bittering or for dry hopping. Its flavor is smooth with balanced floral characteristics, some citrus and a dash of spice.

Homebrewer's Comments

The Belgian style ale I made with Celeia has been a big hit with everyone who has tried it. 1oz Styrian Golding is added at the start of the boil for bittering. 0.5 oz of Celeia is added for the last 15 minutes for flavor. 1 oz of Celeia is added in the last 5 minutes for aroma. The result is a light ale with a very slightly citrus flavor and a pleasing floral aroma. (*Stormrider51 via homebrewtalk.com*)

Also Known As	Wye Challenger
Characteristics	
Purpose	Bittering & Aroma
Alpha Acid Composition	6.5%-9%
Beta Acid Composition	3.2%-4.5%
Cohumulone Composition	20%-25%
Country	UK
Cone Size	Medium to large
Cone Density	Moderate to compact
Seasonal Maturity	Late
Yield Amount	1400-1800 kg/hectare (1240-1610 lbs/acre)
Growth Rate	Moderate
Resistant to	Resistant to downy mildew and powdery mildew
Susceptible to	Susceptible to verticillium wilt

Storability	Retains 70%-85% alpha acid after 6 months storage at 20ºC (68ºF)
Ease of Harvest	Difficult
Total Oil	1-1.7 mL/100g
Myrcene Oil	30%-42%
Humulene Oil	25%-32%
Caryophyllene Oil	8%-10%
Farnesene Oil	1%-3%
Substitutes	Perle (US), Northern Brewer, Admiral
Style Guide	Golden Ale, Barley Wine, Imperial Stout

References
http://beerlegends.com/challenger-hops
https://ychhops.com/varieties/challenger
http://www.britishhops.org.uk/challenger/
http://freshops.com/usda-named-hop-variety-descriptions/#usda_id_21043

Chelan

Chelan is a privately patented bittering hop and daughter to Galena. Developed by John I. Haas, Inc. and grown exclusively in Washington State, it was released in 1994 and has found popular use in male styles of ales – particularly American style ales.

Despite being comparable in style, Chelan enjoys higher yields and a higher alpha percentage than its parent Galena. With very high beta acids also, Chelan imparts a strong, almost brutish bitterness.

Homebrewer's Comments

It is a great hop to work with. I made a dark IPA with 100% Chelan hops "Fall Evening At Lake Chelan", wonderful in a brandy snifter when you allow it to warm to 55. *(Central WA Brewing via northernbrewer.com)*

Also Known As	
Characteristics	Strong, brutish bitterness

Purpose	Bittering
Alpha Acid Composition	12%-15.5%
Beta Acid Composition	8.5%-11.5%
Cohumulone Composition	33%-35%
Country	US
Cone Size	
Cone Density	
Seasonal Maturity	Early to mid
Yield Amount	2460-2910 kg/hectare (2200-2600 lbs/acre)
Growth Rate	
Resistant to	Resistant to verticillium wilt
Susceptible to	Moderately susceptible to downy mildew
Storability	Retains 80% alpha acid after 6 months storage at 20ºC (68ºF)
Ease of Harvest	
Total Oil	1.5-1.9 mL/100g
Myrcene Oil	45%-55%
Humulene Oil	12%-15%
Caryophyllene Oil	9%-12%
Farnesene Oil	<1%
Substitutes	Galena, Nugget
Style Guide	American Ale

References

http://hopunion.com/chelan/
http://www.brewerslair.com/index.php?p=brewhouse&d=hops&id=&v=&term=14
http://www.usahops.org/index.cfm?fuseaction=hop_info&pageID=7
http://www.yakimavalleyhops.com/ChelanLeaf8oz_p/hopsleafchelanl2-2015crop.htm

Chinook

Chinook hops are suitable for any stage of the boil. They're not only a natural for American-style Pale Ales and IPAs, but they also find their way into seasonal ales, barley wine and some porters and stouts.

The variety is a cross between Petham Golding and a USDA male and features a piney, spicy bouquet with robust flavors of grapefruit.

Released in 1985, Chinook has recently grown in popularity, particularly among craft breweries. Currently, they're commercially featured alone in Stone's Arrogant Bastard and in addition to Cascade and Centennial in Sierra Nevada's Celebration Ale – a brew famous for its piney, citrusy character.

Homebrewer's Comments

> Chinook is one of my favorite hops for bittering and flavor/aroma. My experience with dry hopped chinook beers is that when the beer is young they lend a piney flavor and aroma that is very nice, as the beer ages the piney character fades and it becomes more woody/herbal or even smokey but thats after a year or more. (k1v1116 via homebrewtalk.com)

Also Known As	
Characteristics	Bouquet of pine and spice
Purpose	Bittering & Aroma
Alpha Acid Composition	12%-14%
Beta Acid Composition	3%-4%
Cohumulone Composition	29%-34%
Country	
Cone Size	Medium
Cone Density	Compact
Seasonal Maturity	Mid to late
Yield Amount	1700-2230 kg/hectare (1520-2000 lbs/acre)
Growth Rate	Moderate to high
Resistant to	
Susceptible to	

Storability	Retains 68%-70% alpha acid after 6 months storage at 20ºC (68ºF)
Ease of Harvest	Difficult
Total Oil	1.5-2.7 mL/100g
Myrcene Oil	35%-40%
Humulene Oil	18%-25%
Caryophyllene Oil	9%-11%
Farnesene Oil	0%-1%
Substitutes	Galena, Eroica, Nugget, Bullion, Columbus, Northern Brewer, Target
Style Guide	Winter Ale, Pale Ale, India Pale Ale, Porter, Stout, Lager, Barley Wine, American Lager, American Ale

References
http://www.brew365.com/hops_chinook.php
https://ychhops.com/varieties/chinook
http://beerlegends.com/chinook-hops
http://freshops.com/shop/hop/bittering-hop/chinook-hop/
https://www.craftbrewer.com.au/shop/details.asp?PID=606

Cicero

Sister to Cekin, Cicero is a dual use hop with a Styrian-type aroma bred from Aurora, a Yugoslav tetraploid male and a USDA tetraploid male. Developed in Slovenia in the 1980's, Cicero possesses very high vigor and yield potential in home region but has not tested well in the US.

Also Known As	HBC 394
Characteristics	
Purpose	Bittering & Aroma
Alpha Acid Composition	6%-7%
Beta Acid Composition	2.4%
Cohumulone Composition	29%
Country	Slovenia

Cone Size	
Cone Density	
Seasonal Maturity	Late
Yield Amount	810 kg/hectare (720 lbs/acre)
Growth Rate	Moderate to high
Resistant to	Moderately resistant to downy mildew
Susceptible to	
Storability	Retains 80% alpha acid after 6 months storage at 20ºC (68ºF)
Ease of Harvest	
Total Oil	1.05 mL/100g
Myrcene Oil	51%
Humulene Oil	18%
Caryophyllene Oil	7%
Farnesene Oil	3%
Substitutes	
Style Guide	American Pale Ale

References

http://www.ciceros-stl.com/the-first-pour-grand-teton-sweetgrass

http://freshops.com/usda-named-hop-variety-descriptions/#usda_id_21614

https://books.google.com.au/books?id=fctJLwKUzX4C&pg=PT214&lpg=PT214&dq=cicero+hops+slovenia&source=bl&ots=DZvZYTYAsz&sig=CMnPZJzvfqpX5iNg0e1ak2zfLPs&hl=en&sa=X&ved=0ahUKEwjstZiEsMnMAhWBMaYKHRH8Dw8Q6AEINDAF#v=onepage&q=cicero%20hops%20slovenia&f=false

https://translate.google.com.au/translate?hl=en&sl=nl&u=https://nl.wikipedia.org/wiki/Cicero_(hop)&prev=search

Citra®

American aroma hop Citra® was created by John I. Haas, Inc. and Select Botanicals Group joint venture, the Hop Breeding Company. It was released to the brewing world in 2008. Now one of the most coveted high-impact aroma hops in the US, particularly among craft brewers, it boasts a complex lineage that includes the likes of Hallertau Mittelfrüh (father), US Tettnang, Brewer's Gold and East Kent Golding.

Gene Probasco is credited with having first bred Citra® in 1990. After trialing the new variety with iconic craft breweries Deschutes, Sierra Nevada and others, commercial acreage was significantly expanded in the lead up to its official release.

Citra®, as the name implies, has a strong citrusy profile. This is largely credited to its very high myrcene content. It has an extraordinary flavor profile of grapefruit, lime and tropical fruits but despite its high alphas, brewers often warn against its use for bittering, which is considered by some to be harsh and undesirable.

Brewmaster's Comments

Citra hops have become a favourite of craft brewers and consumers alike. They provide awesome grapefruit, tangerine or even catty aromas that have become signature elements in west coast style IPAs. Use in late additions for aroma....first or second addition use of Citra is missing the point. The more used the more the catty quality tends to come out. *(Ryan Schmiege, Assistant Brewmaster at Deschutes Brewery)*

Homebrewer's Comments

To my palette, Citra really shines as an aroma/dry hop. I've done a Citra single hop beer and, while it had an amazing sweet tropical mango aroma, the flavor and bittering were severely lacking. *(hamaien via homebrewtalk.com)*

Also Known As	Citra® Brand HBC 394 cv
Characteristics	Citrus, grapefruit, lime, tropical fruits, harsh bitterness
Purpose	Bittering & Aroma
Alpha Acid Composition	10%-15%
Beta Acid Composition	3%-4.5%
Cohumulone Composition	20%-35%
Country	US
Cone Size	Medium
Cone Density	Tight
Seasonal Maturity	Mid

Yield Amount	1600-1800 kg/hectare (1400-1600 lbs/acre)
Growth Rate	Medium to high
Resistant to	Downy mildew, powdery mildew and verticillium wilt
Susceptible to	Aphids
Storability	Retains 75% alpha acid after 6 months storage at 20°C (68°F)
Ease of Harvest	Easy to moderate
Total Oil	1.5-3 mL/100g
Myrcene Oil	60%-70%
Humulene Oil	7%-12%
Caryophyllene Oil	5%-8%
Farnesene Oil	< 1%
Substitutes	Simcoe®, Cascade, Centennial, Mosaic®
Style Guide	India Pale Ale, American Ales, Amber

References

http://www.UShops.org/index.cfm?fuseaction=hop_info&pageID=8

https://ychhops.com/varieties/citra-brand-hbc-394-cv

http://fifthseasongardening.com/citra-a-brief-history-of-an-exceptional-hop

http://craftbeeracademy.com/hop-of-the-week-citra/

https://www.craftbrewer.com.au/shop/details.asp?PID=3640

http://www.usahops.org/index.cfm?fuseaction=hop_info&pageID=8

http://www.uvm.edu/extension/cropsoil/wp-content/uploads/Hop-Varietal-Guide-2013.pdf

http://learn.kegerator.com/citra-hops/

Cluster (AUS)

Though its official lineage is vague, Australian Cluster is a dual-use hop thought to be of Dutch, English and/or American ancestry. Australian Cluster, grown by HPA is strongly resinous but yields a balanced bitterness with a notable herbal character. Australian's, particularly those in Queensland, might recognize Australian-grown Cluster as the aroma variety in XXXX Bitter.

Also Known As	Australian Cluster
Characteristics	Strongly resinous, herbal character
Purpose	Bittering & Aroma
Alpha Acid Composition	5.5%-8.5%
Beta Acid Composition	4.5%-5.5%
Cohumulone Composition	36%-42%
Country	Australia
Cone Size	
Cone Density	Medium
Seasonal Maturity	Early to mid
Yield Amount	1900-2400 kg/hectare (1695-2141 lbs/acre)
Growth Rate	High
Resistant to	
Susceptible to	Susceptible to downy mildew
Storability	Retains 80-85% alpha acid after 6 months storage at 20ºC (68ºF)
Ease of Harvest	Easy
Total Oil	0.4-1 mL/100g
Myrcene Oil	45%-55%
Humulene Oil	15%-18%
Caryophyllene Oil	6%-7%
Farnesene Oil	<1%
Substitutes	Northern Brewer, Galena
Style Guide	Lager, Stout, Ale

References

http://www.hops.com.au/products/cluster

https://www.craftbrewer.com.au/shop/details.asp?PID=3214

http://www.cheekypeakbrewery.com.au/index.php/hops/australian-hops/product/287-pellet-cluster-hops-aa-7-9-per-gram-price-0-075

Cluster (US)

Cluster (US) is thought to be one of the oldest and most robust hop crops in the US. With its balanced aroma and bittering profile and outstanding storage stability, it has long been a go to hop of large commercial breweries in the US.

So prolific was Cluster's use in fact that at the beginning of the 20th century, Cluster accounted for a whopping 96% of the total acreage of hops grown in the United States. Cluster remained at the top right through until the 1970's.

The exact lineage of Cluster is unknown. It is considered to have a clean, neutral and slightly floral flavor.

Homebrewer's Comments

> I don't find anything in the way of grapefruit in Clusters. They are an older American variety, once very common but replaced for the most part with newer high alpha hops. They sometimes get a bad rep as being 'catty'. I like them a lot in certain beers like CAP and some pale ales. Clusters aren't really known for their flavor and aroma but IMO they would work very well in a Cal Common as a bittering hop. I might switch the additions with the NB or try using something like Willamette as the finisher to get a different beer than an Anchor knockoff. (*Bryan / BigEd via homebrewtalk.com*)

Also Known As	
Characteristics	Clean, neutral, slightly floral
Purpose	Bittering & Aroma
Alpha Acid Composition	5.5%-9%
Beta Acid Composition	4%-6%
Cohumulone Composition	36%-42%
Country	US
Cone Size	Medium
Cone Density	Compact
Seasonal Maturity	Mid

Yield Amount	1600-2140 kg/hectare (1420-1900 lbs/acre)
Growth Rate	Very high
Resistant to	Resistant to prunus necrotic ring-spot virus
Susceptible to	Susceptible to downy mildew and powdery mildew
Storability	Retains 80%-85% alpha acid after 6 months storage at 20°C (68°F)
Ease of Harvest	Difficult
Total Oil	0.4-1 mL/100g
Myrcene Oil	38%-55%
Humulene Oil	15%-20%
Caryophyllene Oil	6%-10%
Farnesene Oil	0%-1%
Substitutes	Eroica, Galena
Style Guide	Barley Wine, Porter, English Pale Ale, Amber Ale, Honey Ale, Cream Ale, American Lager

References

http://beerlegends.com/cluster-hops

https://ychhops.com/varieties/cluster

http://www.agraria.com.br/extranet/arquivos/agromalte_arquivo/producao_de_lupulo_em_varios_paises_-_ing.pdf

http://beervana.blogspot.com.au/2011/06/taste-of-past-cluster-hops.html

Cobb

Cobb, also known as Cobb's Golding, is a product of Canterbury Whitebine. Introduced in 1881 by Mr. John Cobb, it is among the varieties known as Goldings. A high-yielding aroma hop, it bears a classic English flavor and is lightly hoppy. In the past, it was in demand for copper and dry hopping in traditional English ales though its production has been curtailed now due to a susceptibility to wilt and mildew. It is known for its exquisite and delicate aroma.

Also Known As	Cobb's Golding
Characteristics	
Purpose	Aroma
Alpha Acid Composition	4.4%-6.7%
Beta Acid Composition	1.9%-2.8%
Cohumulone Composition	26%-32%
Country	
Cone Size	Medium
Cone Density	
Seasonal Maturity	Mid
Yield Amount	1500-2000 kg/hectare (1330-1780 lbs/acre)
Growth Rate	High
Resistant to	
Susceptible to	Sensitive to wilt, susceptible to downy mildew and powdery mildews
Storability	Retains 46% alpha acid after 6 months storage at 20°C (68°F)
Ease of Harvest	Moderate to difficult
Total Oil	0.8-1.0 mL/100g
Myrcene Oil	
Humulene Oil	
Caryophyllene Oil	
Farnesene Oil	
Substitutes	East Kent Golding, Early Bird
Style Guide	India Pale Ale, English Ales

References

http://www.willingham-nurseries.co.uk/hops/cobb.html
http://www.willingham-nurseries.co.uk/books/Hops/english%20hops.pdf

Coigneau

Originating from the 18th century, Belgian Coigneau hops have largely disappeared. Light on bitterness, Coigneau hops were often employed in Lambic beers and to a lesser extend, Pilsners.

In 1930, the commercial crop of Coigneau was all but replaced by Green Belle with the last plots disappearing in the 1950's. Recently however, the variety has been rediscovered from within the archives at Wye College in Kent, England. Plans exist to resurrect the variety.

Also Known As	Cagneau, Cagnau, Carnau
Characteristics	
Purpose	
Alpha Acid Composition	
Beta Acid Composition	
Cohumulone Composition	
Country	Belgium
Cone Size	
Cone Density	
Seasonal Maturity	
Yield Amount	
Growth Rate	
Resistant to	
Susceptible to	
Storability	
Ease of Harvest	
Total Oil	
Myrcene Oil	
Humulene Oil	
Caryophyllene Oil	
Farnesene Oil	
Substitutes	
Style Guide	Labic, Pilsner

References

https://translate.google.com/translate?hl=en&sl=nl&u=https://nl.wikipedia.org/wiki/Coigne au_(hop)&prev=search

Columbia

Columbia enjoyed limited production in the 1980's but was later discontinued in favor of Willamette. However, as craft brewers have started to discover Columbia's unique, pungent kick of hoppiness and notable twist of lemon citrus, it seems to have come back in to fashion. Columbia was returned to production in 2011. Now it's used in Widmer Bros. Columbia Common Spring Ale among others.

Also Known As	
Characteristics	Pungent hoppy kick, twist of lemon citrus
Purpose	Aroma
Alpha Acid Composition	8.8%
Beta Acid Composition	4%
Cohumulone Composition	40%
Country	
Cone Size	Medium
Cone Density	
Seasonal Maturity	Late
Yield Amount	1710 kg/hectare (1520 lbs/acre)
Growth Rate	
Resistant to	Resistant to downy mildew and verticillium wilt
Susceptible to	
Storability	Retains 72% alpha acid after 6 months storage at 20ºC (68ºF)
Ease of Harvest	
Total Oil	1.21 mL/100g
Myrcene Oil	55%
Humulene Oil	17%
Caryophyllene Oil	7%
Farnesene Oil	4.1%
Substitutes	
Style Guide	

References

http://www.ars.usda.gov/SP2UserFiles/person/2450/hopcultivars/21040.html

Columbus

The exact lineage of the proprietary hop Columbus is unknown. Its namesake was created in part as the result of a legal dispute between Hopunion and Yakima Chief when both parties attempted to patent the same hop. Yakima Chief's variety was named Tomahawk®. After an agreement was reached, both names were registered. They are technically the same hop however.

Originally bred by Charles (Chuck) Zimmerman as part of a USDA breeding program sometime in the 1970's, Columbus is sometimes referred to at CTZ (Columbus, Tomahawk® and Zues) though it is genetically distinct from Zues hops.

It features a punchy hoppiness and deep, pensive aroma with understated citrus notes—perfect as a dual use hop. Commonly used late in the boil and, when fresh, Columbus has a herbal flavor with a lemon citrus back note. Usable in a number of styles, notably American-style ales.

Homebrewer's Comments

I really like Columbus but you can easily over do it if you're not careful. As a bittering hop, it isn't clean at all. But that can be a good thing since it's character withstands a full boil. Dank and pungent is how I would describe them. They work really well in an American stout. (*jmo88 via homebrewtalk.com*)

Also Known As	Tomahawk®, CTZ
Characteristics	Pensive aroma with notes of citrus
Purpose	Bittering & Aroma
Alpha Acid Composition	14%-18%
Beta Acid Composition	4.5%-6%
Cohumulone Composition	28%-35%
Country	US
Cone Size	Medium to large

Cone Density	Compact
Seasonal Maturity	Mid to late
Yield Amount	2000-2500 kg/hectare (1780-2230 lbs/acre)
Growth Rate	Moderate to high
Resistant to	
Susceptible to	Susceptible to downy mildew and powdery mildew
Storability	Retains 50%-60% alpha acid after 6 months storage at 20ºC (68ºF)
Ease of Harvest	Difficult
Total Oil	1.5-4.5 mL/100g
Myrcene Oil	25%-55%
Humulene Oil	9%-25%
Caryophyllene Oil	6%-12%
Farnesene Oil	0%-1%
Substitutes	Zeus, Chinook, Northern Brewer, Nugget, Target, Warrior®, Millenium, Bullion
Style Guide	Imperial Brown Ale, Barley Wine, Imperial Stout, American Ales, Stout

References
http://beerlegends.com/columbus-hops
https://ychhops.com/varieties/columbus
http://learn.kegerator.com/columbus-hops/

Comet

Comet has an intriguing parentage of English Sunshine and a native American hop, bringing out a "wild American" flavor. Released in 1974 by the USDA, Comet was originally bred to address the needs for higher alpha hops. Today, it is no longer in commercial production and is somewhat difficult to find.

Comet's flavor profile rests heavily on a strong accent of grapefruit. It does feature solid bittering capabilities and traditionally brewers considered it best suited as a bittering agent for American-style lagers. Recently however, there has been a surge in its use as a dry-hop in ales and IPA's.

Homebrewer's Comments

Bought a pound last year and it was my favorite hop. Hoping that pellets get released by HD soon. Made a comet only pale ale and the flavor is straight grapefruit juice. I mean strong ruby red juice. The dankness really didn't come through with dry hopping, just grapefruit. If you're a grapefruit fan then rock it hard and don't be afraid, otherwise use sparingly with other citrus hops because it's pretty intense. Currently conditioning a comet dry hopped sour that's got the same grapefruit flavor. I'm a fan. (*pohldogg via homebrewtalk.com*)

This is an older variety that originally was largely ignored because people didn't like dank resiny flavors in their beers. Now its gaining popularity. Strong grapefruit zest flavor but extremely pungent aroma of dank resin with a touch of citrus. I love using it as a dry hop in my black IPAs. (*m00ps via email*)

Also Known As	
Characteristics	Strong grapefruit, dank resin flavors
Purpose	Bittering & Aroma
Alpha Acid Composition	9.4%-12.4%
Beta Acid Composition	3%-6.1%
Cohumulone Composition	41%
Country	US
Cone Size	
Cone Density	
Seasonal Maturity	Late
Yield Amount	1900-2240 kg/hectare (1700-2000 lbs/acre)
Growth Rate	Very high
Resistant to	Resistant to verticillium wilt
Susceptible to	Susceptible to downy mildew

Storability	Retains 49% alpha acid after 6 months storage at 20°C (68°F)
Ease of Harvest	
Total Oil	1.98 mL/100g
Myrcene Oil	67%
Humulene Oil	1%
Caryophyllene Oil	10%
Farnesene Oil	0.1%
Substitutes	Galena, Summit™
Style Guide	Lager, American Ale, India Pale Ale, Ale

References
http://www.homebrewtalk.com/wiki/index.php/Comet
https://www.hopunion.com/comet/
http://dangerousmanbrewing.com/beers/single-hop-ser?ParentPageID=4

Crystal

Despite a relatively low yield, Crystal's has made it a fairly popular hop. It's woodsy, green, floral and fruity with herb and spice notes of cinnamon, nutmeg and black pepper. Extremely versatile, it's even used for its notable aromatic qualities in IPAs and Bitters despite its low alpha acid content.

First bred in 1983, it has an interesting lineage with roots extending back to Hallertau, Cascade, Brewer's Gold and Early Green. Commercially it is used in a great variety of beers from RogueBrutal Bitters to Mountain Sun's Belgian Dip Chocolate Stout.

Homebrewer's Comments

I use a lot of crystal hops. I like them a lot. They are kinda like a slightly lemony version of Hallertauer hops. I also used them once in a all FWH kolsch and I thought it was fantastic. It was easily one of the best kolsches I ever made. *(majorvices via homebrewersassociation.org)*

Also Known As	
Characteristics	Woody, floral and fruity with spice notes of cinnamon, nutmeg and black pepper
Purpose	Aroma
Alpha Acid Composition	2.8%-4.4%
Beta Acid Composition	5.8%-7%
Cohumulone Composition	21%-26%
Country	
Cone Size	
Cone Density	
Seasonal Maturity	Late
Yield Amount	2020-2460 kg/hectare (1800-2200 lbs/acre)
Growth Rate	Very high
Resistant to	Resistant to verticillium wilt
Susceptible to	Moderately susceptible to downy mildew
Storability	Retains 65% alpha acid after 6 months storage at 20°C (68°F)
Ease of Harvest	
Total Oil	0.82 mL/100g
Myrcene Oil	47%
Humulene Oil	26%
Caryophyllene Oil	7%
Farnesene Oil	Trace Amounts
Substitutes	Liberty, Mount Hood, Hallertau, Ultra, Strisselspalter, Hersbrucker
Style Guide	Bitter, Pilsner, Light Lager, Golden Ale, Nut Brown Ale, Pale Ale, India Pale Ale, Stout, Chocolate Stout, American Lager

References

http://beerlegends.com/crystal-hops
http://www.ars.usda.gov/SP2UserFiles/person/2450/hopcultivars/21490.html

Czech Premiant

Premiant, meaning prized or prizewinning, is moderately bittering with a low cohumulone ratio. This makes it an ideal neutral bittering agent, especially for Pilsners. Released in 1996, it is a descendant of Northern Brewer and often employed by brewers in Belgian Pilsners and is also well suited to Belgian, French and German Ales as well. This versatility is perhaps one reason that breweries dabbling in Czech or Belgian styles have a strong preference for Premiant.

Homebrewer's Comments

> Homebrewing Czech beer has been a real challenge.. I've recently had fantastic results though with using 1 oz of Czech Premiant hops. Very neutral and slightly spicy, other Czech beers use it as a bittering hop such as Zatec Bright Lager. *(1Pivoman via northernbrewer.com)*

Also Known As	
Characteristics	Neutral bittering, slightly spicy
Purpose	Aroma
Alpha Acid Composition	8%-12.5%
Beta Acid Composition	4.5%-8%
Cohumulone Composition	22%-23%
Country	Czech Republic
Cone Size	
Cone Density	
Seasonal Maturity	Early
Yield Amount	2000-2300 kg/hectare (1784-2052 lbs/acre)
Growth Rate	
Resistant to	Tolerant to downy and powdery mildew
Susceptible to	
Storability	
Ease of Harvest	
Total Oil	1.1-1.8 mL/100g

Myrcene Oil	35%-50%
Humulene Oil	25%-35%
Caryophyllene Oil	7%-13%
Farnesene Oil	1%-1.5%
Substitutes	
Style Guide	Pilsner, Ale, Pale Ale, Belgian Ales, Belgian Pilsners

References

http://www.hopsteiner.de/info/nc/en/pdf/hop-variety-finder/variety-information/sdb/premiant-1.html?filename=Premiant.pdf

http://hopsteiner.com/wp-content/uploads/2014/03/Premiant.pdf

Dana

Dana, or Extra Styrian Dana as it is often known, is a Slovenian hop bred from a German Hallertau Magnum and a wild Slovenian male. A product of the Institute of Hop Research in Zalec, Solvenia, it is said to feature quality and harmonious bittering properties alongside a slightly floral and citrus flavor profile.

Also Known As	Styrian Dana, Ekstra Styrian Dana, Extra Styrian Dana
Characteristics	Subtle floral and citrus flavors
Purpose	Bittering & Aroma
Alpha Acid Composition	11%-16%
Beta Acid Composition	4%-6%
Cohumulone Composition	28%-31%
Country	Slovenia
Cone Size	Medium
Cone Density	
Seasonal Maturity	
Yield Amount	
Growth Rate	
Resistant to	

Susceptible to	
Storability	
Ease of Harvest	
Total Oil	2.4-3.9 mL/100g
Myrcene Oil	50%-59%
Humulene Oil	15%-21.6%
Caryophyllene Oil	5.7%-7.6%
Farnesene Oil	6.9%-8.7%
Substitutes	
Style Guide	India Pale Ale

References
http://www.hopsdirect.com/dana-pellets/
http://www.hmezad.si/hops/hop-varieties/ekstra-styrian-dana
http://stravale.com/2013/04/14/47/

Defender

Defender has an interesting heritage. Bred from a New Mexico Wild American female, Eastwell Golding and other English hops it was selected in the early 1960's by Dr R. A. Neve at Wye College in England. Despite its significant humulene and farnesene content, Defender's very low alpha percentage and low yield potential has significantly hindered its commercial viability. It may show promise in breeding though with a promisingly high alpha to beta ratio. It is said to impart a pleasant, European-style aroma.

Also Known As	
Characteristics	Pleasant, European-style aroma
Purpose	Aroma
Alpha Acid Composition	3.3%-6%
Beta Acid Composition	1.1%-2.5%
Cohumulone Composition	27%
Country	UK
Cone Size	

Cone Density	
Seasonal Maturity	Early
Yield Amount	1120-1340 kg/hectare (1000-1200 lbs/acre)
Growth Rate	Moderate
Resistant to	Moderately resistant to downy mildew and resistant to verticillium wilt
Susceptible to	
Storability	Retains 59% alpha acid after 6 months storage at 20ºC (68ºF)
Ease of Harvest	
Total Oil	0.5 mL/100g
Myrcene Oil	31%
Humulene Oil	35%
Caryophyllene Oil	14%
Farnesene Oil	3.7%
Substitutes	Density
Style Guide	

References

http://www.ars.usda.gov/SP2UserFiles/person/2450/hopcultivars/62053.html

Delta

Released in 2009, aroma variety Delta is a relatively new kid on the block. It is a Fuggle-type hop, similar to a Willamette, but with a kick. It features a mild and pleasantly spicy aroma of with notes of melon and citrus. Delta is considered ideal for ale finishing.

Hopsteiner first offered Delta to Boston's Harpoon Brewery as a cross between an English-style Fuggle and a Cascade derived male. Harpoon brewed it into an English-style single hop ESB. Delta has a much more emphatic flavor than its Fuggle parent—a truly American punch.

Homebrewer's Comments

I just brewed up a special bitter with these in three weeks ago. I bottled it two weeks ago and will be serving to guests this weekend. I am VERY happy with the character I got from the hop. It's very subdued but nice. I used 1oz at 20 min and then another .5oz at 5 min. I did not dry hop the beer, but it's a nice brew. *(smokinghole via homebrewtalk.com)*

Also Known As	Hopsteiner 04188
Characteristics	Spicy with notes of melon and citrus
Purpose	Aroma
Alpha Acid Composition	5.5%-7%
Beta Acid Composition	5.5%-7%
Cohumulone Composition	22%-24%
Country	US
Cone Size	
Cone Density	
Seasonal Maturity	Early to mid
Yield Amount	1600-2000 kg/hectare (1400-1800 lbs/acre)
Growth Rate	
Resistant to	Resistant to downy mildew
Susceptible to	Susceptible to powdery mildew
Storability	Retains 80%-90% alpha acid after 6 months storage at 20ºC (68ºF)
Ease of Harvest	
Total Oil	0.5-1.1 mL/100g
Myrcene Oil	25%-40%
Humulene Oil	25%-35%
Caryophyllene Oil	9%-15%
Farnesene Oil	0%-1%
Substitutes	Cascade, Delta, Nelson Sauvin, Fuggle, Willamette

References
http://hopsteiner.com/wp-content/uploads/vpdf/Delta.pdf
http://www.usahops.org/graphics/File/HGA%20BCI%20Reports/Variety%20Manual%207-24-12.pdf

Density

Density shares the same interesting heritage as its sibling, Defender. Selected by Dr R. A. Neve at Wye College in England, Density was born as a cross from a New Mexico Wild American female hop, Eastwell Golding and other English hops. However, its very low alpha content and low yield potential has caused it to be discontinued from commercial production in England. Like it's sibling, it is said to also feature a pleasant, European-style aroma.

Also Known As	
Characteristics	
Purpose	Aroma
Alpha Acid Composition	4.4%-6.6%
Beta Acid Composition	3.3%
Cohumulone Composition	36%
Country	UK
Cone Size	Small to medium
Cone Density	
Seasonal Maturity	Mid
Yield Amount	1120-1570 kg/hectare (1000-1400 lbs/acre)
Growth Rate	Moderate to high
Resistant to	Resistant to verticillium wilt
Susceptible to	Susceptible to downy mildew
Storability	Retains 72% alpha acid after 6 months storage at 20ºC (68ºF)
Ease of Harvest	

Total Oil	0.44 mL/100g
Myrcene Oil	57%
Humulene Oil	17%
Caryophyllene Oil	7%
Farnesene Oil	0.3%
Substitutes	Defender
Style Guide	

References
http://www.ars.usda.gov/SP2UserFiles/person/2450/hopcultivars/62052.html

Dr Rudi

Originally known as Super Alpha, the variety was renamed to Dr Rudi in 2012. It was bred from New Zealand Smooth Cone and is largely grown in New Zealand. It was originally released in 1976.

Originally considered a bittering hop, Dr Rudi is now widely regarded as dual-use and features a grassy, piney, citrus character. It is also well known for its clean and crisp bittering despite its high cohumulone content. Works well in single-hopped beers.

Homebrewer's Comments

I made an 'Oceanic' IPA double batch and dry hopped with Dr Rudi for 5 days, a whole 135g of it. I used Topaz during the boil at 60, 30 ,5 and 0 to a 58 IBU target. It was a great beer, very punchy with a 11.8 kg grain bill and I used crystal 60 and a lick of carapils, with a mash temperature at 67. There was so much going on in that beer it was hard to discern the dry hop impact with specific flavours though independent palates picked out passionfruit as well as grapefruit with usual citrus undertones. The aroma was incredible, but perhaps my grain bill dominated the flavour profile a bit much. (*Goose via aussiehomebrewer.com*)

I've dry hopped with it in a dark ale and found it [quite] clean. (*Midnight Brew via aussiehomebrewer.com*)

Also Known As	SuperAlpha
Characteristics	Grass, pine and citrus flavors
Purpose	Bittering & Aroma
Alpha Acid Composition	10%-12%
Beta Acid Composition	7%-8.5%
Cohumulone Composition	36%-39%
Country	New Zealand
Cone Size	Medium
Cone Density	Compact
Seasonal Maturity	Early to mid
Yield Amount	1940-1940 kg/hectare (1730-1730 lbs/acre)
Growth Rate	Moderate to high
Resistant to	
Susceptible to	
Storability	Retains 60%-70% alpha acid after 6 months storage at 20ºC (68ºF)
Ease of Harvest	Difficult
Total Oil	1.3-1.6 mL/100g
Myrcene Oil	29%-48%
Humulene Oil	22%-33%
Caryophyllene Oil	6%-10%
Farnesene Oil	0%-1%
Substitutes	Green Bullet
Style Guide	Lager, India Pale Ale

References

http://beerlegends.com/super-alpha-hops
https://bsgcraftbrewing.com/dr-rudi-super-alpha
https://ychhops.com/varieties/dr-rudi
http://www.nzhops.co.nz/variety/dr-rudi
https://www.craftbrewer.com.au/shop/details.asp?PID=592

Dunav

Originating in the former Yugoslavia, Dunav was bred in the 1960's with the intent of replacing the low-yielding Backa. However, it has never truly been accepted commercially and remains in limited production in Serbia. It is a triploid cross from Northern Brewer, Styrian Golding and a wild male. Sibling to Neoplanta and Vojvodina, Dunav tends to exhibit a variable alpha acid rate but enjoys good storage stability.

Also Known As	
Characteristics	
Purpose	Aroma
Alpha Acid Composition	5.1%-9.6%
Beta Acid Composition	2.8%-4.6%
Cohumulone Composition	30%
Country	Serbia
Cone Size	
Cone Density	
Seasonal Maturity	Late
Yield Amount	1565 kg/hectare (1400 lbs/acre)
Growth Rate	Very high
Resistant to	Moderately resistant to downy mildew
Susceptible to	
Storability	Retains 74% alpha acid after 6 months storage at 20°C (68°F)
Ease of Harvest	
Total Oil	1.19 mL/100g
Myrcene Oil	19%
Humulene Oil	19%
Caryophyllene Oil	6%
Farnesene Oil	6.2%
Substitutes	
Style Guide	

References

http://www.ars.usda.gov/SP2UserFiles/person/2450/hopchem/21081.html

Early Bird

Early Bird, or Amos's Early Bird as it was formerly known, is a Goldings variety and considered one of England's premier aroma hops. While not terribly disease and wilt tolerant, it is bred for its immensely pleasing aroma and gentle hoppiness.

Discovered in 1887 by Alfred Amos, the owner of Spring Grove farm in Wye, Early Bird was hand-selected from a field of Bramlings. Early Bird can definitely be a go-to hop when a delicate aroma is required. Commercially it has been featured by Britain's oldest brewer, Shepherd Neame in their gently bitter and lightly malted Early Bird Spring Hop Ale.

Also Known As	Amos's Early Bird
Characteristics	Pleasing, delicate aroma
Purpose	Aroma
Alpha Acid Composition	4.4%-6.7%
Beta Acid Composition	1.9%-2.8%
Cohumulone Composition	26%-32%
Country	UK
Cone Size	Medium
Cone Density	
Seasonal Maturity	Early
Yield Amount	1500-2000 kg/hectare (1340-1780 lbs/acre)
Growth Rate	Moderate to high
Resistant to	
Susceptible to	Susceptible to wilt, downy mildew and powdery mildew
Storability	
Ease of Harvest	

Total Oil	0.8 mL/100g
Myrcene Oil	
Humulene Oil	
Caryophyllene Oil	
Farnesene Oil	
Substitutes	Kent Golding, Cobb, Bramling Cross
Style Guide	India Pale Ale, Ales

References
http://www.willingham-nurseries.co.uk/hops/earlyb.html

Early Green

Developed in the UK, Early Green arrived in the US in the early 1930's. To this day, little analytical data can be found on the variety. Despite gaining almost no traction as a brewing hop in its own right, it was chosen as a parent in the breeding of many classic varieties like Crystal, Horizon, Nugget and Mount Hood, among others.

Also Known As	
Characteristics	
Purpose	Aroma
Alpha Acid Composition	
Beta Acid Composition	
Cohumulone Composition	
Country	UK
Cone Size	
Cone Density	
Seasonal Maturity	
Yield Amount	
Growth Rate	
Resistant to	
Susceptible to	
Storability	

Ease of Harvest

Total Oil

Myrcene Oil

Humulene Oil

Caryophyllene Oil

Farnesene Oil

Substitutes

Style Guide

References

http://inhoppursuit.blogspot.com.au/2010/02/hop-talk-with-hopmeister-al-haunold-buy.html

http://www.homebrewstuff.com/hop-profiles

http://agales.com/?page_id=69

Early Prolific

Originating from Wye College in England, Early Prolific has a pleasant continental-style aroma but is not currently produced commercially as a result of its poor growth rate and lackluster yield. It received USDA accession in 1980. Despite having little commercial impact as a brewing variety, Early Prolific may however exhibit some breeding potential on the basis of its aromatic characteristics and impressive storage stability.

Also Known As	
Characteristics	Pleasant continental-style aroma
Purpose	Aroma
Alpha Acid Composition	4.7%
Beta Acid Composition	2.2%
Cohumulone Composition	23%
Country	UK
Cone Size	
Cone Density	
Seasonal Maturity	Early
Yield Amount	560-670 kg/hectare (500-600 lbs/acre)
Growth Rate	Low to moderate

Resistant to	Moderately resistant to downy mildew
Susceptible to	
Storability	Retains 80% alpha acid after 6 months storage at 20ºC (68ºF)
Ease of Harvest	
Total Oil	0.5 mL/100g
Myrcene Oil	<50%
Humulene Oil	21.2%
Caryophyllene Oil	7%
Farnesene Oil	4.6%
Substitutes	
Style Guide	

References
http://www.freshops.com/hops/usda-named-hop-variety-descriptions#usda_id_21276
http://www.ars.usda.gov/SP2UserFiles/person/2450/hopcultivars/21276.html

Early Promise

Early Promise was originally selected at Wye College, England, most likely from an old English variety through mass selection. Though originally slated for use as an aroma hop in the US, its poor yield in its USDA Corvallis plot eventually led to its discontinuation as a commercial prospect. Like Early Prolific, Early Promise may be useful for breeding aroma hops with a continental-style aroma.

Also Known As	
Characteristics	Continental-style aroma
Purpose	Aroma
Alpha Acid Composition	6.1%
Beta Acid Composition	1.7%
Cohumulone Composition	30%
Country	UK
Cone Size	

Cone Density	
Seasonal Maturity	Early
Yield Amount	670-900 kg/hectare (600-800 lbs/acre)
Growth Rate	Low to moderate
Resistant to	Moderately resistant to downy mildew
Susceptible to	Susceptible to powdery mildew
Storability	
Ease of Harvest	
Total Oil	0.5 mL/100g
Myrcene Oil	<42%
Humulene Oil	18.4%
Caryophyllene Oil	
Farnesene Oil	
Substitutes	
Style Guide	

References

http://www.freshops.com/hops/usda-named-hop-variety-descriptions#usda_id_21277

http://www.ars.usda.gov/SP2UserFiles/person/2450/hopcultivars/21277.html

East Kent Golding

East Kent Golding is often thought of as the ultimate English hop. Grown exclusively in Kent, England and descended from Canterbury Whitebine, it is a centuries old variety. Despite claims to the contrary, it is identical to Canterbury Golding. The two names have been used interchangeably for some time with the confusion likely stemming from its namesake. Canterbury is a town in East Kent and the hop was first brought to market there in 1790. Some, however, charge to this day that East Kent Golding and Cantebury Golding are two distinct varieties though there is no clear evidence to support this. The variety began to be known exclusively as East Kent Golding in 1838.

It has a good yield in England, but has shown to have an even better yield in Oregon after its introduction there in 1994. It has an amazing aroma profile with lavender, spice, honey and notes of thyme. Flavor-wise it is earthy and mildly bittering with a sweet, silky, honey-like character. East Kent Golding is considered to be the quintessential English hop, long held as one of the island's favorites for ales and pale ales.

Brewmaster's Comments

East Kent Golding is the original hop of the leading style of craft beer, India Pale Ale and is still a great hop after hundreds of years. It's very nostalgic for me, as I "grew up" on British bitters suffused with Fuggle and Golding. Best as a late kettle hop.
(Garrett Oliver, Brewmaster at Brooklyn Brewery)

Also Known As	Kent Golding, EKG, Canterbury Golding
Characteristics	Aromas of lavender, spice, honey, thyme, earthy flavors
Purpose	Aroma
Alpha Acid Composition	5%-6%
Beta Acid Composition	2%-3%
Cohumulone Composition	29%
Country	
Cone Size	Large
Cone Density	Loose
Seasonal Maturity	Early
Yield Amount	640 kg/hectare (570 lbs/acre)
Growth Rate	High
Resistant to	Moderately resistant to downy mildew
Susceptible to	Susceptible to hop mosaic virus
Storability	Retains 78% alpha acid after 6 months storage at 20ºC (68ºF)
Ease of Harvest	
Total Oil	0.85 mL/100g
Myrcene Oil	42%
Humulene Oil	27%
Caryophyllene Oil	9%

Farnesene Oil	0%-1%
Substitutes	Golding (UK), Whitbread Golding, Progress, Fuggle, First Gold
Style Guide	Pale Ale, Extra Special English Ale, English Dark Ale, English Light Ale, Belgian Ale, Christmas Ale

References

http://beerlegends.com/east-kent-golding-hops
http://www.ars.usda.gov/SP2UserFiles/person/2450/hopcultivars/21681.html
http://www.ars.usda.gov/SP2UserFiles/person/2450/hopcultivars/21680.html

Eastern Gold

Eastern Gold is a Super Alpha variety developed in Japan by Kirin Brewing Co. Ltd Hops Research from Kirin No. 2 and OB79, an open-pollinated wild American hop. Despite its yield potential, high alpha acids and storage stability, it seems it is not currently being grown in any significant commercial capacity.

Very little is known about the history of its use and its flavor profile but it was originally bred in a similar vein to Toyomidori and Kitamidori as an effort to replace Kirin No. 2 with a similar, yet higher-alpha variety.

Also Known As	
Characteristics	
Purpose	Bittering
Alpha Acid Composition	11%-14%
Beta Acid Composition	5%-6%
Cohumulone Composition	27%
Country	Japan
Cone Size	
Cone Density	
Seasonal Maturity	Late
Yield Amount	
Growth Rate	Very high

Resistant to	Moderately resistant to downy mildew
Susceptible to	
Storability	Retains 81% alpha acid after 6 months storage at 20ºC (68ºF)
Ease of Harvest	
Total Oil	1.43 mL/100g
Myrcene Oil	42%
Humulene Oil	19%
Caryophyllene Oil	7%-8%
Farnesene Oil	3%
Substitutes	Kirin No. 2, Brewer's Gold
Style Guide	

References

http://www.freshops.com/hops/usda-named-hop-variety-descriptions#usda_id_21678

http://www.ars.usda.gov/SP2UserFiles/person/2450/hopcultivars/21678.html

http://onlinelibrary.wiley.com/store/10.1002/j.2050-0416.2000.tb00052.x/asset/j.2050-0416.2000.tb00052.x.pdf;jsessionid=E3298EDF879F970F4C173E5EEBCEDCFF.f02t03?v=1&t=ijthodjk&s=238e092ab8ada076e9298d0aab52920435a94456

http://www.britishhops.org.uk/wp-content/uploads/2014/08/fact-sheet-press-day.-wye-hops.pdf

Eastern Green

Eastern Green is an aroma variety developed and tested in the 1980's by the Kirin Brewery Co. Ltd. Hop Research Center in Iwate, Japan. It was conceived via an open pollination cross with named parent varietal, Toyomidori. In addition to its high vigor and yield, it is said to have desirable continental-style aroma traits.

Also Known As	
Characteristics	Pleasant continental-style aroma
Purpose	Aroma
Alpha Acid Composition	5.15%
Beta Acid Composition	1.9%-2%
Cohumulone Composition	25.5%

Country	Japan
Cone Size	
Cone Density	
Seasonal Maturity	Mid to late
Yield Amount	2110 kg/hectare (1875 lbs/acre)
Growth Rate	Very high
Resistant to	
Susceptible to	
Storability	Retains 83% alpha acid after 6 months storage at 20ºC (68ºF)
Ease of Harvest	
Total Oil	0.45mL/100g
Myrcene Oil	25%
Humulene Oil	25%
Caryophyllene Oil	8%
Farnesene Oil	4.9%-5%
Substitutes	
Style Guide	

References
http://www.ars.usda.gov/SP2UserFiles/person/2450/hopchem/21700.html
http://allgrain.beer/hops/eastern-green/

Eastwell Golding

Created via clonal selection in 1889 in Kent, England, Eastwell Golding is one of the many varieties of Golding aroma hops. Exhibiting a typical English hop aroma, it is currently in demand for copper and dry hopping and usually employed in English and Belgian Ales.

Also Known As	
Characteristics	
Purpose	Aroma
Alpha Acid Composition	6%

Beta Acid Composition	3%
Cohumulone Composition	30%
Country	UK
Cone Size	
Cone Density	
Seasonal Maturity	Mid to late
Yield Amount	810 kg/hectare (720 lbs/acre)
Growth Rate	
Resistant to	Tolerant of verticillium wilt
Susceptible to	Moderately susceptible to downy mildew
Storability	Retains 70% alpha acid after 6 months storage at 20ºC (68ºF)
Ease of Harvest	
Total Oil	1.50 mL/100g
Myrcene Oil	50%
Humulene Oil	25%
Caryophyllene Oil	8%
Farnesene Oil	0.2%
Substitutes	Pentham Golding
Style Guide	English Ales, Belgian Ales

References

http://www.freshops.com/hops/usda-named-hop-variety-descriptions#usda_id_21669
https://books.google.com.au/books?id=oWQdjnVo2B0C&pg=PA316&lpg=PA316&dq=%2
2eastwell+golding%22&source=bl&ots=wmP6dQUiF-
&sig=7Cr2Gt7H3SHFvRhfLWHG7t9BIoc&hl=en&sa=X&ved=0CEUQ6AEwCGoVChMIlI
mV1L7kyAIVwSemCh2OQwob#v=onepage&q=%22eastwell%20golding%22&f=false

El Dorado®

El Dorado® is a relatively new kid on the block. Created by Moxee Valley-based CLS Farms, LLC in 2008, it was released to the public in 2010. A product of the Yakima Valley's cooler climate, it features a uniquely fruity flavor profile in addition to desirable bittering and aromatic properties.

High vigor, high alpha acids, lots of oils and resins, good storage stability and an exceptional yield also make this, on paper at least, an outstanding commercial variety. It exhibits bold tropical fruit flavors, said to be reminiscent of pineapple and mango, in addition to a resinous back note. On the nose, it imbues aromas of pear, watermelon, stone fruits and even candy. To date, it has seen use in wheat beers, Pale Ales and IPA's.

Homebrewer's Comments

My Cascade/Centennial/El Dorado IPA has now reached maturity. I used an even mix of each, with summit for bittering, for about 10 oz of hops overall. Against the background of Cascade and Centennial, the El Dorado is definitely noticeable. But I wouldn't say that this has the same "holy crap" kind of tropical fruit impression I would get from 3 oz of Citra. There is a much more subtle note, especially on the nose, where I feel Citra can be extreme. Anyway, it's a good hop and a good combination. I think I'd like to try an all-Dorado APA at some point to get a purer idea. (*motorneuron via homebrewtalk.com*)

I did a SMaSH brew with El Dorado last fall. Very good flavor and aroma, not so strong on bittering -- even with the high AA content. If you're looking for a hoppy IPA, maybe throw in some neutral bittering hops like Magnum or Northern Brewer and then pile in more of the El Dorado at the 5 minute or steeping steps. This should give you a real full melon/tropical fruit aroma and flavors while giving you a strong bittering finish. (*Oginme via homebrewtalk.com*)

Also Known As	
Characteristics	Flavors of tropical fruit, pineapple, mango. Aromas of pear, watermelon, stone fruit and candy.
Purpose	Bittering & Aroma
Alpha Acid Composition	13%-17%
Beta Acid Composition	7%-8%
Cohumulone Composition	28%-33%
Country	US
Cone Size	

Cone Density	
Seasonal Maturity	
Yield Amount	2650-2880 kg/hectare (2300-2500 lbs/acre)
Growth Rate	
Resistant to	
Susceptible to	
Storability	Retains 60%-75% alpha acid after 6 months storage at 20°C (68°F)
Ease of Harvest	
Total Oil	2.50-3.3 mL/100g
Myrcene Oil	55%-60%
Humulene Oil	10%-15%
Caryophyllene Oil	6%-8%
Farnesene Oil	0.1%
Substitutes	Galena, Simcoe®
Style Guide	Wheat, India Pale Ale

References

http://www.usahops.org/graphics/File/HGA%20BCI%20Reports/Variety%20Manual%207-24-12.pdf

http://clsfarms.com/hops.php

http://brooklynbrewshop.com/themash/hop-of-the-month-el-dorado/

Ella

Ella™ hops, formally known as Stella, is an Australian aroma variety. It is half-sister to Galaxy® and the progeny of Spalt and a tetraploid female and was developed in the state of Victoria in the early 2000's. By 2007, Ella™ was ready for release in brewing trials. An immediate hit, the variety was fast-tracked into commercial production.

Due to its high level of oils, Ella™ can significantly change character depending on how it is utilized. When used in low quantities, it displays a spicy, floral character like star anise. When used in greater quantities or in dry hopping, it holds its own with any robust malt and conveys a decided tropical and grapefruit flavor.

Homebrewer's Comments

Ella is generally a milder hop overall and I haven't really ever gotten grapefruit from it. Maybe grape or plum are comparable fruits. Try it solo in a pale ale, or even better in a strong stout at 15 minutes to get that sharp anise aspect. *(wileaway via homebrewtalk.com)*

Also Known As	Stella
Characteristics	Tropical flavors, grapefruit, star anise
Purpose	Aroma
Alpha Acid Composition	13.3%-16.3%
Beta Acid Composition	4.8%-7.8%
Cohumulone Composition	34% - 38%
Country	Australia
Cone Size	
Cone Density	Compact
Seasonal Maturity	Late
Yield Amount	
Growth Rate	
Resistant to	
Susceptible to	
Storability	
Ease of Harvest	
Total Oil	2.4-3.4 mL/100g
Myrcene Oil	40%-50%
Humulene Oil	16%-22%
Caryophyllene Oil	12%-18%
Farnesene Oil	0%-1%
Substitutes	
Style Guide	Lager, Pilsner, Pale Ale, Stout

References

https://bellsbeer.com/store/products/Ella-%28AU%29-Hops-%252d-1-lb-Pellets.html

http://www.hops.com.au/products/ella-

Elsaesser

The Elsaesser's commercial production is confined to very limited acreage in the Alsace region of France. It most likely originated from an old land race in the same area. Elsaesser has an aroma akin to that of noble European varieties. Charlemagne's father, Peppin the Younger, was said to have had a hops garden in the 7th century. Even though the use of hops in beer isn't recorded until the 9th century, perhaps todays Elsaesser hops are a descendant of the same variety that graced that very garden.

Also Known As	Elsasser
Characteristics	European noble aroma
Purpose	Aroma
Alpha Acid Composition	4.65%
Beta Acid Composition	5.78%
Cohumulone Composition	20%-30%
Country	France
Cone Size	
Cone Density	
Seasonal Maturity	Early
Yield Amount	810 kg/hectare (720 lbs/acre)
Growth Rate	Low
Resistant to	Moderately resistant to downy mildew
Susceptible to	
Storability	Retains 63% alpha acid after 6 months storage at 20ºC (68ºF)
Ease of Harvest	
Total Oil	0.28-1.13 mL/100g
Myrcene Oil	38%
Humulene Oil	32%
Caryophyllene Oil	116.3%

Farnesene Oil	1.7%
Substitutes	
Style Guide	

References
http://www.ars.usda.gov/SP2UserFiles/person/2450/hopcultivars/21170.html
https://nl.wikipedia.org/wiki/Elsasser

Equinox

Developed by The Hop Breeding Company, a joint venture between John I Haas and the Select Botanicals Group, Equinox is a distinctive aroma hop. Planted originally in Toppenish, Washington and officially unveiled in 2014, its use is said to bring with it notes of lemon and lime citrus, fruits like papaya and apple as well as green peppers and herbs.

Homebrewer's Comments

I just brewed a single hop IPA with equinox. Love that hop! Grapefruity citrus, a little tropical fruit, a little bit of spice. *(singybrue via homebrewtalk.com)*

Equinox have this green, raw vegetable (think raw zucchini, celery), fresh herbs component that would work well with other hops like mosaic or simcoe. *(fab80 via homebrewtalk.com)*

Also Known As	HBC 366 Cv.
Characteristics	Notes of lemon and lime citrus, fruits like papaya and apple, green peppers and herbs
Purpose	Aroma
Alpha Acid Composition	14.5%-15.5%
Beta Acid Composition	4.5%-5.5%
Cohumulone Composition	32%-38%
Country	US
Cone Size	
Cone Density	

Seasonal Maturity	
Yield Amount	
Growth Rate	
Resistant to	
Susceptible to	
Storability	
Ease of Harvest	
Total Oil	2.5-4.5 mL/100g
Myrcene Oil	
Humulene Oil	
Caryophyllene Oil	
Farnesene Oil	
Substitutes	
Style Guide	IPA, American Ale, Pilsner

References

http://www.hopbreeding.com/#q1
http://hopunion.com/Equinox/
http://www.yakimavalleyhops.com/Equinox8oz_p/hopsequinox2-2014crop.htm
http://www.rebelbrewer.com/shop/what-s-new/equinox-hops-1oz-pellets
http://www.northernbrewer.com/equinox-hop-pellets
http://www.craftbrewingbusiness.com/ingredients-supplies/brooklyn-brewmaster-garrett-oliver-explains-hbc-366-hop/
https://ychhops.com/varieties/equinox-brand-hbc-366-cv
http://www.brew-dudes.com/equinox-hops/5604

Eroica

Despite Eroica hops enjoying a high alpha acid percentage, they are, on paper at least, overshadowed by their sister Galena. It appears this comparison is also moving them toward denouement of commercial production along with their cones being considered difficult to harvest and it's susceptibility to Ringspot and Mosaic virus.

Developed by both the Idaho and Oregon Agricultural Experiment Stations in conjunction the USDA, Eroica is directly descended from Brewer's Gold. Though the seedling was selected in 1968, the variety wasn't officially registered until 1982. Flavor-wise, they feature a sharp fruity essence and fortunately can still be obtained for home brewing experimentation.

Homebrewer's Comments

> I got Eroica in a hop sampler and used it in a very hoppy APA due to the high alpha. It came out so nice and I've used it a few times but only for bittering. It might be a bit too much for flavoring. (*HD4Mark via northernbrewer.com*)

Also Known As	
Characteristics	Sharp fruity essence
Purpose	Bittering
Alpha Acid Composition	12.3%
Beta Acid Composition	4.5%
Cohumulone Composition	40%
Country	
Cone Size	Medium
Cone Density	Compact
Seasonal Maturity	Late to very late
Yield Amount	2020-2470 kg/hectare (1800-2200 lbs/acre)
Growth Rate	Very high
Resistant to	Moderately resistant to downy mildew and resistant to verticillium wilt
Susceptible to	Susceptible to prunus necrotic ringspot, apple mosaic virus and hop mosaic virus
Storability	Retains 77% alpha acid after 6 months storage at 20°C (68°F)
Ease of Harvest	Easy
Total Oil	0.8-1.3 mL/100g
Myrcene Oil	55%-65%
Humulene Oil	0%-1%
Caryophyllene Oil	7%-13%
Farnesene Oil	0%-1%

| Substitutes | Bullion, Brewer's Gold, Galena, Glacier |
| Style Guide | Bitter, Pale Ale, Amber Ale, Porter, India Pale Ale |

References
http://beerlegends.com/eroica-hops
https://www.hopunion.com/eroica/
http://www.ars.usda.gov/SP2UserFiles/person/2450/hopcultivars/21183.html

Eureka

With similarities to Simcoe® and Summit™ hops, Eureka is a fairly new variety with very strong bittering qualities and a complex and robust flavor and aroma profile. It is said to impart flavors of citrus, resin, tropical and dark fruit along with aromas of grapefruit rind, citrus and tangerine. It is the progeny of varietals Apollo and Merkur.

Also Known As	EXP #: 05256, Exp Pine Fruit
Characteristics	Falvors of citrus, peach and pine, aromas of stone fruit and mandarin
Purpose	Bittering & Aroma
Alpha Acid Composition	18%-19%
Beta Acid Composition	5%-6%
Cohumulone Composition	27%
Country	
Cone Size	
Cone Density	
Seasonal Maturity	
Yield Amount	
Growth Rate	
Resistant to	
Susceptible to	
Storability	
Ease of Harvest	
Total Oil	3.10 mL/100g

Myrcene Oil	43%
Humulene Oil	29.8%
Caryophyllene Oil	14.2%
Farnesene Oil	0.2%
Substitutes	
Style Guide	Imperial India Pale Ale, India Pale Ale, American Ales, American Red, Saison

References

http://www.vetterbrew.com/uploads/4/9/6/4/49642653/pilot_this!_hop_data.pdf
http://brulosophy.com/2015/08/20/the-hop-chronicles-eureka-aka-experimental-pine-fruit/

Falconer's Flight®

Falconer's Flight® is a proprietary blend of Pacific Northwest hops. These include 7 "C" hops, Cascade, Centennial, Chinook, Citra®, Cluster, Columbus and Crystal in addition to experimental varieties developed by Hopunion LLC.

Launched in 2010, it is considered a dual-purpose blend particularly suited to IPAs, but also Pale Ales and Lagers. Falconer's Flight® is listed has having distinct tropical, floral, lemon and grapefruit attributes.

The blend was named in honor of Glen Hay Falconer, a popular and up-and-coming American professional brewer who tragically passed away in 2002.

Homebrewer's Comments

I'm a fan of Falconer's Flight. Good bittering with a nice blend of citrus and pine for flavor and aroma. It aint no Citra, but its got a nice well rounded Pacific NW style feel to it. I've made a few single hop IPAs with FF and each one has been a winner with me and those I shared them with. I've started using all FF in my Cascadian Dark Ales as well and it fits in perfect with a half pound of Carafa in the grain bill. I usually go with 1 oz at 60 minutes, 1 oz somewhere around 7-15 minutes, 2-2.5 oz whirlpool/hopstand and then 2-2.5 oz dry hop. It starts out with more pine, but soon rounds into shape with the citrus moving

Also Known As	
Characteristics	Distinct tropical, floral, lemon and grapefruit attributes
Purpose	Bittering & Aroma
Alpha Acid Composition	9.5%-12%
Beta Acid Composition	4%-5%
Cohumulone Composition	20%-25%
Country	US
Cone Size	
Cone Density	
Seasonal Maturity	
Yield Amount	
Growth Rate	
Resistant to	
Susceptible to	
Storability	
Ease of Harvest	
Total Oil	1.6-4.6 mL/100g
Myrcene Oil	
Humulene Oil	
Caryophyllene Oil	
Farnesene Oil	
Substitutes	Cascade, Columbus, Centennial Technical
Style Guide	India Pale Ale, Pale Ale, Lager

References

http://www.phillybeerscene.com/2012/04/falconers-flight/
http://www.glenfalconerfoundation.org
https://www.craftbrewer.com.au/shop/details.asp?PID=4271
https://ychhops.com/varieties/falconers-flight

Fantasia

A proprietary blend created by the Barth-Haas group, Fantasia claims to bring a cream and caramel character to your brew. Other observations have suggested that while this might be the case on some level, it has a much more significant profile of fruit and classic European noble characteristics.

Also Known As	
Characteristics	Fruit, noble aromas, cream, caramel
Purpose	Bittering & Aroma
Alpha Acid Composition	4.3%
Beta Acid Composition	
Cohumulone Composition	
Country	
Cone Size	
Cone Density	
Seasonal Maturity	
Yield Amount	
Growth Rate	
Resistant to	
Susceptible to	
Storability	
Ease of Harvest	
Total Oil	0.9 mL/100g
Myrcene Oil	
Humulene Oil	
Caryophyllene Oil	
Farnesene Oil	
Substitutes	
Style Guide	

References

http://www.barthhaasgroup.com/images/pdfs/cp/Fantasia.pdf

Feux-Coeur

Cheekily named Feux-Coeur (aka Feux-Coeur Francais) is an Australian bittering hop with genetic roots in Burgundian France. First harvested in 2010, the breed is considered rare and bred specifically to be grown in the cooler, southern state of Victoria. Unfortunately little has been written about its best utilization or flavor profile at this stage.

Also Known As	Feux-Coeur Francais
Characteristics	
Purpose	Bittering
Alpha Acid Composition	12%-16%
Beta Acid Composition	3.1%-6%
Cohumulone Composition	
Country	Australia
Cone Size	
Cone Density	
Seasonal Maturity	
Yield Amount	
Growth Rate	
Resistant to	
Susceptible to	
Storability	
Ease of Harvest	
Total Oil	
Myrcene Oil	
Humulene Oil	
Caryophyllene Oil	
Farnesene Oil	
Substitutes	
Style Guide	

References

http://www.brewunited.com/hop_database.php

https://en.wikipedia.org/wiki/List_of_hop_varieties#Feux-Coeur_Francais

http://everything.explained.today/List_of_hop_varieties/

https://static1.squarespace.com/static/5121589de4b06840010ad949/t/513e3070e4b07325d70f5abc/1363030128128/HopBook.pdf

First Choice

First Choice is a New Zealand variety that was grown commercially for 20 years between the 1960s and the 1980s. It is no longer in commercial production, likely a result of its low alpha content. It was selected by Dr R.H.J. Roborgh at the Riwaka Research Station, much like its parent, California Cluster. It possesses high yield and growth potential but little is known about its flavor and aroma profile.

Also Known As	
Characteristics	
Purpose	Aroma
Alpha Acid Composition	4.8%-6.7%
Beta Acid Composition	3.5%-6.7%
Cohumulone Composition	39%
Country	New Zealand
Cone Size	
Cone Density	
Seasonal Maturity	Late
Yield Amount	900-1570 kg/hectare (800-1400 lbs/acre)
Growth Rate	
Resistant to	
Susceptible to	Moderately susceptible to downy mildew
Storability	Retains 74% alpha acid after 6 months storage at 20°C (68°F)
Ease of Harvest	
Total Oil	0.51-1.25 mL/100g
Myrcene Oil	71%

Humulene Oil	1%
Caryophyllene Oil	1.3%
Farnesene Oil	
Substitutes	
Style Guide	

References
https://www.freshops.com/hops/usda-named-hop-variety-descriptions#usda_id_66055

First Gold

First Gold is a Golding variety, bred from Whitbread Golding and a dwarf variety at Wye College in England. It was released in 1996 and has the distinction of being England's first hedgerow hop. For brewers, it is useful in just about any style.

Exceptionally versatile, First Gold can be added at any point in the boil in addition to dry hopping. It features a sweet tangerine and orange aroma with a trace of cinnamon. Its flavor is considered floral and fruity, like marmalade and magnolia.

Homebrewer's Comments

I use them for bittering in nearly all my British type beers, they are quite like goldings. *(enderwig via homebrewtalk.com)*

Also Known As	
Characteristics	Tangerine, orange, cinnamon aroma, marmalade flavors
Purpose	Bittering & Aroma
Alpha Acid Composition	5.6%-9.3%
Beta Acid Composition	2.3%-4.1%
Cohumulone Composition	31%-36%
Country	UK
Cone Size	Medium to large
Cone Density	Moderate to compact

Seasonal Maturity	Mid
Yield Amount	1100-1700 kg/hectare (980-1500 lbs/acre)
Growth Rate	Moderate
Resistant to	Resistant to powdery mildew and verticillium wilt
Susceptible to	Susceptible to downy mildew
Storability	Retains 80%-85% alpha acid after 6 months storage at 20ºC (68ºF)
Ease of Harvest	Difficult
Total Oil	0.7-1.5 mL/100g
Myrcene Oil	24%-28%
Humulene Oil	20%-24%
Caryophyllene Oil	6%-7%
Farnesene Oil	2%-4%
Substitutes	Willamette, East Kent Golding, Styrian Golding
Style Guide	Porter, English Bitter, Wheat Beer, Celtic Ale, Summer Ale, Amber Ale, Dark Amber Ale, India Pale Ale, Imperial India Pale Ale

References

https://ychhops.com/varieties/first-gold
http://www.britishhops.org.uk/first-gold-class-tall/
https://www.craftbrewer.com.au/shop/details.asp?PID=840
http://www.charlesfaram.co.uk/hop-varieties/first-gold/
http://beerlegends.com/first-gold-hops

Fuggle

The Fuggle hop originates in England and was first discovered in 1861 in a hop yard owned by George Stace in Kent. Some 14 years later it was officially named and introduced by Richard Fuggle of Benchley in 1875. Similar to a Styrian Golding, is noted for its distinct European aroma and has enjoyed a long, versatile run. At its peak nearly 100 years ago Fuggle was known as a dual-use hop. Today however, as other higher alpha acid varieties have become more prevalent, it's now more prominently used for its aroma.

Homebrewer's Comments

UK Fuggle is good for English pale ales, flavor hops for American apa's, bitters, brown ales, most European beers and a slew of other ales. *(lumpher via homebrewtalk.com)*

Fuggle is my favorite hop along with East Kent Goldings. I love the earthy smell and the great flavor of Fuggle. It pairs really well with EKG which is floral so I will often use a 50/50 mix of them. *(bradsul via homebrewtalk.com)*

Also Known As	
Characteristics	
Purpose	Aroma
Alpha Acid Composition	2.4%-6.1%
Beta Acid Composition	2.1%-2.8%
Cohumulone Composition	25%-29%
Country	UK
Cone Size	
Cone Density	
Seasonal Maturity	Early
Yield Amount	1008-1233 kg/hectare (900-1100 lbs/acre)
Growth Rate	Low to moderate
Resistant to	Resistant to downy mildew
Susceptible to	Moderately susceptible to verticillium wilt, carries the apple and cherry strain of Prunus Necrotic Ringspot virus and the Hop Mosaic virus
Storability	Retains 75% alpha acid after 6 months storage at 20°C (68°F)
Ease of Harvest	
Total Oil	0.44-0.83 mL/100g
Myrcene Oil	43.4%
Humulene Oil	26.6%

Caryophyllene Oil	9.1%
Farnesene Oil	4.3%
Substitutes	Fuggle (US), Willamette, Styrian Golding, Tettnanger, Newport
Style Guide	English Ale, Porter, Mild Ale, Bitter, Extra Special Bitter, Lambic, Amber Ale, Cask Ale, Stout, Oatmeal Stout, Strong Ale, Nut Brown Ale, Golden Ale, Christmas Ale

References

http://beerlegends.com/fuggle-uk-hops
https://www.freshops.com/hops/usda-named-hop-variety-descriptions#usda_id_19209

Fuggle (US)

Fuggle (US) has slightly less aroma impact than its English counterpart. Grown at first in Oregon and now in Washington, it features a more balanced oil profile and higher alpha acid content than the original UK variety giving it a fruitier flavor profile. In commercial circles, it has now largely been replaced by Willamette.

Homebrewer's Comments

> I have made some pretty good milds and bitters with US Fuggles. Definitely not as spicy and earthy, but in a pinch, they make a good beer. Willamette is also good, though UK Fuggles and EKG are really the best. (bierhaus15 via *homebrewtalk.com*)

Also Known As	US Fuggle
Characteristics	
Purpose	Aroma
Alpha Acid Composition	4%-5.5%
Beta Acid Composition	1.5%-2%
Cohumulone Composition	25%-33%
Country	US
Cone Size	Small
Cone Density	Moderate to compact

Seasonal Maturity	Early
Yield Amount	1070-1600 kg/hectare (955-1420 lbs/acre)
Growth Rate	Moderate
Resistant to	Resistant to downy mildew and prunus necrotic ring-spot virus
Susceptible to	
Storability	Retains 60%-65% alpha acid after 6 months storage at 20ºC (68ºF)
Ease of Harvest	
Total Oil	0.7-1.4 mL/100g
Myrcene Oil	24%-28%
Humulene Oil	35%-40%
Caryophyllene Oil	11%-13%
Farnesene Oil	4%-5%
Substitutes	Fuggle, Willamette, Styrian Golding, Tettnanger (GR)
Style Guide	English Pale Ale, Belgian India Pale Ale, Extra Special Bitter, Brown Ale, Red Ale

References
http://beerlegends.com/fuggle-us-hops

Fuggle H

Fuggle H is one of several Fuggle hybrids. Selected in 1961 at Corvallis, Oregon, from the original Fuggle, it carries the same alpha acids content as Fuggle (US) and is known to bear a robust woody and fruity aroma. With the announcement in 1997 that Anheiser Beusch was phasing out Fuggle, production in the US has declined.

Also Known As	
Characteristics	Robust woody and fruity aroma
Purpose	Aroma
Alpha Acid Composition	4.1%-7.7%
Beta Acid Composition	2.1%-3.9%

Cohumulone Composition	26%
Country	
Cone Size	
Cone Density	
Seasonal Maturity	Early
Yield Amount	1120-1570 kg/hectare (1000-1400 lbs/acre)
Growth Rate	Poor to moderate
Resistant to	Resistant to downy mildew
Susceptible to	Moderately susceptible to Verticillium wilt
Storability	Retains 73% alpha acid after 6 months storage at 20°C (68°F)
Ease of Harvest	
Total Oil	0.41-1.89 mL/100g
Myrcene Oil	47%
Humulene Oil	24%
Caryophyllene Oil	8.1%
Farnesene Oil	4.1%
Substitutes	
Style Guide	Stout, English Pale Ale, Belgian India Pale Ale, Extra Special Bitter, Brown Ale, Red Ale

References

http://www.ars.usda.gov/SP2UserFiles/person/2450/hopcultivars/48209.html

Fuggle N

Fuggle N is a clonal selection from the original Fuggle. It was selected in 1943 as part of a trial that began in 1931 at the East Malling Research Station. It is not produced commercially; rather it is used for breeding.

Also Known As

Characteristics	
Purpose	Aroma, Breeding
Alpha Acid Composition	5.6%
Beta Acid Composition	3%
Cohumulone Composition	26.4%
Country	UK
Cone Size	
Cone Density	
Seasonal Maturity	
Yield Amount	974 kg/hectare (869 lbs/acre)
Growth Rate	
Resistant to	Resistant to downy mildew
Susceptible to	
Storability	Retains 72% alpha acid after 6 months storage at 20°C (68°F)
Ease of Harvest	
Total Oil	0.95 mL/100g
Myrcene Oil	48%
Humulene Oil	24%
Caryophyllene Oil	8%
Farnesene Oil	4.2%
Substitutes	
Style Guide	

References

http://www.ars-grin.gov/npgs/pi_books/scans/200pt3/pi200pt3_526.pdf

https://books.google.com.au/books?id=B2ymbXkJAf4C&pg=PA120&lpg=PA120&dq=%22fuggle+N%22&source=bl&ots=KYXoPI45o5&sig=THqhqJWUyKV3FBJeSR0J6kJLvBg&hl=en&sa=X&ved=0CC4Q6AEwBGoVChMIgZWImtfkyAIVwymmCh01Lg98#v=onepage&q=%22fuggle%20N%22&f=false

https://books.google.com.au/books?id=_H1yBgAAQBAJ&pg=PA199&lpg=PA199&dq=%22fuggle+N%22&source=bl&ots=O9VHVGdClj&sig=x9Lb3hkp5uzGK2wYxo8bHOObYP0&hl=en&sa=X&ved=0CCYQ6AEwAmoVChMIgZWImtfkyAIVwymmCh01Lg98#v=onepage&q=%22fuggle%20N%22&f=false

http://www.ars.usda.gov/SP2UserFiles/person/2450/hopchem/21016.html

Furano Ace

Furano Ace is an aroma hop originally cultivated by Sapporo Brewing Co. Ltd. in the late 1980's. Bred from a mix of Saaz and Brewer's Gold, it has a pleasing European-style aroma but it is no longer grown in any significant commercial capacity. It was primarily grown in an effort to create a Saaz-like aroma variety that would outperform the then common Shinshuwase hops variety.

Also Known As	
Characteristics	European-style aroma
Purpose	Aroma
Alpha Acid Composition	7%-8%
Beta Acid Composition	5%-8%
Cohumulone Composition	21%
Country	Japan
Cone Size	
Cone Density	
Seasonal Maturity	Late
Yield Amount	1040 kg/hectares (925 lbs/acre)
Growth Rate	Very good
Resistant to	Resistant to downy mildew and botrytis
Susceptible to	
Storability	Retains 70% alpha acid after 6 months storage at 20°C (68°F)
Ease of Harvest	
Total Oil	1.53 mL/100g
Myrcene Oil	50%
Humulene Oil	19%
Caryophyllene Oil	7%
Farnesene Oil	12%
Substitutes	
Style Guide	

References

http://www.ars.usda.gov/SP2UserFiles/person/2450/hopcultivars/21701.html

https://books.google.com.au/books?id=fctJLwKUzX4C&pg=PT399&lpg=PT399&dq=furan
o+ace+hops&source=bl&ots=DZt1SU1CrB&sig=lUTP3Tz5x06H7i4yc29n66cyX2c&hl=en
&sa=X&ved=0CEkQ6AEwCWoVChMIs9rI59jmyAIV4yCmCh3p_wa9#v=onepage&q=fura
no%20ace%20hops&f=false

Galaxy®

Descended from German variety Perle, Galaxy® is a unique Australian breed of hops that has the distinction of sporting the highest percentage of essential oils in the industry.

It has an amazing citrus, peach and passionfruit aroma, especially when used as a late addition. The flavor is often quite intense upon production but mellows as it matures. Galaxy® enjoyed her first commercial production in 2009 after nine years of testing and quickly became popular both in Australia and overseas.

Brewmaster's Comments

It's a fantastic hop, full of incredible passionfruit and clean citrus notes. It's pretty important to us as our Pacific Ale is 100% Galaxy, but I love experimenting in other brews too – it's a versatile partner to other hops. The real luxury of GalaxyTM is its intense aromatics and high concentration of alpha acids. It's a solid, reliable, effortless hop to use. You can throw a fair amount into the kettle in the confidence the consistency remains the best. *(Brad Rogers, Assistant Brewmaster at Stone & Wood)*

We've enjoyed brewing with Galaxy since first using it at Goat about six years ago. It's been a component of our flagship Hightail Ale and the star of our recent Fancy Pants can. We find it really emphasizes the citrus, fruity nature of the beers.

Galaxy has a fantastic unique character, boasting heaps of tropical fruit, passionfruit and pineapple notes, and is really versatile to use in with other hops, as well as a standalone ingredient. It's also great to use an Australian-grown hop, helping to support local farmers." *(Dave Bonighton, Head Brewer at Mountain Goat)*

Homebrewer's Comments

I've just done an ESB with all galaxy and am going to dry hop it today with more galaxy. Passionfriut aroma, hell yes! *(Fents via aussiehomebrewer.com)*

This one's a bit weird for me. The first time I used it was from a 2013 harvest and it was very tropical mango. The newer harvests have had the same flavor, but are much more resinous than I remember the first batch I got was. I also noticed this in commercial IPAs that use exclusively Galaxy. Maybe its just my tastebuds though. *(m00ps via email)*

Also Known As	
Characteristics	Citrus, peach and passionfruit aromas
Purpose	Bittering & Aroma
Alpha Acid Composition	11%-16%
Beta Acid Composition	5%-6.9%
Cohumulone Composition	32%-42%
Country	Australia
Cone Size	
Cone Density	
Seasonal Maturity	Mid to late
Yield Amount	
Growth Rate	
Resistant to	
Susceptible to	
Storability	
Ease of Harvest	
Total Oil	3-5 mL/100g
Myrcene Oil	33%-69%
Humulene Oil	1%-2%
Caryophyllene Oil	7%-9%
Farnesene Oil	2%-4%
Substitutes	Citra®, Amarillo®, Centennial

References

http://www.hops.com.au/products/galaxy-

https://www.craftbrewer.com.au/shop/details.asp?PID=1161

https://ychhops.com/varieties/galaxy

https://bsgcraftbrewing.com/galaxy-hop

http://www.hops.com.au/media/W1siZiIsIjIwMTUvMDUvMjEvMTFfMzJfMDJfMTMyXzI
wMTVfSFBBX0dhbGF4eV9Qcm9kdWN0X1NoZWV0LnBkZiJdXQ/2015%20HPA%20Gal
axy%20Product%20Sheet.pdf

Galena

Super alpha Galena has edged out California Cluster as the most widely used bittering hop variety in the US and is also an excellent dual-use hop. It is thought to have ousted Cluster because brewers tend to like Galena's fruitier aroma over Cluster's reputed "cattiness". Super Galena was created to address these concerns.

Galena's flavor profile really kicks with clean and very agreeable notes of citrus. Some brewers have noted its better when boiled in smaller quantities and that later additions bring forth stronger aromas of blackcurrant.

Directly descended from Brewer's Gold, Galena was brought about via open pollination and was officially selected in 1968 by agricultural scientist Richard R. Romanko in the state of Idaho. Commercially, Galena is most noted for it's purported use as the only hop in pale lager, Corona Extra.

Homebrewer's Comments

> I used Galena for bittering in a huge RIS. It seemed quite neutral with some definite resinous qualities to it. It's a fairly clean hop as well. Reminds me of Magnum to a degree. *(brewinhard via thebrewingnetwork.com)*

Also Known As	
Characteristics	Fruity aroma
Purpose	Bittering & Aroma
Alpha Acid Composition	12%
Beta Acid Composition	7.5%
Cohumulone Composition	39%
Country	US
Cone Size	Medium
Cone Density	Compact
Seasonal Maturity	Mid
Yield Amount	1790-2240 kg/hectare (1600-2000 lbs/acre)
Growth Rate	Moderate
Resistant to	Resistant to downy mildew and peronospera
Susceptible to	Susceptible to prunus necrotic ring-spot virus, powdery mildew and aphids
Storability	Retains 75%-80% alpha acid after 6 months storage at 20°C (68°F)
Ease of Harvest	Easy
Total Oil	0.9-1.3 mL/100g
Myrcene Oil	55%-60%
Humulene Oil	10%-15%
Caryophyllene Oil	3%-6%
Farnesene Oil	0%-1%
Substitutes	Nugget, Columbus, Zeus, Chinook, Pride of Ringwood, Eroica, Newport, Cluster, Brewers Gold
Style Guide	Imperial Stout, Stout, India Pale Ale, Barley Wine

References

http://beerlegends.com/galena-hops
http://hopunion.com/galena/
http://www.ars.usda.gov/SP2UserFiles/person/2450/hopcultivars/21182.html

Gargoyle

Gargoyle, along with Ivanhoe, is a new generation of California Cluster and the first to be grown commercially in over half a century. Revived by organic hop farm Hops-Mesiter, LLC near Clearlake, California, it is similar to Ivanhoe but tends more toward a citrusy-mango bouquet.

Homebrewer's Comments

> A gargoyle is a device that funnels water away from vertical stone walls, preventing otherwise rapid erosion due to potentially acidic water sheeting over the stone...I have no idea how this applies to their performance as hops. (*TimpanogosSlim via homebrewtalk.com*)

Also Known As	
Characteristics	Citrusy-mango aroma
Purpose	Aroma
Alpha Acid Composition	7.50%
Beta Acid Composition	
Cohumulone Composition	
Country	US
Cone Size	
Cone Density	
Seasonal Maturity	
Yield Amount	
Growth Rate	
Resistant to	
Susceptible to	
Storability	
Ease of Harvest	
Total Oil	
Myrcene Oil	

Humulene Oil

Caryophyllene Oil

Farnesene Oil

Substitutes   California Cluster, Ivanhoe

Style Guide

References

http://www.hopsmeister.com

http://www.homebrewtalk.com/f39/gargoyle-hops-347692/

Glacier

Developed by Washington State University and released in 2000, Glacier is a high yielding, dual-purpose hop characterized by low cohumulone levels, giving it a moderate and pleasant bitterness. Glacier's aroma and flavor notes are herby, woody and citrusy.

Glacier's popularity in the brewing sector is growing. It is highly suited for IPAs, ESBs and APAs, but has been used in many other styles as well. It is the progeny of Elsasser, Northern Brewer and Brewer's Gold.

Homebrewer's Comments

My Glacier APA is on now. It was a extract brew and finished very high at 1.020. Sweet aroma, not a lot of flavor and dry finish. I think it's a good bittering hop but really needs something extra to carry a whole beer. It's lacking in flavor and aroma. *(Malticulous via homebrewtalk.com)*

I've used glacier a few times, and I'm quite happy with it. I don't think its flavor is as distinctive as Willamette, I'd liken it more to US Goldings. *(gxm via homebrewtalk.com)*

Also Known As

Characteristics   Herbs, wood and citrus

Purpose   Bittering & Aroma

Alpha Acid Composition   3.3%-9.7%

Beta Acid Composition	5.4%-10%
Cohumulone Composition	11%-16%
Country	
Cone Size	Medium
Cone Density	Compact
Seasonal Maturity	Mid
Yield Amount	2400-2600 kg/hectare (2140-2320 lbs/acre)
Growth Rate	Moderate
Resistant to	
Susceptible to	Susceptible to powdery mildew and downy mildew
Storability	Retains 70%-75% alpha acid after 6 months storage at 20°C (68°F)
Ease of Harvest	Easy
Total Oil	0.7-1.6 mL/100g
Myrcene Oil	33%-62%
Humulene Oil	24%-36%
Caryophyllene Oil	7%-13%
Farnesene Oil	0%-1%
Substitutes	Willamette, Fuggle (US), Tettnanger (GR), Golding (US)
Style Guide	Extra Special Bitter, India Pale Ale, Wheat Beer, American Pale Ale

References

http://beerlegends.com/glacier-hops
https://ychhops.com/varieties/glacier

Golden Star

Golden Star is an aroma hop that is commercially grown only in Japan. It is, in essence, a mutant form of Shinshuwase that was selected by Dr. Y. Mori from the Sapporo Brewery some time in the late 1960's or early 1970's. Like many other Japanese varieties, it is the offspring of Saaz and

White Vine conceived through open pollination. It is considered superior to Shinshuwase only because of it's increased yield and improved mildew resistance.

Also Known As	
Characteristics	
Purpose	Aroma
Alpha Acid Composition	5.4%
Beta Acid Composition	4.6%
Cohumulone Composition	50%
Country	Japan
Cone Size	
Cone Density	
Seasonal Maturity	Late
Yield Amount	1790-2240 kg/hectare (1600-2000 lbs/acre)
Growth Rate	Very good
Resistant to	Resistant to downy mildew
Susceptible to	
Storability	Retains 64% alpha acid after 6 months storage at 20ºC (68ºF)
Ease of Harvest	
Total Oil	0.63 mL/100g
Myrcene Oil	57%
Humulene Oil	13%
Caryophyllene Oil	5%
Farnesene Oil	None
Substitutes	
Style Guide	

References

http://www.ars.usda.gov/SP2UserFiles/person/2450/hopcultivars/21039.html

https://books.google.com.au/books?id=_H1yBgAAQBAJ&pg=PA202&lpg=PA202&dq=%22golden+star%22+hops&source=bl&ots=O9VHVO6Bqk&sig=LcokZnKNM6yXzFNeVqI09SKpZw8&hl=en&sa=X&ved=0CCEQ6AEwATgKahUKEwjq7dz75ubIAhUmlKYKHYQrDLY#v=onepage&q=%22golden%20star%22%20hops&f=false

Golding (US)

Golding (US) hops are descended from the original East Kent Golding. In North America, they were first grown in British Columbia, and then appeared in the state of Washington in 1993 and Oregon after that. They are no longer grown commercially in Canada. They feature a subtle bitterness when used as a early addition but are predominantly used for their quintessentially 'English' flavor and aroma.

Golding's use is primarily in English-style Ales, though they also see wide use in Barley Wines and Belgian Ales as well. It is low yielding, susceptible to disease and difficult to harvest, but their delicate and typical English aroma keeps the variety popular.

Homebrewer's Comments

I'd use these in place of anything you'd use UK Goldings for. They are not exactly the same, but close enough. I'd easily use them in Bitters, Porters, Stouts, Amber Ales, Blondes, Scottish or Irish beers and they would still work great in any American beer were you are not looking for a citrus note. They would even work in just about any belgian where all you want is a bittering addition. *(Brewsmith via homebrewtalk.com)*

Also Known As	US Golding, US Goldings, Northwest Goldings
Characteristics	Delicate English-style aromas, fruit, herbs
Purpose	Aroma
Alpha Acid Composition	4%-6%
Beta Acid Composition	2%-3%
Cohumulone Composition	20%-20%
Country	US
Cone Size	Small
Cone Density	Loose
Seasonal Maturity	Early to mid
Yield Amount	900-1500 kg/hectare (802-1338 lbs/acre)
Growth Rate	Moderate

Resistant to	
Susceptible to	
Storability	Retains 66% alpha acid after 6 months storage at 20°C (68°F)
Ease of Harvest	Moderate to difficult
Total Oil	0.4-1.0 mL/100g
Myrcene Oil	25%-35%
Humulene Oil	35%-45%
Caryophyllene Oil	13%-16%
Farnesene Oil	<1%
Substitutes	East Kent Golding, Fuggle, Willamette, Savinjski Golding, Progress, Whitbread Golding
Style Guide	Bitter, Pale Ale, Belgian Ale, Belgian IPA, Barley Wine, Imperial Stout, Red Ale, Irish Stout, American Pale Ale

References

https://www.hopunion.com/golding/
http://beerlegends.com/goldings-us-hops

Goldings (NZ)

New Zealand Goldings are said to have a subtle flavor and an enjoyable perfume with a nicely rounded bittering. It differs from the English Kent Goldings in its delicate touch. In fresh beers, its flavor will only hold for about a month. Good traditional aroma hop used late in the boil or for dry hopping.

Homebrewer's Comments

I've tried the NZ Goldings a few times (as flowers) and found them as per the vague description but very pleased with the subtle flavour and enjoyable perfume while bittering was quite rounded and not aggressive or objectionable. The late/dry hops addition in a SMaSH English pale was quite delicate and had an optimum window peaking about a month from bottling for savouring but tailed off a few more months thereafter, which was a little bit disappointing.

I quite like them as a traditional aroma/late and all of the Goldings derivatives I've tried seem to have that slightly sweet, flowery base profile which I find quite agreeable. If I had to distinguish between them and EKG, the NZ Goldings are more delicate and not quite as robust, whereas EKG have a perhaps more pronounced spiciness, although differing rates would obviously dictate. If you wanted to zing up parts of the flavour spectrum or add some diversity, EKG would lend much more spiciness and perhaps mint than NZG, but they are in a roughly similar vein.

I enjoy the subtlety of NZG to be honest as I readily tire of being smacked in the face by hops. It depends to some extent on the desired style too, I'd suggest being prepared for these easily-swamped characteristics, they're certainly not muted or absent, it just takes a little fore-thought to get the best out of them.
(RdeVjun via aussiehomebrewer.com)

Also Known As	
Characteristics	
Purpose	Bittering & Aroma
Alpha Acid Composition	4%-4.2%
Beta Acid Composition	4.6%-4.8%
Cohumulone Composition	20%-25%
Country	New Zealand
Cone Size	Small
Cone Density	Loose
Seasonal Maturity	Early to mid
Yield Amount	
Growth Rate	Moderate
Resistant to	
Susceptible to	
Storability	
Ease of Harvest	
Total Oil	0.3 mL/100g

Myrcene Oil	13.8%
Humulene Oil	48.4%
Caryophyllene Oil	13.3%
Farnesene Oil	0.3%
Substitutes	East Kent Golding
Style Guide	English Pale Ale, Pale Ale

References
http://www.baylandsbrewery.com/store/nz-goldings-hop-pellets-50g
http://aussiehomebrewer.com/topic/41951-nz-golding-hops/?p=593771
http://nzhl.info-prime.co.nz/variety/golding

Green Bullet

Green Bullet is a New Zealand hops variety, one of the first generation of new crosses attempted when Black Root Rot descended on New Zealand hops in 1949.

Bred from Fuggle and an unspecified native parent, it has a special zing that has become New Zealand's stock-in-trade. It's a dual-use hop with high alpha acids, yet it has a smooth taste and aroma of raisins and fruits, possibly due to its high myrcene content.

Homebrewer's Comments

Great clean bittering hop, I've been using it to bitter saisons, a couple ipas, some brett beers and sours. The new thing I've been trying is using it for aroma. I did a SMaSH with Vienna and Green Bullet, and it was very nice, esp. as a subtle dry hop. It is floral. I get some fruit, like pear, but part of that may have been the WLP530 yeast. I will be dry hopping a winter warmer IPA with that and Mosaic soon. Green Flash makes a Triple IPA called Green Bullet that is all Green Bullet and Pacific Gem, but the Gem takes over a bit (strong dark berry/oak). I like Green Bullet and I think you can have a lot of fun with it. *(youreanimpulse via homebrewtalk.com)*

Also Known As	
Characteristics	Aromas of raisin and fruit
Purpose	Bittering & Aroma
Alpha Acid Composition	11%-15%
Beta Acid Composition	2.9%-7%
Cohumulone Composition	38%-43%
Country	New Zealand
Cone Size	Medium to Large
Cone Density	Compact
Seasonal Maturity	Late
Yield Amount	2100-2400 kg/hectare (1875-2140 lbs/acre)
Growth Rate	Moderate to high
Resistant to	Resistant to downy mildew
Susceptible to	
Storability	Retains 60%-70% alpha acid after 6 months storage at 20°C (68°F)
Ease of Harvest	Easy
Total Oil	0.46-1.13 mL/100g
Myrcene Oil	38.3%-53%
Humulene Oil	19%-28.2%
Caryophyllene Oil	9.2%-20%
Farnesene Oil	19%-20%
Substitutes	Liberty, Hallertauer, Crystal, Mount Hood, Ultra
Style Guide	Bock, Saison, India Pale Ale

References

http://beerlegends.com/green-bullet-hops
http://www.nzhops.co.nz/variety/green-bullet
https://ychhops.com/varieties/green-bullet

Greenburg

Greensburg is an American aroma hop grown mainly in southern Idaho and is used primarily by microbreweries. It has both fruity and woody notes. Its beta acids actually supersede its alpha acid content. Best when added to the end of a boil for aroma.

Also Known As	
Characteristics	Fruity, woody aromas
Purpose	Bittering & Aroma
Alpha Acid Composition	5.2%
Beta Acid Composition	7.2%
Cohumulone Composition	
Country	US
Cone Size	
Cone Density	
Seasonal Maturity	
Yield Amount	
Growth Rate	
Resistant to	
Susceptible to	
Storability	
Ease of Harvest	
Total Oil	
Myrcene Oil	
Humulene Oil	
Caryophyllene Oil	
Farnesene Oil	
Substitutes	
Style Guide	

References

http://www.brewunited.com/hop_database.php

Groene Bel

Groene Bel or Green Belle as it is otherwise known, is a long-lost Belgian hop that likely came about via clonal selection from native Aalst hops in the late 19th century or early 20th century. After World War II, Groene Bel all but vanished from hop production in Belgium after it was replaced by German favorites, Saaz and Hallertau. Although Groene Bel is no longer commercially produced, it has been used for breeding aroma hops in Zalec, Slovenia during the 1970's. Its high humulene content is said to result in a pleasing, continental aroma.

Also Known As	Green Belle, Green Bubble Belle
Characteristics	Pleasing continental aroma
Purpose	Aroma
Alpha Acid Composition	4.9%
Beta Acid Composition	3.5%
Cohumulone Composition	27%
Country	Belgium
Cone Size	
Cone Density	
Seasonal Maturity	Mid to late
Yield Amount	825 kg/hectare (740 lbs/acre)
Growth Rate	Low to moderate
Resistant to	
Susceptible to	
Storability	Retains 58% alpha acid after 6 months storage at 20°C (68°F)
Ease of Harvest	
Total Oil	0.98 mL/100g
Myrcene Oil	39%
Humulene Oil	32%
Caryophyllene Oil	18%
Farnesene Oil	2.41%
Substitutes	

References

http://www.ars.usda.gov/SP2UserFiles/person/2450/hopcultivars/21216.html

https://nl.wikipedia.org/wiki/Groene_Belle

Hallertau (Hallertauer Mittelfrüh)

Hallertau, Hallertauer and Hallertauer Mittelfrüher are all names for the original German Hallertau variety. Dating back more than 100 years, it stems from an old German landrace and is one of the original four "noble" hops. It features a lightly flowery and spicy aroma.

Though its popularity has been steadily declining over the past 50 years, primarily as a result of grave susceptibility to verticillium wilt and poor yields, it has been used to create a multitude of offspring – most of which are more wilt tolerant. It is now only grown on one farm in Germany.

Brewmaster's Comments

I love Saaz, Hallertau and Tettnang when brewing pilsners or a traditional kolsch. The spicy, peppery, herbal qualities are unmatched for such styles. They can be used early, middle and/or late for these beers. *(Ryan Schmiege, Assistant Brewmaster at Deschutes Brewery)*

Homebrewer's Comments

I managed to score a pound of Mittelfruh while in Germany last fall. I haven't noticed any difference between them and the German Hallertau hops I've bought from HopsDirect. Which doesn't mean they are the same, just that any differences are more refined than my crude palate. *(gxm via homebrewtalk.com)*

Also Known As	Hallertauer, Mittelfrüh, Mittelfrüher, Hallertauer Mittelfrüher, Hallertau Mittelfruh
Characteristics	Lightly flowery and spicy aroma
Purpose	Aroma

Alpha Acid Composition	3.5%-3.5%
Beta Acid Composition	3.5%-4.5%
Cohumulone Composition	20%-26%
Country	Germany
Cone Size	Small
Cone Density	Loose
Seasonal Maturity	Early to mid
Yield Amount	800-1100 kg/hectare (700-980 lbs/acre)
Growth Rate	Moderate to high
Resistant to	
Susceptible to	Susceptible to german wilt, downy mildew, powdery mildew and verticillium wilt
Storability	Retains 52%-58% alpha acid after 6 months storage at 20°C (68°F)
Ease of Harvest	Easy
Total Oil	0.6-1.2 mL/100g
Myrcene Oil	35%-44%
Humulene Oil	30%-55%
Caryophyllene Oil	10%-15%
Farnesene Oil	0%-1%
Substitutes	Liberty, Hallertauer, German Tradition
Style Guide	German Pilsner, Pale Ale, Wheat, American Lager

References
http://www.ars.usda.gov/SP2UserFiles/person/2450/hopcultivars/21014.html
https://www.freshops.com/hops/usda-named-hop-variety-descriptions#usda_id_21014
http://www.ars.usda.gov/SP2UserFiles/person/2450/hopcultivars/56001.html

Hallertau (US)

Hallertau (US) is definitely a tenacious, Bavarian-style hop. It long dominated its heritage region and is still in demand by craft brewers for Bavarian-style ales. As an American hop, it is outperformed by Mt. Hood and Liberty but is still holding its own. Its low alpha acids and high humulene contribute to a mild, flowery and delicately spicy aroma and flavor profile. The original German-grown Hallertau has long been the staple of German and European lagers.

Homebrewer's Comments

I made a hop bomb IPA and added US Hallertau at 25 min and backed it up at knockout. It really cut through a mountain of Citrusy, American hops. If just using one aroma addition, you will need a lot. If you re-enforce the flavors by layering, you can use less hops. *(Geoff Henderson via northernbrewer.com)*

Also Known As	US Hallertau
Characteristics	Flowery, delicately spicy
Purpose	Aroma
Alpha Acid Composition	3.5%-5.5%
Beta Acid Composition	3.5%-5.5%
Cohumulone Composition	18-24%
Country	US
Cone Size	Small
Cone Density	Loose
Seasonal Maturity	Early
Yield Amount	1900-1400 kg/hectare (1695-1240 lbs/acre)
Growth Rate	
Resistant to	
Susceptible to	Necrotic ring-spot virus, downey mildew, verticillium wilt and insects
Storability	Retains 52%-58% alpha acid after 6 months storage at 20°C (68°F)
Ease of Harvest	
Total Oil	0.6-1.0 mL/100g
Myrcene Oil	35-44%
Humulene Oil	30-38%
Caryophyllene Oil	10-12%

Farnesene Oil	< 1%
Substitutes	Mount Hood, Liberty, Crystal, Hallertauer Mittelfrüh, Hallertauer Tradition, Ultra
Style Guide	Lager, Pilsner, Bock, Wheat Beer, Kölsch, Munich Helles, Belgian Ale, American Lager

References
http://beerlegends.com/hallertau-aroma-hops

Hallertau Blanc

Hallertau Blanc, daughter of Cascade, was released to the world in 2012. Established on the Hüll farm in the German Hallertau region, it was grown primarily for use in American-style Ales. Hallertau Blanc's flavor profile is said to be fruity, with wine-like qualities of gooseberry and grass, similar to that of Sauvignon Blanc. It also features a complex aroma profile with notes of cassis and elderflower in addition to grapes, grapefruit and lemongrass. Other notes detected in trials have been passionfruit, pineapple and gooseberry.

Homebrewer's Comments

Hallertau Blanc is one of my favorite hops. It's like Nelson, Galaxy and Hallertau had an orgy and nine months later this guy was born. Awesome, awesome blonde ale and saison hop. Also good in pale ales and IPAs. *(ArcaneXor via homebrewtalk.com)*

This is a great new hop from Germany. Along with Huell Melon and Mandarina Bavaria, Germany is cranking out some surprisingly potent fruity hops given their tendency towards more traditional noble hops. Very unique gooseberry character that is closest to Nelson Sauvin IME. Its like a cleaner, more floral, less funky Nelson Sauvin. *(m00ps via email)*

Also Known As	
Characteristics	Flavors of white-wine and fruit, aromas of cassis, elderflower, grapes, grapefruit and lemongrass.
Purpose	Aroma
Alpha Acid Composition	9%-12%
Beta Acid Composition	4%-6%
Cohumulone Composition	22%-26%
Country	Germany
Cone Size	
Cone Density	
Seasonal Maturity	Late
Yield Amount	1150-1600 kg/hectare (1020-1420 lbs/acre)
Growth Rate	
Resistant to	Resistant to downy and powdery mildew
Susceptible to	
Storability	
Ease of Harvest	
Total Oil	0.8-1.5 mL/100g
Myrcene Oil	50%-75%
Humulene Oil	0%-3%
Caryophyllene Oil	0%-2%
Farnesene Oil	0%-3.5%
Substitutes	Nelson Sauvin
Style Guide	American Ale, Blonde Ale, Saison

References

https://www.hopunion.com/german-hallertau-blanc/

http://www.orpheusbrewing.com/beers/hop-experiment-1/?ao_confirm

http://www.baywa.eu/fileadmin/media/relaunch/Downloads/.EU/Hopfenvertrieb/081358_Agrar_Flyer_Hallertau_Blanc_EN_A4_lay3.pdf

https://www.hopsteiner.de/info/nc/en/pdf/hop-variety-finder/variety-information/sdb/hallertau-blanc-1.html?filename=Hallertau%20Blanc.pdf

Hallertauer (New Zealand)

Hallertau (New Zealand) is a triploid hop bred from Hallertau Mittelfrüher and a New Zealand male cultivar. First introduced in 1988 by HortResearch (now the New Zealand Institute for Plant and Food Research), it is purported to impart a distinct lime 'zing' beneath a delicately floral top.

Despite being bred from Hallertau Mittelfrüher, its New Zealand parent has modified the aroma and flavor profile enough that it isn't considered a "true" Hallertau. Despite this, Hallertau (New Zealand) has been popular among brewers and boasts good vigor, yield and storage stability and has no known susceptibility to viruses. It is characterized as clean tasting with staying power.

Homebrewer's Comments

> I really liked NZ Hallertau and would use them again. I thought they had a little bit of a buttery/pastry aroma to them. I didn't get any lime character, but that might vary a bit between harvests. *(Doppelganger via ratebeer.com)*

Also Known As	NZ Hallertau
Characteristics	Clean taste, notes of lime and a distinct floral bouquet
Purpose	Aroma
Alpha Acid Composition	7%-9%
Beta Acid Composition	5.8%-8.5%
Cohumulone Composition	28%-35%
Country	New Zealand
Cone Size	Medium
Cone Density	Loose
Seasonal Maturity	Early
Yield Amount	2300-2400 kg/hectare (2052-2141 lbs/acre)
Growth Rate	High
Resistant to	

Susceptible to	
Storability	Retains 80%-85% alpha acid after 6 months storage at 20ºC (68ºF)
Ease of Harvest	Moderate
Total Oil	0.9-1.1 mL/100g
Myrcene Oil	35%-48%
Humulene Oil	10%-16.8%
Caryophyllene Oil	6%-8.2%
Farnesene Oil	5%-6.7%
Substitutes	Hallertauer Mittelfrüh, Perle
Style Guide	Pale Ale, Lager, Pilsner, Bitter, Bock, American Lager

References

http://beerlegends.com/hallertau-aroma-hops
https://en.wikipedia.org/wiki/HortResearch

Hallertauer Gold

A varietal of the German Institute for Hop Research in Huell, Germany, Hallertauer Gold is a descendant of Hallertau Mittelfrüher and is often marketed under various, similar names. Developed in the mid-1970s, it was released to the public in the late 1980s. A lot of commercially sold Hallertau is usually Hallertauer Gold or Hallertauer Gold combined with Hallertau Mittelfrüher. Its aroma is continental but with higher alpha acids and low cohumulone. This hop was bred to be more wilt resistant than its parent after persistent wilt became an issue in Germany.

Also Known As	Hallertau Gold
Characteristics	Pleasing continental aroma
Purpose	Aroma
Alpha Acid Composition	7%-10%
Beta Acid Composition	5%-7%
Cohumulone Composition	20%
Country	Germany

Cone Size	
Cone Density	
Seasonal Maturity	Early
Yield Amount	1345-1565 kg/hectare (1200-1400 lbs/acre)
Growth Rate	Moderate to high
Resistant to	Resistant to downy mildew and moderately resistant to powdery mildew
Susceptible to	Susceptible to Verticillium wilt
Storability	Retains 47% alpha acid after 6 months storage at 20ºC (68ºF)
Ease of Harvest	
Total Oil	1.78 mL/100g
Myrcene Oil	63%
Humulene Oil	17%
Caryophyllene Oil	4.8%
Farnesene Oil	0.2%
Substitutes	Hallertauer Mittelfrüh, Tettnanger, East Kent Golding, Crystal, Mount Hood
Style Guide	American Lager

References
http://www.ars.usda.gov/SP2UserFiles/person/2450/hopcultivars/21671.html

Hallertauer Taurus

German born Hallertau Taurus features an earthy, strong aroma with hints of chocolate and banana, spice and pepper and finishes with a zesty curry undertone. It was released in 1995.

Interestingly, it carries the highest xanthohumol content of any hop. Xanthohumol is a potent antioxidant, 200 times more powerful than antioxidants found in red wine. Used in Paulaner's hop selection for their Oktoberfest bier.

Also Known As	German Taurus, Taurus
Characteristics	Chocolate, banana, spice, pepper, curry
Purpose	Bittering & Aroma
Alpha Acid Composition	12.3%-17.9%
Beta Acid Composition	4%-6%
Cohumulone Composition	23%-25%
Country	Germany
Cone Size	Medium
Cone Density	Moderate
Seasonal Maturity	Late
Yield Amount	1600-2000 kg/hectare (1260-1420 lbs/acre)
Growth Rate	Moderate
Resistant to	Resistant to verticillium wilt
Susceptible to	Susceptible to powdery mildew
Storability	Retains 60%-70% alpha acid after 6 months storage at 20ºC (68ºF)
Ease of Harvest	Difficult
Total Oil	0.9-1.5 mL/100g
Myrcene Oil	30%
Humulene Oil	30%-31%
Caryophyllene Oil	8%
Farnesene Oil	0%-1%
Substitutes	Hallertauer Magnum, Merkur, Hercules
Style Guide	Schwarzbier, Oktoberfest

References

http://beerlegends.com/hallertauer-taurus-hops

http://fis.org/xanthohumol/

https://www.hopsteiner.de/info/nc/en/pdf/hop-variety-finder/variety-information/sdb/hallertauer-taurus-1.html?filename=Hallertauer%20Taurus.pdf

Hallertauer Tradition

Hallertau Tradition is a Hüll-bred fine aroma hop originating from
Hallertau Mittelfrüher, Hallertauer Gold and Saaz. Bred specifically for
fungus and disease resistance, it succeeded in that effort and also features
higher alpha acids than its parent varieties, low cohumulone and higher
myrcene. It was released for commercial production in 1989.

Its oil profile contributes to a wonderfully earthy and grassy character
atop a nose of nectar fruits. It is best used late in the boil, or for dry
hopping. This utilization is preferential since its humulene content has
been noted to dissipate rapidly when heated.

Also Known As	Tradition, German Tradition
Characteristics	Earthy, grassy, aromas of nectar fruits
Purpose	Aroma
Alpha Acid Composition	4.6%-7%
Beta Acid Composition	4%-5%
Cohumulone Composition	23%-29%
Country	Germany
Cone Size	Medium
Cone Density	Compact
Seasonal Maturity	
Yield Amount	1560-1780 kg/hectare (1390-1580 lbs/acre)
Growth Rate	High
Resistant to	Resistant to verticillium wilt, downy mildew and powdery mildew
Susceptible to	
Storability	Retains 65%-70% alpha acid after 6 months storage at 20°C (68°F)
Ease of Harvest	Difficult
Total Oil	0.9-1.9 mL/100g
Myrcene Oil	20%-25%
Humulene Oil	40%-55%

Caryophyllene Oil	10%-15%
Farnesene Oil	0%-1%
Substitutes	Hallertau Mittlefrüher, Liberty, Ultra, Crystal
Style Guide	American Lager

References

http://beerlegends.com/hallertauer-tradition-hops
https://www.freshops.com/hops/usda-named-hop-variety-descriptions#usda_id_21672

Helga

Helga is an Australian cultivar, formerly known as Southern Hallertau. Helga was bred by Hop Products Australia from Hallertau Mittelfrüher in an effort to dissect and retain its Hallertau's characteristic noble aroma. Helga is easy to work with—no matter at what point she is added into the brew, even when dry hopping, the results are said to be ever pleasant. It is mildly floral and spicy. Helga made a quiet debut, established in 1996 it took nearly 10 years to catch on commercially. Currently, production is being increased as craft brewers take interest.

Also Known As	Southern Hallertau
Characteristics	Noble-style aroma, mildly floral and spicy
Purpose	Aroma
Alpha Acid Composition	5.4%-7.3%
Beta Acid Composition	5%-7%
Cohumulone Composition	20%-23%
Country	Australia
Cone Size	
Cone Density	
Seasonal Maturity	
Yield Amount	
Growth Rate	
Resistant to	
Susceptible to	

Storability	
Ease of Harvest	
Total Oil	0.6-1.0 mL/100g
Myrcene Oil	1%-13%
Humulene Oil	35%-55%
Caryophyllene Oil	10%-15%
Farnesene Oil	
Substitutes	Hallertau Mittelfrüher
Style Guide	Ales

References
https://bellsbeer.com/store/products/Helga-%28AU%29-Hops-%252d-1-oz-Pellets.html
http://www.hops.com.au/products/helga
http://www.hops.com.au/media/W1siZiIsIjIwMTMvMDUvMjkvMTdfNDJfMTJfMzU4X0h
QQV9IZWxnYV9Qcm9kdWN0X1NoZWV0LnBkZiJdXQ/HPA_Helga_Product_Sheet.pdf
https://www.hopunion.com/australian-helga/

Herald

Herald hops were one of a first wave of dwarf hops introduced to the industry. It was released in 1996 alongside sisters Pilgrim and Pioneer. Some brewers were initially reluctant to use Herald despite its clean bitterness and a nice nose of orange and grapefruit. Today Herald is employed by a multitude of craft breweries, particularly in the UK.

Also Known As	
Characteristics	
Purpose	Bittering & Aroma
Alpha Acid Composition	11.9%-12.8%
Beta Acid Composition	4.8%-5.5%
Cohumulone Composition	35%-37%
Country	UK
Cone Size	Large
Cone Density	Moderate to compact
Seasonal Maturity	Early

Yield Amount	1200-1250 kg/hectare (1070-1120 lbs/acre)
Growth Rate	Moderate
Resistant to	Resistant to verticillium wilt, powdery mildew and downy mildew
Susceptible to	
Storability	Retains 60%-70% alpha acid after 6 months storage at 20ºC (68ºF)
Ease of Harvest	Difficult
Total Oil	1-1.9 mL/100g
Myrcene Oil	40%-40%
Humulene Oil	15%-15%
Caryophyllene Oil	7%
Farnesene Oil	0%-1%
Substitutes	Pioneer
Style Guide	Pale Ale, Golden Ale

References

http://beerlegends.com/herald-hops

https://books.google.com.au/books?id=cdVpCgAAQBAJ&pg=PA269&lpg=PA269&dq=herald+hops&source=bl&ots=U-D2tUriXn&sig=7Lx_a8c6Y1aCXpcqqG63S6B4IBY&hl=en&sa=X&ved=0ahUKEwiF2caR2MnMAhXDJ5QKHTbUAjsQ6AEIUDAI#v=onepage&q=herald&f=false

Herkules

Strong and robust in flavor and aroma, German Herkules lives up to it's name. The Hüll-bred offspring of Hallertauer Taurus, Herkules is a high alpha acid bittering hop, known to be spicy and floral, tangy and hoppy, with notes of melon, black pepper, with hints of pine. It was released in 2005.

Homebrewer's Comments

For me its a good high alpha hop that I will only use in beers that are going to be aged. I will not be using it any quick turn around beers, due to that harsh edge. (*awalker via jimsbeerkit.co.uk*)

Also Known As	
Characteristics	Notes of melon, black pepper and pine
Purpose	Bittering & Aroma
Alpha Acid Composition	12%-17%
Beta Acid Composition	4%-5.5%
Cohumulone Composition	32%-38%
Country	Germany
Cone Size	
Cone Density	
Seasonal Maturity	
Yield Amount	2500-2700 kg/hectare (2230-2408 lbs/acre)
Growth Rate	
Resistant to	Wilt
Susceptible to	Downy and powdery mildew
Storability	
Ease of Harvest	
Total Oil	1.4-2.4 mL/100g
Myrcene Oil	30%-50%
Humulene Oil	28%-45%
Caryophyllene Oil	7%-12%
Farnesene Oil	< 1%
Substitutes	
Style Guide	German Ale

References

https://ychhops.com/varieties/herkules

https://www.hopsteiner.de/info/nc/en/pdf/hop-variety-finder/variety-information/sdb/herkules-1.html?filename=Herkules.pdf

http://www.hopsteiner.com/wp-content/uploads/vpdf/en/Herkules.pdf

https://en.wikipedia.org/wiki/List_of_hop_varieties#Hallertauer_Herkules

Hersbrucker

Hersbrucker was originally bred with the intention of producing a variety resistant to verticillium wilt that could act as a replacement for Hallertau Mittelfrüh. Hersbrucker reached the height of it's popularity in the 1970's and 1980's but despite that, Germany's overall production of this hop today still exceeds 1000 metric tons each year. It can even be found organically grown on several boutique hop farms.

With low alpha acids and low cohumulone, it exhibits a pleasant aroma with a balanced, fruity, spicy and floral character. It has commonly been used in German lagers, however this variety is now making its way into some fine English cask ales. It has been cloned several times in an attempt to improve its alpha acid content, but without success.

Also Known As	Hersbrucker-G, Hersbrucker Late, Hersbrucker Spaet, Hersbrucker Spat
Characteristics	Floral, fruity and spicy aromas
Purpose	Aroma
Alpha Acid Composition	2%-5%
Beta Acid Composition	4%-6%
Cohumulone Composition	19%-25%
Country	Germany
Cone Size	Medium
Cone Density	Moderate
Seasonal Maturity	Late
Yield Amount	1400-1800 kg/hectare (1240-1610 lbs/acre)
Growth Rate	Very high
Resistant to	Resistant to verticillium wilt
Susceptible to	Susceptible to downy mildew
Storability	Retains 55%-65% alpha acid after 6 months storage at 20ºC (68ºF)
Ease of Harvest	Difficult
Total Oil	0.5-1.3 mL/100g
Myrcene Oil	10%-25%

Humulene Oil	15%-35%
Caryophyllene Oil	7%-15%
Farnesene Oil	0%-1%
Substitutes	Hallertauer Tradition, Spalt Select, Mt Hood, Strisselspalter, Hallertau, Liberty
Style Guide	Dunkel, Strong Ale, Pilsner, Altbier, Weizenbock, Golden Ale, Marzen, Pale Ale, Wheat, Specialty Ale, Hefeweizen, Light Ale, Lager

References

http://beerlegends.com/hersbrucker-hops

http://www.ars.usda.gov/SP2UserFiles/person/2450/hopcultivars/21185.html

Hersbrucker E

Hersbrucker E (for England) was planted and grown at Wye College, England in the 1970's. It is largely identical to the original Hersbrucker variety grown in the Hersbruck Mountains. The storage stability, especially of its soft resins, is low.

Also Known As	
Characteristics	
Purpose	Aroma
Alpha Acid Composition	4%-6%
Beta Acid Composition	5%-7%
Cohumulone Composition	22%-24%
Country	UK
Cone Size	
Cone Density	
Seasonal Maturity	Late
Yield Amount	700 kg/hectare (620 lbs/acre)
Growth Rate	Very high
Resistant to	
Susceptible to	Moderately susceptible to downy mildew

Storability	Retains 58% alpha acid after 6 months storage at 20ºC (68ºF)
Ease of Harvest	
Total Oil	0.63 mL/100g
Myrcene Oil	46%
Humulene Oil	29%
Caryophyllene Oil	9%
Farnesene Oil	0.2%
Substitutes	Strisselspalter, Mount Hood
Style Guide	Lager, Pilsner, Bock, Weizenbock, Wheat Beer, Belgian Ale, Kölsch, Munich Helles

References

http://www.ars.usda.gov/SP2UserFiles/person/2450/hopcultivars/21179.html

Hersbrucker Pure

The offspring of Hallertauer Mittelfrüh, Saaz and a wild German hop, Hersbrucker Pure was originally tested by brewing giant Anheuser Busch as a replacement for Hersbrucker. After their interest waned in the variety, it failed to catch on as a viable commercial prospect. It has an noble aroma and flavor profile similar to that of its parents.

Also Known As	
Characteristics	Pleasing noble aroma
Purpose	Aroma
Alpha Acid Composition	4.7%-6%
Beta Acid Composition	2%-3%
Cohumulone Composition	20%-28%
Country	
Cone Size	Medium
Cone Density	Moderate
Seasonal Maturity	

Yield Amount	1500-1550 kg/hectare (1330-1390 lbs/acre)
Growth Rate	Moderate
Resistant to	Resistant to verticillium wilt, downy and powdery mildew and pernaspora
Susceptible to	
Storability	Retains 60%-70% alpha acid after 6 months storage at 20ºC (68ºF)
Ease of Harvest	Difficult
Total Oil	0.6-1.2 mL/100g
Myrcene Oil	24%-50%
Humulene Oil	10%-27%
Caryophyllene Oil	4%-11%
Farnesene Oil	0%-1%
Substitutes	Hersbrucker, Hallertauer Mittelfrüh
Style Guide	Pilsner, Hefeweizen, Lager

References

http://beerlegends.com/hersbrucker-pure-hops
http://www.ars.usda.gov/SP2UserFiles/person/2450/hopcultivars/21673.html

Hersbrucker Red-Stem

Hersbrucker Red-Stem is, as I'm sure you guessed, so named due to its red stem. All Hersbruckers have red stems, but in this variety it is even more distinct. It is a clonal offshoot of Hersbrucker, supposedly with a higher alpha acid potential. Hersbrucker clones have declined in production over the years since their introduction in the 1980's. This is mainly due to the rise of Hallertauer Tradition and Spalter Select, which exhibit much higher alpha percentages.

Also Known As	Hersbrucker Alpha
Characteristics	Pleasing noble characteristics
Purpose	Aroma
Alpha Acid Composition	5%-6%

Beta Acid Composition	5%-6%
Cohumulone Composition	18%
Country	Germany
Cone Size	
Cone Density	
Seasonal Maturity	Late
Yield Amount	1110 kg/hectare (990 lbs/acre)
Growth Rate	High
Resistant to	
Susceptible to	Moderately susceptible to downy mildew
Storability	Retains 60% alpha acid after 6 months storage at 20ºC (68ºF)
Ease of Harvest	
Total Oil	1.20 mL/100g
Myrcene Oil	55%
Humulene Oil	10%
Caryophyllene Oil	9%
Farnesene Oil	175%
Substitutes	
Style Guide	

References

http://www.ars.usda.gov/SP2UserFiles/person/2450/hopcultivars/21517.html

Horizon

Horizon is a versatile hop with some star qualities. Created in Oregon in 1970, Horizon is a diploid hop and half-sister to Nugget.

Considered dual-use it has high alpha acids, but also low cohumulone – a trait considered highly favorable when bittering. Its high myrcene and high farnesene content give it some great aroma and flavor notes too, both floral and citrusy.

It has been picked up by several craft brewers and is a star at North by Northwest brewery in Austin, Texas where it is used in its top three classic brews, as well as in their specialty beers from time to time.

Homebrewer's Comments

I used Horizon in an IPA alongside Amarillo. It was a nice combination. Very tropical/citrus, almost like pineapple. *(treehousebrewing via homebrewtalk.com)*

Also Known As	
Characteristics	Floral, citrusy
Purpose	Bittering & Aroma
Alpha Acid Composition	8.8%-16.5%
Beta Acid Composition	5.5%-8.5%
Cohumulone Composition	16%-22%
Country	US
Cone Size	Medium
Cone Density	Compact
Seasonal Maturity	Mid to late
Yield Amount	2017-2241 kg/hectare (1800-2000 lbs/acre)
Growth Rate	Moderate to high
Resistant to	Resistant to verticillium wilt
Susceptible to	Susceptible to downy mildew
Storability	Retains 80%-85% alpha acid after 6 months storage at 20ºC (68ºF)
Ease of Harvest	Difficult
Total Oil	0.5-2 mL/100g
Myrcene Oil	45%-70%
Humulene Oil	8%-20%
Caryophyllene Oil	8%-14%
Farnesene Oil	3%-5%
Substitutes	Hallertauer Magnum
Style Guide	Light Ale, Red Ale, Pumpkin Ale

References

http://beerlegends.com/horizon-hops

https://ychhops.com/varieties/horizon

https://www.craftbrewer.com.au/shop/details.asp?PID=608

http://www.usahops.org/graphics/File/HGA%20BCI%20Reports/Variety%20Manual%207-24-12.pdf

http://www.greatlakeshops.com/horizon.html

Hüll Melon

Relatively new on the market, Hüll Melon made its debut in 2012. A daughter of Cascade, it has some interesting flavor characteristics not commonly associated with hops. It is noted to be intensely fruity with flavors and aromas of honeydew melon and strawberry.

Homebrewer's Comments

I just finished bottling an American Wheat with Huell Melon hops. It has a very bright, aromatic sweet melon aroma, reminiscent of cantaloupe. *(Oginme via homebrewtalk.com)*

I got my hands on this very cool German hop variety and wanted to make a summer beer that would let it shine. Hull Melon smells a bit like Citra, but with melon notes instead of citrusy/tropical. *(slymaster via homebrewtalk.com)*

Also Known As	Huell Melon
Characteristics	Intensely fruity, flavors and aromas of honeydew melon, strawberry
Purpose	Aroma
Alpha Acid Composition	6.9%-7.5%
Beta Acid Composition	7.3%-7.9%
Cohumulone Composition	25%-30%
Country	Germany
Cone Size	
Cone Density	
Seasonal Maturity	

Yield Amount	
Growth Rate	
Resistant to	
Susceptible to	
Storability	
Ease of Harvest	
Total Oil	0.8 mL/100g
Myrcene Oil	36%
Humulene Oil	10%-20%
Caryophyllene Oil	5%-10%
Farnesene Oil	< 1%
Substitutes	
Style Guide	

References
http://www.hopunion.com/german-hull-melon/
http://www.barthhaasgroup.com/johbarth/images/pdfs/hop-varieties/en/Sortenblatt_Engl_GERMANY_HuellMelon.pdf

Hüller Bitterer

Developed in the late 1960's and released in 1978, Hüller Bitterer has the distinction of being the first wilt resistant variety to come from the German Hüll hop breeding program. Descended from Northern Brewer, it is an excellent dual-use hop and is still known for its clean bittering character. In commercial use, it has now largely been replaced with other wilt resistant varieties, specifically Perle.

Also Known As	
Characteristics	
Purpose	Bittering & Aroma
Alpha Acid Composition	4.5%-7%
Beta Acid Composition	4.5%-5.5%
Cohumulone Composition	26%-31%
Country	Germany

Cone Size	Medium
Cone Density	Moderate
Seasonal Maturity	
Yield Amount	1150-1370 kg/hectare (1020-1220 lbs/acre)
Growth Rate	Moderate
Resistant to	Resistant to verticillium wilt, peronospora, powdery mildew
Susceptible to	
Storability	Retains 60% alpha acid after 6 months storage at 20ºC (68ºF)
Ease of Harvest	Difficult
Total Oil	1-1.5 mL/100g
Myrcene Oil	28%-51%
Humulene Oil	9%-21%
Caryophyllene Oil	5%-8%
Farnesene Oil	0%-1%
Substitutes	
Style Guide	Schwarzbier, Lager

References

http://beerlegends.com/h%C3%BCller-bitterer-hops

https://books.google.com.au/books?id=gcJQAwAAQBAJ&pg=PA112&lpg=PA112&dq=Hüller+Bitterer&source=bl&ots=u-bnoItnFt&sig=8i7twCcwfauqud-phHBEi2u71_w&hl=en&sa=X&ved=0ahUKEwje0OPv38nMAhWhK6YKHT_kCuo4ChDoAQgaMAA#v=onepage&q=Hüller%20Bitterer&f=false

https://bsgcraftbrewing.com/Resources%5CCraftBrewing%5CPDFs%5CAgricultural_Reports_and_Papers/TheBreeding_Varieties.pdf

http://freshops.com/usda-named-hop-variety-descriptions/#usda_id_21097

https://books.google.com.au/books?id=ZZPTBwAAQBAJ&pg=PA408&lpg=PA408&dq=Hüller+Bitterer+released&source=bl&ots=ShoeGCrU3a&sig=wpxP7ulBsnO9SbrLeUFlv5iq8Uc&hl=en&sa=X&ved=0ahUKEwiUhrGX4cnMAhUCGpQKHaqGDJcQ6AEINjAG#v=onepage&q=Hüller%20Bitterer%20released&f=false

Hybrid-2

Hybrid-2 was developed in South Africa in the early 1940's. Thought to be an open-pollinated seedling of California Cluster, it was discontinued in South Africa in 1964 due to low yields. It is however still produced commercially in Cashmere, India where it shows significantly better yields.

Also Known As	Hybrid
Characteristics	
Purpose	Aroma
Alpha Acid Composition	10.2%
Beta Acid Composition	6.3%
Cohumulone Composition	32%
Country	South Africa
Cone Size	
Cone Density	
Seasonal Maturity	Mid to late
Yield Amount	1570-2240 kg/hectare (1400-2000 lbs/acre)
Growth Rate	High
Resistant to	
Susceptible to	Moderately susceptible to downy mildew
Storability	Retains 60% alpha acid after 6 months storage at 20ºC (68ºF)
Ease of Harvest	
Total Oil	0.91 mL/100g
Myrcene Oil	52%
Humulene Oil	3%
Caryophyllene Oil	9%
Farnesene Oil	3.9%
Substitutes	Yakima Cluster, California Cluster
Style Guide	

References
http://www.ars.usda.gov/SP2UserFiles/person/2450/hopcultivars/21167.html

Ivanhoe

Ivanhoe is one of the first revivals of California Cluster in more than 50 years. Revived by organic hop farm Hops-Mesiter, LLC near Clearlake, California, it is a European aroma type and has been compared to a more moderate Cascade. It features a lovely, mellow aroma of citrus and pine, but with heady floral and herbal notes.

Homebrewer's Comments

I did a barley wine with all ivanhoe back in January. It's very fruity, from gravity and taste tests during fermentation there was a HUGE pineapple character (both my wife and I thought it was like drinking pineapple juice and rum) that settled down into a more subdued tropical / pineapple / passionfruit character. It's a good multipurpose hop as the AA% is around 8-9 but it has lots or aroma and flavor as well. I am thinking of trying a cali common with it at some point. It is a cluster type hop so it's related to northern brewer. *(morticaixavier via homebrewersassociation.org)*

Also Known As	
Characteristics	Mellow aroma of citrus and pine. Heady floral and herbal notes.
Purpose	Aroma
Alpha Acid Composition	7.3%-8%
Beta Acid Composition	4.60%
Cohumulone Composition	
Country	US
Cone Size	
Cone Density	
Seasonal Maturity	
Yield Amount	
Growth Rate	
Resistant to	
Susceptible to	
Storability	

Ease of Harvest	
Total Oil	
Myrcene Oil	
Humulene Oil	
Caryophyllene Oil	
Farnesene Oil	
Substitutes	Galena, Cluster, Northern Brewer
Style Guide	American Ale, California Common, Stout, India Pale Ale

References
http://www.brewerganic.com/california-ivanhoe-organic-whole-hops.aspx
http://www.hopsmeister.com

Janus

Selected at Wye College, England in the 1950's, Janus was originally praised for its early harvest qualities. Its extremely low yield however led it to being discarded as a commercial prospect in 1992. To date, it has never been used for breeding either. It is a cross between a Eastwell Golding, a New Mexico Wild American hop and other unspecified English hops. Janus exhibits very high myrcene potential and is said to have a pleasant, European aroma.

Also Known As	
Characteristics	Pleasing European aroma
Purpose	Aroma
Alpha Acid Composition	5.1%
Beta Acid Composition	2.3%
Cohumulone Composition	32%
Country	UK
Cone Size	
Cone Density	
Seasonal Maturity	Very early
Yield Amount	< 1120 kg/hectare (< 1000 lbs/acre)

Growth Rate	Low
Resistant to	Resistant to downy mildew and Verticillium wilt
Susceptible to	
Storability	Retains 68% alpha acid after 6 months storage at 20°C (68°F)
Ease of Harvest	
Total Oil	0.58 mL/100g
Myrcene Oil	40%
Humulene Oil	34%
Caryophyllene Oil	10.9%
Farnesene Oil	None
Substitutes	
Style Guide	

References

http://www.ars.usda.gov/SP2UserFiles/person/2450/hopcultivars/62051.html

Keyworth's Early

Keyworth's Early is a venerable old English hop which was, for a while, discontinued from production due to low yield. Raised at Wye College, England in the 1920's, it was rushed into production on the back of Dr. W. G. Keyworth's research in the 1940's after Verticillium wilt became a major problem in parts of Kent. Due to its promising resistance, it gained in popularity for a while but fell out of favor with both brewers and growers.

Bred from a New Mexico wild male in open pollination, it has recently seen somewhat of a revival and is said to impart lemon and grapefruit notes seen as desirable in todays brews.

Also Known As	OJ47
Characteristics	Lemon and grapefruit notes
Purpose	Aroma

Alpha Acid Composition	8.6%
Beta Acid Composition	3.3%
Cohumulone Composition	33%
Country	UK
Cone Size	
Cone Density	
Seasonal Maturity	
Yield Amount	710 kg/hectare (630 lbs/acre)
Growth Rate	Moderate to high
Resistant to	
Susceptible to	Moderately suceptible to downy mildew
Storability	Retains 72% alpha acid after 6 months storage at 20°C (68°F)
Ease of Harvest	
Total Oil	1.39 mL/100g
Myrcene Oil	45%
Humulene Oil	22%
Caryophyllene Oil	7%
Farnesene Oil	Trace Amounts
Substitutes	Keyworth's Midseason
Style Guide	American Ales

References

http://www.ars.usda.gov/SP2UserFiles/person/2450/hopcultivars/21278.html

http://onlinelibrary.wiley.com/store/10.1002/j.2050-0416.1949.tb01496.x/asset/j.2050-0416.1949.tb01496.x.pdf;jsessionid=DDB9199FA0E951B83865219A71B873F8.f02t04?v=1&t=igc23uew&s=7ede43687d71a805915362ff94a4ba91154e99b1

http://edsbeer.blogspot.com.au/2013/02/changing-tastes-in-hops.html

Keyworth's Midseason

Keyworth's Midseason was produced alongside Keyworth's Early in the 1940's for the same desired wilt resistance. A cross between Fuggle and a wild American female, Keyworth's Midseason proved more popular than Keyworth's Early and reached a cultivation close to 600 acres in 1954. It is the parent of Density and Defender.

Homebrewer's Comments

> ...if you can't get true fresh UK Fuggles, then Keyworth
> Midseason is indistinguishable, just as dreamy. *(seymour via
> jimsbeerkit.co.uk)*

Also Known As	
Characteristics	
Purpose	Aroma
Alpha Acid Composition	7.5%
Beta Acid Composition	3.1%
Cohumulone Composition	46%
Country	UK
Cone Size	
Cone Density	
Seasonal Maturity	
Yield Amount	1680-2460 kg/hectare (1500-2200 lbs/acre)
Growth Rate	High to very high
Resistant to	Moderately resistant to downy mildew
Susceptible to	
Storability	Retains 45% alpha acid after 6 months storage at 20ºC (68ºF)
Ease of Harvest	
Total Oil	0.89 mL/100g
Myrcene Oil	56%
Humulene Oil	13%
Caryophyllene Oil	10%
Farnesene Oil	Trace Amounts
Substitutes	Fuggle
Style Guide	

References

http://cropandsoil.oregonstate.edu/hopcultivars/21279.html

https://books.google.com.au/books?id=_H1yBgAAQBAJ&pg=PA199&lpg=PA199&dq=key
worths+midseason&source=bl&ots=O9VHWG8zik&sig=aWzpbt6oeCdMkmIVirli1NfNxg
8&hl=en&sa=X&ved=0CDQQ6AEwBWoVChMIy4fm8LfnyAIVRa2mCh12sAED#v=onepa
ge&q=keyworths%20midseason&f=false

Kirin II

Kirin II is one of a few Japanese hops to spring up since the Japanese governments decision to reduce the importation of beer hops. The variety is grown domestically and solely under government contract. The variety was developed by Kirin Brewery Co. as a clonal selection from Shinshuwase and as such is directly descended from Saaz and open pollinated White Vine.

Also Known As	
Characteristics	
Purpose	Bittering & Aroma
Alpha Acid Composition	8%
Beta Acid Composition	6.4%
Cohumulone Composition	43%-45%
Country	Japan
Cone Size	
Cone Density	
Seasonal Maturity	Very late
Yield Amount	1860 kg/hectare (1660 lbs/acre)
Growth Rate	
Resistant to	
Susceptible to	
Storability	Retains 70% alpha acid after 6 months storage at 20°C (68°F)
Ease of Harvest	
Total Oil	1.18mL/100g
Myrcene Oil	50%
Humulene Oil	14%

Caryophyllene Oil	9.4%
Farnesene Oil	0.2%
Substitutes	
Style Guide	

References

https://www.ars.usda.gov/SP2UserFiles/person/2450/hopcultivars/21286.html

https://books.google.com.au/books?id=_H1yBgAAQBAJ&pg=PA202&lpg=PA202&dq=kiri
n+ii+hops&source=bl&ots=O9XD-Nbxpk&sig=ER93hbu-
Yp59rVo2MUxANDtYngY&hl=en&sa=X&ved=0ahUKEwjt1InR4snMAhWJHJQKHY5FC
M44ChDoAQgjMAI#v=onepage&q=kirin%20ii%20hops&f=false

Kitamidori

Developed by the Kirin Brewery Company in Tokyo, Japan, Kitamidori is no longer grown commercially there or anywhere else. It was bred alongside Toyomidori and Eastern Gold as a potential super alpha replacement for Kirin No. 2, which was itself a replacement for Shinshuwase hops. It sports an oil composition with remarkable similarities to Saaz.

Also Known As	
Characteristics	
Purpose	Bittering
Alpha Acid Composition	9%-12%
Beta Acid Composition	5%-6%
Cohumulone Composition	22%
Country	Japan
Cone Size	
Cone Density	
Seasonal Maturity	Late
Yield Amount	1490 kg/hectare (1330 lbs/acre)
Growth Rate	
Resistant to	
Susceptible to	

Storability	Retains 75% alpha acid after 6 months storage at 20°C (68°F)
Ease of Harvest	
Total Oil	1.35 mL/100g
Myrcene Oil	34%
Humulene Oil	31%
Caryophyllene Oil	8%-10%
Farnesene Oil	6%-7%
Substitutes	Kirin No. 2, Saaz, Toyomidori, Eastern Gold
Style Guide	

References

http://www.ars.usda.gov/SP2UserFiles/person/2450/hopcultivars/21677.html

http://www.asbcnet.org/publications/journal/vol/abstracts/50-03.htm

https://books.google.com.au/books?id=fctJLwKUzX4C&pg=PT528&lpg=PT528&dq=kitam idori+hops&source=bl&ots=DZu_ZM_yjx&sig=WrGssNZldelx6JOi5gvVZcAKJD0&hl=en &sa=X&redir_esc=y#v=onepage&q=kitamidori%20hops&f=false

https://books.google.com.au/books?id=mROkAgAAQBAJ&pg=PA251&lpg=PA251&dq=ki tamidori+hops&source=bl&ots=9Uo9sO72vU&sig=m1dpsWCxYHCPb28hLzH0lAaMi-M&hl=en&sa=X&redir_esc=y#v=onepage&q=kitamidori%20hops&f=false

Kohatu

Kohatu, meaning stone or rock in Maori, was released alongside Wai-iti in 2011. It was named after Kohatu, a small town nestled by the Motueka River, south west of Nelson, New Zealand. Kohatu is not as fruity as Wai-iti, but with its intense aroma of tropical fruit and freshly crushed pine needles, it adds a wonderfully fresh character to beer. Even with a low alpha, when used as an early addition it features a pleasant, rounded bitterness.

Homebrewer's Comments

Kohatu didn't quite live up to its commercial description for me. It was definitely fruity, but it reminded me of a mixed red fruit juice similar to Hawaiian Punch. I couldn't distinguish individual fruits. The pine character was subtle. The bitterness was soft. The 75ibu beer drank like a 35ibu beer. Overall, I wasn't too impressed with Kohatu, but might give it another chance someday in a fruit beer. *(Kinetic via homebrewersassociation.org)*

Also Known As	
Characteristics	Intense tropical fuit and pine needle aroma
Purpose	Aroma
Alpha Acid Composition	6%-8.1%
Beta Acid Composition	4%-6%
Cohumulone Composition	21%
Country	New Zealand
Cone Size	
Cone Density	Loose
Seasonal Maturity	Early to mid
Yield Amount	
Growth Rate	
Resistant to	
Susceptible to	
Storability	
Ease of Harvest	
Total Oil	0.12-1.0 mL/100g
Myrcene Oil	35.5%
Humulene Oil	36.5%
Caryophyllene Oil	11.5%
Farnesene Oil	0.3%
Substitutes	
Style Guide	Ale, Pale Ale, India Pale Ale

References

http://www.reddit.com/r/Homebrewing/comments/1xpv5q/kohatu_initial_impressions_on_a_lesser_known_new/

http://www.farmhousebrewingsupply.com/kohatu-4-oz-2013/

http://www.brew-dudes.com/kohatu-hops/5624

http://beertravl.com/portfolio/new-zealand-hop-strains/

http://hopco.com.au/f.ashx/Kohatu.pdf

Landhopfen

A low growth rate and yield in addition to a susceptibility to viruses are all reasons why the old German Landhopfen variety is no longer grown commercially. While it's exact date of creation remains illusive, it has been documented as a variety as far back as 1851. It is said to have good European aroma characteristics and is thought to be a cultivar of an old German land race created via clonal selection.

Also Known As	
Characteristics	Pleasing European aroma
Purpose	Aroma
Alpha Acid Composition	3.2%-4.1%
Beta Acid Composition	2.5%-3.5%
Cohumulone Composition	21%-25%
Country	Germany
Cone Size	
Cone Density	
Seasonal Maturity	Early
Yield Amount	< 1120 kg/hectare (< 1000 lbs/acre)
Growth Rate	Moderate
Resistant to	Moderately resistant to downy mildew
Susceptible to	Susceptible to Yellow Fleck, Hop Mosaic virus and Hop Latent virus
Storability	Retains 66% alpha acid after 6 months storage at 20°C (68°F)
Ease of Harvest	
Total Oil	0.25 -0.45 mL/100g
Myrcene Oil	37%
Humulene Oil	22%
Caryophyllene Oil	6.3%
Farnesene Oil	13.3%
Substitutes	
Style Guide	

References

http://www.ars.usda.gov/SP2UserFiles/person/2450/hopcultivars/21172.html

http://allgrain.beer/hops/landhopfen/

https://translate.google.com.au/translate?hl=en&sl=de&u=https://books.google.com.au/books%3Fid%3DM7VDAAAAcAAJ%26pg%3DPA1268%26lpg%3DPA1268%26dq%3Dlandhopfen%2Byear%26source%3Dbl%26ots%3DJfpR-H81f3%26sig%3DQiZtpR1RHVkmR-YXpR2cuTXtzXU&prev=search

Legacy™

Legacy™ has been grown in Washington State for over 50 years. Despite this, Hops Direct, LLC registered the variety in 2013 and named it Legacy.

The variety displays some lovely wild notes such as blackberry, black currant, orange and grapefruit as well as floral and spicy notes. Legacy is about as far from a noble-style hop aroma as you can get.

Homebrewer's Comments

> The black currant (flavor) is a little stronger than I anticipated, especially in the dry hop. I did a winter ale that was about 50/50 legacy and serebrianka and the black currant pretty much took over the beer. What I'm really excited about though, I (also) used them in a pale ale in combination with amarillo and citra, where legacy was slighty under half of the total hops. Insane! Never tasted a beer quite like it, I've been trying to keep my hands off it as it still tastes a bit green/watery, but the hoppy-fruitiness is just crazy.   *(markg388 via homebrewtalk.com)*

Also Known As	
Characteristics	Notes of blackberry, black currant, orange and grapefruit. Floral and spicy.
Purpose	Bittering & Aroma
Alpha Acid Composition	7.8%-8.4%
Beta Acid Composition	
Cohumulone Composition	
Country	US
Cone Size	
Cone Density	

Seasonal Maturity	
Yield Amount	
Growth Rate	
Resistant to	
Susceptible to	
Storability	
Ease of Harvest	
Total Oil	
Myrcene Oil	
Humulene Oil	
Caryophyllene Oil	
Farnesene Oil	
Substitutes	Cluster, Galena, Northern Brewer
Style Guide	Ale, Lager, Stout, India Pale Ale

References

http://www.hopsdirect.com/legacy-leaf/
http://www.hopsdirect.com/legacy-hop-pellets/
http://www.brew-dudes.com/legacy-hops/4840

Liberty

Born in 1983, Liberty is half-sister to Crystal, Ultra and Mt. Hood. It originates from Hallertau Mittelfrüher and a disease resistant German aroma male. Liberty's yield is low but it still enjoys popularity, especially in the US. It is a genetically sterile variety and not suitable for breeding.

Harvest Moon Brewery uses Liberty liberally in their Full Moon Pale Ale along with Cascade. Given its heritage, it's no wonder Liberty is likened characteristically to noble hops. Brewers should be advised that, due to Liberty's very poor storage stability, they should be obtained and used fresh where possible.

Homebrewer's Comments

Liberty is my favorite Hallertau Mittelfrueh-derived triploid hop. If you like the hop flavor found in Sam Adams Boston

Lager, you will love Liberty. Of the four Hallertau Mittelfrueh-derived triploid hop cultivars that were released by Dr. Al Haunold (the other three are Mt. Hood, Ultra and Crystal), Liberty comes the closest to matching the real thing. However, it does so while bringing its own thing to the party. Liberty is best used in pale to very pale beers. It's a great all pale base malt, single hop beer hop. *(EarlyAmateurZymurgist via homebrewtalk.com)*

Also Known As	
Characteristics	Noble hop characteristics
Purpose	Aroma
Alpha Acid Composition	3%-6%
Beta Acid Composition	3.5%
Cohumulone Composition	24%-28%
Country	US
Cone Size	Medium
Cone Density	Compact
Seasonal Maturity	Early
Yield Amount	1200-2000 kg/hectare (1070-1780 lbs/acre)
Growth Rate	Very high
Resistant to	Moderately resistant to downy mildew
Susceptible to	
Storability	Retains 35%-55% alpha acid after 6 months storage at 20ºC (68ºF)
Ease of Harvest	Moderate to easy
Total Oil	1.3 mL/100g
Myrcene Oil	46%
Humulene Oil	31%
Caryophyllene Oil	9%-12%
Farnesene Oil	< 1%
Substitutes	Hallertau, Mount Hood, Traditon
Style Guide	Bock, Lager, Pale Ale

References

http://beerlegends.com/liberty-hops
http://www.ars.usda.gov/SP2UserFiles/person/2450/hopcultivars/21457.html

Lubelska

Often thought to be a Polish hop, Lubelska actually originates in Zatec, Czechoslovakia. Sometimes marketed as Lublin or Lubelski, Lubelska's high humulene content is trumped only by its rare, high levels of farnesene. This oil profile results in interesting aromas of magnolia and lavender. It is considered to very noble-like in character. Thought to be a landrace cultivar of Saaz, it is now a mainstay of Polish breweries.

Also Known As	Lublin, Lubelski
Characteristics	Noble-like character
Purpose	Aroma
Alpha Acid Composition	3%-5%
Beta Acid Composition	2.5%-4%
Cohumulone Composition	25%-28%
Country	Czechoslovakia
Cone Size	Medium
Cone Density	Loose
Seasonal Maturity	Early
Yield Amount	900-1250 kg/hectare (800-1120 lbs/acre)
Growth Rate	Moderate
Resistant to	
Susceptible to	
Storability	Retains 70%-75% alpha acid after 6 months storage at 20°C (68°F)
Ease of Harvest	Difficult
Total Oil	0.5-1.2 mL/100g
Myrcene Oil	22%-35%
Humulene Oil	30%-40%
Caryophyllene Oil	6%-11%

Farnesene Oil	10%-14%
Substitutes	Saaz, Sterling
Style Guide	Pilsner, Lager

References
http://beerlegends.com/lublin-lubelski-hops
https://www.freshops.com/hops/usda-named-hop-variety-descriptions#usda_id_21113

Lubelska-Pulawy

First entering commercial production in 1964, Lubelska-Pulawy is a Polish-grown variety descended from the original Czech hop Lubelski, or Lublin as it is sometimes known. It was grown by the Hop Institute in Pulawy, Poland in an effort to better mold the variety to local conditions and increase alpha potential. It is said to have pleasant European characteristics, unsurprising given its Saaz roots.

Also Known As	Lubelski-Pulawy, Polish Lublin
Characteristics	Pleasant European characteristics
Purpose	Aroma
Alpha Acid Composition	5%-7%
Beta Acid Composition	3%-5%
Cohumulone Composition	23%-25%
Country	Poland
Cone Size	
Cone Density	
Seasonal Maturity	Early
Yield Amount	340 kg/hectare (310 lbs/acre)
Growth Rate	
Resistant to	
Susceptible to	
Storability	Retains 55% alpha acid after 6 months storage at 20ºC (68ºF)
Ease of Harvest	

Total Oil	0.88 mL/100g
Myrcene Oil	52%
Humulene Oil	14%
Caryophyllene Oil	4%-6%
Farnesene Oil	12%
Substitutes	Brewer's Gold, Nugget Glacier
Style Guide	

References
https://www.freshops.com/hops/usda-named-hop-variety-descriptions#usda_id_21523
http://www.barthhaasgroup.com/johbarth/images/pdfs/Hops_1967-68.pdf

Lucan

Developed at the Hop Research Institute in Zatec, Czechoslovakia, and officially registered in 1941, Lucan was created via clonal selection of the Czech Zatecky Krajovy variety. Known as being one of the Czech Rebublic's oldest varieties, it is also thought likely to be a close relative of Saaz. Noted for its commercially desirable noble aroma qualities and mild bitterness, its yield is marginal in the US, but decent in its native Czech Republic.

Also Known As	Saazer, Bohemian Early Red
Characteristics	Mild bitterness, noble aroma
Purpose	Aroma
Alpha Acid Composition	4%
Beta Acid Composition	3.3%
Cohumulone Composition	21%
Country	Czech Republic
Cone Size	
Cone Density	
Seasonal Maturity	Early
Yield Amount	340 kg/hectare (300 lbs/acre)
Growth Rate	Low
Resistant to	

Susceptible to   Moderately susceptible to downy mildew

Storability

Ease of Harvest

Total Oil

Myrcene Oil

Humulene Oil

Caryophyllene Oil

Farnesene Oil

Substitutes

Style Guide

References

http://www.ars.usda.gov/SP2UserFiles/person/2450/hopcultivars/21528.html

https://books.google.com.au/books?id=W2oDHNDpmjkC&pg=PA77&lpg=PA77&dq=Zatecky+krajovy+hops&source=bl&ots=Y8l-1K8hSu&sig=GNZzw1uwI4ptfxrby0FmAMH0akM&hl=en&sa=X&ved=0CB4Q6AEwAGoVChMImbL-8Y_pyAIVhCyICh2trQR_#v=onepage&q=Zatecky%20krajovy%20hops&f=false

https://books.google.com.au/books?id=fctJLwKUzX4C&pg=PT941&lpg=PT941&dq=lucan+myrcene&source=bl&ots=DZt1TTXDrz&sig=_vnQJOtew3JHHlHVIBvmPBu3pcY&hl=en&sa=X&ved=0CCUQ6AEwAmoVChMIqZy4jJLpyAIVFjGICh3ncwDB#v=onepage&q=lucan%20myrcene&f=false

Magnum

German-grown Magnum is fast becoming a brewing favorite in Europe and towards being one of the most widely grown high alpha varieties in the US. Used predominately as a base bittering hop it features an exceptional growth rate, yield and superlative storage stability and is said to result in squeaky clean bitterness and subtle citrus-like flavors.

Originally created at the German Hop Institute in Hull, Magnum was released to the brewing world in 1980 and has since been recognized as being most suited to pale ales and lagers where a clean bitterness is desired. It is the result of a cross between Galena and an unnamed German male variety.

Homebrewer's Comments

I use US and German Magnum interchangeably in some of my beers as the bittering hop. I can't tell any difference in the finished product. *(SacoDeToro via thebrewingnetwork.com)*

Also Known As	Hallertau Magnum
Characteristics	Clean bitterness, subtle citrus flavors
Purpose	Bittering
Alpha Acid Composition	12%-14%
Beta Acid Composition	4.5%-5.5%
Cohumulone Composition	24%-25%
Country	Germany
Cone Size	Large
Cone Density	Moderate
Seasonal Maturity	Late
Yield Amount	1340-1700 kg/hectare (1200-1520 lbs/acre)
Growth Rate	Moderate
Resistant to	Resistant to verticillium wilt and peronospora
Susceptible to	
Storability	Retains 80%-85% alpha acid after 6 months storage at 20ºC (68ºF)
Ease of Harvest	Difficult
Total Oil	1.9-2.3 mL/100g
Myrcene Oil	30%-35%
Humulene Oil	34%-40%
Caryophyllene Oil	8%-12%
Farnesene Oil	0%-1%
Substitutes	Hallertauer Taurus, Columbus, Nugget, Horizon

India Pilsner, Belgian India Pale Ale, American Ale, Blonde Ale, Pale Ale, Nut Brown Ale, Dark Ale, Pilsner, Bright Ale, Hefeweizen

References
http://beerlegends.com/magnum-hops
https://www.hopunion.com/magnum/
http://beerlegends.com/hallertauer-magnum-hops

Magnum (US)

Magnum is grown on limited acreage in the US but what is produced has an excellent bittering profile and a nice, hoppy, floral aroma and subtle characters of citrus. Though genetically indistinguishable from the original German Magnum, some subtleties undoubtedly exist through varied growing conditions between the two countries. Both hops however are largely considered to be totally interchangeable.

The original German-grown Magnum was released in 1980 and hails from the German Hop Institute in Hull. It is considered to be notably good for strong ales like IPA's and Imperial beers but is also said to shine well in Lagers and Pilsners.

Homebrewer's Comments

I use Magnum to bitter pretty much all of my Belgian and German style brews, as well as many other styles. It's my go-to bittering hop due to its smoothness and the fact that it's a lot more economical to bitter with higher alpha hops than it is for lower alpha varieties. *(LLBeanJ via homebrewtalk.com)*

Avery's Maharaja uses Magnum for flavor if you wanna know what it's like. For bittering it's super squeaky clean. *(Saccharomyces via homebrewtalk.com)*

Also Known As   Yakima Magnum

Characteristics   Clean bittering, light citrus flavor

Purpose	Bittering
Alpha Acid Composition	10%-14%
Beta Acid Composition	4.5%-7%
Cohumulone Composition	24%-30%
Country	US
Cone Size	
Cone Density	
Seasonal Maturity	
Yield Amount	
Growth Rate	
Resistant to	
Susceptible to	
Storability	
Ease of Harvest	
Total Oil	1.9-3.0 mL/100g
Myrcene Oil	
Humulene Oil	
Caryophyllene Oil	
Farnesene Oil	
Substitutes	German Magnum, Horizon, Northdown, Northern Brewer
Style Guide	American Pale Ale, American India Pale, Ale, Strong Ale, American Lager, Lager, Pilsner, India Pale Ale

References
http://www.brew365.com/hops_magnum.php
http://www.midwestsupplies.com/us-magnum-pellet-hops.html
http://www.homebrewtalk.com/showthread.php?t=190388

Mandarina Bavaria

Daughter of Cascade, Hallertau Blanc and Hüll Melon, Mandarina Bavaria originated in Hüll, Germany and was released to the brewing masses in 2012. It is useful for both flavor and aroma and imparts slightly sweet notes of tangerine and citrus, especially when used for dry hopping.

Homebrewer's Comments

It's great. Not quite like an American hop; it tastes and smells exactly the way you might expect it to: like a cross between a citrusy fruity American hop and a German noble(think hersbrucker.) In the nose there's a nice subtle fruitiness with a bit of the herbal grassy notes that you get from German varieties. On the palate it's a little juicier and fruitier(oranges, of course mandarin) with the grassy herbal flavors more in the background. Not too in your face, but helped make a great balanced pale ale. *(justclancy via homebrewtalk.com)*

Like it sounds, its pure tangerine. Not nearly as much bite or floral character as most traditional citrusy hops like cascade and centennial. More of a sweet citrus flavor. *(m00ps via email)*

Also Known As	
Characteristics	Tangerine, Citrus
Purpose	Aroma
Alpha Acid Composition	8.5%-10.5%
Beta Acid Composition	5%-6.5%
Cohumulone Composition	33%
Country	Germany
Cone Size	
Cone Density	
Seasonal Maturity	
Yield Amount	
Growth Rate	
Resistant to	
Susceptible to	
Storability	
Ease of Harvest	
Total Oil	2.0 mL/100g
Myrcene Oil	70%

Humulene Oil	5%
Caryophyllene Oil	2%
Farnesene Oil	1%
Substitutes	Columbus, Nugget, Cascade
Style Guide	Belgian Ale, French Ale

References

http://www.baywa.eu/fileadmin/media/relaunch/Downloads/.EU/Hopfenvertrieb/14384_Flyer_Mandarina_eng_DIN_A5_k1.pdf
https://www.hopunion.com/german-mandarina-bavaria/
https://bsgcraftbrewing.com/german-mandarina-bavaria

Marynka

Marynka hops are another widely produced Polish hop from the region as Lublin. It is moderate in most things: yield, growth, stability, but her flavor profile is way above average. Despite being used primarily for bittering, Marynka features a forward, earthy and herbal flavors and aromas. It is the offspring of Brewer's Gold and was official registered in 1988.

Homebrewer's Comments

> This would make a nice clean bittering hop, since you won't need as much due to the high alpha (bitterness) %, but it also has a good full "noble" flavor and aroma that would be good in most continental (German, Belgian, Czec, etc) beers. It will give a spicy note and flavor, opposed to the citrusy american or floral English hop character. *(javedian via homebrewtalk.com)*

Also Known As	
Characteristics	Earthy and herbal flavors and aromas
Purpose	Bittering & Aroma
Alpha Acid Composition	9%-12%
Beta Acid Composition	10.2%-13%
Cohumulone Composition	26%-33%
Country	Poland

Cone Size	Medium
Cone Density	Compact
Seasonal Maturity	Early to mid
Yield Amount	1940-2200 kg/hectare (1730-1970 lbs/acre)
Growth Rate	Moderate
Resistant to	
Susceptible to	
Storability	Retains 60%-70%alpha acid after 6 months storage at 20°C (68°F)
Ease of Harvest	Difficult
Total Oil	1.8-2.2 mL/100g
Myrcene Oil	28%-31%
Humulene Oil	36%-33%
Caryophyllene Oil	10%-13%
Farnesene Oil	1.8%-2.2%
Substitutes	Tettnanger (GR)
Style Guide	Bitter, India Pale Ale, Pale Ale, Pilsner

References
http://beerlegends.com/marynka-hops
https://www.craftbrewer.com.au/shop/details.asp?PID=5157
http://brewandwinesupply.com/index.php?route=product/product&product_id=855

Mathon

The pedigree of the Mathon hop is a bit of a mystery. Early writings about hops indicate that both Mathon and Goldings were growing side by side as early as the late 1700's. Writings today appear to suggest that it may have hailed specifically from Farnham Whitebine or Canterbury Whitebine in much the same way the Goldings varieties did. One this is for sure, it solidly features the pleasant aroma for which most Goldings hops are well known.

Also Known As	Mathon-White, Mathon Whitebine

Characteristics	Goldings-style aroma
Purpose	Aroma
Alpha Acid Composition	4.4%-6.7%
Beta Acid Composition	1.9%-2.8%
Cohumulone Composition	26%-32%
Country	UK
Cone Size	Medium
Cone Density	Compact
Seasonal Maturity	Mid to late
Yield Amount	
Growth Rate	
Resistant to	
Susceptible to	Susceptible to downy and powdery mildew
Storability	
Ease of Harvest	Moderate
Total Oil	0.8 - 1.0 mL/100g
Myrcene Oil	
Humulene Oil	
Caryophyllene Oil	
Farnesene Oil	
Substitutes	Bramling, East Kent Golding, Progress, Whitbread Golding
Style Guide	ESB, Bitter, Pale Ale, Porter

References
http://edsbeer.blogspot.com.au/2012/02/genesis-of-goldings.html
http://www.aplus-hops.co.uk/ProductDetails.asp?ProductCode=EM2LPO
http://www.meadowplant.co.uk/mathonhopsprofile.html

Melba

Bred by Ellerslie Hop Australia, Melba or "The Dame of Hops" as it is affectionately known, is a dual-use variety with high oil content and similarities to Galaxy. When used as an early addition, it is said to impart a clean and somewhat spicy bitterness. When used as a flavor or aroma addition though, properties of passionfruit, grapefruit and citrus come to the fore.

Homebrewer's Comments

> Definitely, an alternative for those who weren't able to obtain Galaxy this year. There's a few slight differences. There's some other fruity notes that come through. Tropical fruit, but passion fruit is still dominant. There's no grassy notes. I think it will be a hop worth looking for... enough difference for those who find Galaxy a little harsh and grassy, but similar enough for those who love the passionfruit. (*HBHB via aussiehomebrewer.com*)

Also Known As	
Characteristics	Clean spicy bitterness, aromas of passionfruit, grapefruit and citrus.
Purpose	Bittering & Aroma
Alpha Acid Composition	7%-10%
Beta Acid Composition	2.5%-5%
Cohumulone Composition	25%-35%
Country	Australia
Cone Size	
Cone Density	Compact
Seasonal Maturity	Early
Yield Amount	2200-2800 kg/hectare (1962-2498 lbs/acre)
Growth Rate	
Resistant to	
Susceptible to	
Storability	
Ease of Harvest	
Total Oil	2.0-4.0 mL/100g
Myrcene Oil	
Humulene Oil	

Caryophyllene Oil

Farnesene Oil

Substitutes   Galaxy

Style Guide

References

http://www.ellersliehop.com.au/melba™.html

http://www.ellersliehop.com.au/assets/ehe_melba.pdf

https://www.craftbrewer.com.au/shop/details.asp?PID=5999

Merkur

Merkur or Hallertau Merkur as it is sometimes known, is a high alpha bittering hop developed at the Hull Hops Research Institute in Germany. It was released in 2000. It's not all about bittering potential though; Merkur boasts high myrcene and humulene oil content giving it an earthy grounding and citrus zing. It works especially well in the early to mid-stages of brewing. Merkur is a descendant of Hallertau Magnum.

Homebrewer's Comments

Really good, clean and somewhat spicyish bittering. Pairs very well with fruit/citrus yeast and hops. In the future I plan on using these for bittering most of my beers and playing around more in late additions. *(chuckstout via homebrewtalk.com)*

Also Known As	Hallertau Merkur
Characteristics	Earthy, spicy bitterness, citrus zing
Purpose	Bittering & Aroma
Alpha Acid Composition	12%-16.2%
Beta Acid Composition	5%-7.3%
Cohumulone Composition	17.8%-19%
Country	Germany
Cone Size	Medium
Cone Density	Moderate
Seasonal Maturity	Late

Yield Amount	1760-1940 kg/hectare (1570-1730 lbs/acre)
Growth Rate	Moderate
Resistant to	Resistant to verticillium wilt, peronospora and powdery mildew
Susceptible to	
Storability	Retains 60%-70% alpha acid after 6 months storage at 20°C (68°F)
Ease of Harvest	Difficult
Total Oil	2.6-3 mL/100g
Myrcene Oil	48%-49%
Humulene Oil	29%-32%
Caryophyllene Oil	8%-9%
Farnesene Oil	0%-1%
Substitutes	Hallertau Magnum
Style Guide	

References

http://beerlegends.com/merkur-hops

https://ychhops.com/varieties/merkur

https://translate.google.com.au/translate?hl=en&sl=nl&u=https://nl.wikipedia.org/wiki/Merkur_(hop)&prev=search

Millennium

Millennium was, unsurprisingly, released in the year 2000. Emanating from the John I. Haas Breeding Program, Millennium hops are directly descended from Nugget and are considered similar in many ways to Columbus. They were born largely out of a desire for greater disease resistance and storage stability. They work well as a bittering agent in American-style ales, Stouts and are considered mild in character with an ability to impart herbaceous notes and elements of resin.

Homebrewer's Comments

I use them as my "standard" bittering hop - nice and clean (cleaner and less harsh than the nugget/columbus they are bred from IMHO) and with an adjustment for AA% I directly sub them into any recipe that calls for Magnum or Northern Brewer or any of the other relatively "clean" bittering hops. I have even used them in light lagers and such like beers with good results. *(Thirsty Boy via thebrewingnetwork.com)*

Also Known As	
Characteristics	Mild, herbaceous, elements of resin
Purpose	Bittering
Alpha Acid Composition	14.5%-16.5%
Beta Acid Composition	4.3%-5.3%
Cohumulone Composition	28%-32%
Country	
Cone Size	
Cone Density	
Seasonal Maturity	
Yield Amount	2464-2913 kg/hectare (2200-2600 lbs/acre)
Growth Rate	
Resistant to	
Susceptible to	
Storability	Retains 76% alpha acid after 6 months storage at 20°C (68°F)
Ease of Harvest	
Total Oil	1.8-2.2 mL/100g
Myrcene Oil	30%-40%
Humulene Oil	23%-27%
Caryophyllene Oil	9%-12%
Farnesene Oil	< 1%
Substitutes	Columbus, Nugget, Summit™, CTZ
Style Guide	Stout, Ale, American Ale

References

https://www.hopunion.com/millennium/

http://www.usahops.org/graphics/File/HGA%20BCI%20Reports/Variety%20Manual%207-

Mosaic®

Released in 2012 by the Hop Breeding Company, LLC, Mosaic® features complex but clean flavor characteristics and is known for its triple-use profile encompassing bittering, flavor and aroma. It has high alpha acids but low cohumulone which makes it pleasantly hoppy, carrying flavors of mango, pine, citrus and herbs and aromas of tropical and stone fruit. Mosaic® is the first daughter of Simcoe® and Nugget as has been humorously referred to by some as "Citra® on steroids".

Brewmaster's Comments

Mosaic is a newer fun hop. Lots going on with it and it can really hold its own if looking to use just a single hop variety. Deep, complex tropical flavors and aromas. *(Jeremy S Kosmicki, Brewmaster at Founders Brewing Co.)*

Homebrewer's Comments

Citra and Mosaic may have some similar qualities, but i don't get any of the Citra problems - catpee, sweat, BO, whatever you prefer - in Mosaic. *(ddrrseio via homebrewtalk.com)*

Also Known As	HBC369
Characteristics	Mango, pine, citrus, herbs, aromas of tropical and stone fruit
Purpose	Bittering & Aroma
Alpha Acid Composition	11.5%-13.5%
Beta Acid Composition	3.2%-3.9%
Cohumulone Composition	24%-26%
Country	
Cone Size	
Cone Density	
Seasonal Maturity	
Yield Amount	

Growth Rate	
Resistant to	
Susceptible to	
Storability	Retains 75% alpha acid after 6 months storage at 20ºC (68ºF)
Ease of Harvest	
Total Oil	1-1.5 mL/100g
Myrcene Oil	47%-53%
Humulene Oil	13%-16%
Caryophyllene Oil	5%-8%
Farnesene Oil	None
Substitutes	Citra®
Style Guide	India Pale Ale, Pale Ale

References
http://www.rebelbrewer.com/shop/american-hops/mosaic-hops-1oz-pellets
https://www.hopunion.com/mosaic-hbc-369-cv/

Motueka

Formerly known as Belgian Saaz or B Saaz, Motueka is a premier New Zealand hop. Developed by HortResearch, this triploid was bred from Saaz and an unnamed New Zealand breeding strain and lends itself well to Lagers, Pilsners and Belgian Ales.

It makes an excellent dual-use hop, carrying an exciting fruit aroma with refreshing notes of tropical fruit and citrus. It can be used at any point during the brewing process and works well in sweet, malty and fruity beers. Massachusettsu2019 Brewmaster Jack brews a special Motueka in a fresh, hoppy Maibock style. Sierra Nevada brewery also debuted their Southern Hemisphere Harvest fresh hops ale in April 2014 using Motueka, along with Southern Cross, as its finishing hops.

Homebrewer's Comments

I have a Belgian blond on tap right now that is hopped exclusively with motueka. It does have a bit of lemon citrus to it, but I would say it's rather more exotic than that - notes of hibiscus and passionfruit. I've also used it in a saison where the citrus and spice plays beautifully with the peppery earthiness of the yeast. I really like these hops. *(BeerLogic via homebrewtalk.com)*

Also Known As	B Saaz, Belgian Saaz
Characteristics	Tropical fruit and citrus
Purpose	Bittering & Aroma
Alpha Acid Composition	6.5%-8.5%
Beta Acid Composition	5%-5.5%
Cohumulone Composition	29%
Country	New Zealand
Cone Size	Small to medium
Cone Density	Loose
Seasonal Maturity	Early
Yield Amount	1200-1500 kg/hectare (1071-1338 lbs/acre)
Growth Rate	Very high
Resistant to	
Susceptible to	
Storability	Retains 60%-70% alpha acid after 6 months storage at 20ºC (68ºF)
Ease of Harvest	Moderate to difficult
Total Oil	0.8 mL/100g
Myrcene Oil	47.7%
Humulene Oil	3.6%
Caryophyllene Oil	2%
Farnesene Oil	12.2%
Substitutes	Saaz, Saaz (US), Sterling
Style Guide	European Ale, English Ale, Dark Lager, Pilsner, Belgian Ales, Lager, Maibock, Ales

References

Mount Hood

Released in 1989, Mount Hood is an American-bred cultivar stemming from Hallertau Mittelfrüher. Popular among American craft brewers, it makes a good aroma hop, with characteristics similar to a Hallertau or Hersbrucker and is also half-sister to Crystal, Ultra and Liberty.

It features a pleasant noble hop aroma and has been noted to impart somewhat of a flavor "punch" when freshly brewed – at least in comparison to true noble hops.

Homebrewer's Comments

> Mt Hood hops are pretty well-rounded dual purpose IMO. Can be used as a noble hop sub. But the styles they lend themselves to dont usually use dry hopping very much. I'd most likely use them in a stout/porter/brown ale or something German as flavor additions but that's just me. (m00ps via homebrewtalk.com)

Also Known As	Mt. Hood, Mt Hood
Characteristics	Noble hop aroma
Purpose	Aroma
Alpha Acid Composition	4%-8%
Beta Acid Composition	5%-8%
Cohumulone Composition	21%-23%
Country	US
Cone Size	Medium
Cone Density	Moderate to compact
Seasonal Maturity	Early to mid
Yield Amount	1450-1960 kg/hectare (1290-1750 lbs/acre)
Growth Rate	Moderate to high
Resistant to	

Susceptible to

Storability	Retains 50%-60% alpha acid after 6 months storage at 20°C (68°F)
Ease of Harvest	Difficult
Total Oil	1-1.7 mL/100g
Myrcene Oil	30%-40%
Humulene Oil	12%-38%
Caryophyllene Oil	7%-16%
Farnesene Oil	0%-1%
Substitutes	Crystal, Strisselspalter, Hersbrucker
Style Guide	Hefeweizen, Doppelbock, Russian Imperial Stout, Brown Ale, Golden Ale, Pale Ale, Amber Ale, Weizenbock, India Pale Ale, Holiday Lager, Bock, American Wheat, Alt Munich Helles, American Lager

References
https://www.hopunion.com/mt-hood/
http://beerlegends.com/mount-hood-hops

Mount Rainier

Like Mount Hood, Mount Rainier is named after one of the many active volcanoes in Washington State. Born out of the USDA-ARS hop breeding program in collaboration with Oregon State University, Mount Rainier is the progeny of Magnum and a USDA male. It has noble, Hallertau-like aroma characteristics alongside notes of citrus and a hint of licorice. It is excellent for both aroma and bittering.

Homebrewer's Comments

I just made a blonde ale with only Mt. Rainier hops. I've only tasted the FG sample so far. My initial impression is it's very much like Hallertauer. Clean bittering with spicy aroma and flavor. Like Magnum with more flavor. (*Malticulous via homebrewtalk.com*)

Also Known As	Mt. Rainier

Characteristics	Hallertau-like aroma, notes of citrus and licorice
Purpose	Bittering & Aroma
Alpha Acid Composition	5%-8.1%
Beta Acid Composition	5%-7%
Cohumulone Composition	21%-24%
Country	
Cone Size	
Cone Density	
Seasonal Maturity	
Yield Amount	
Growth Rate	
Resistant to	Resistant to downy and powdery mildew
Susceptible to	
Storability	
Ease of Harvest	
Total Oil	
Myrcene Oil	
Humulene Oil	
Caryophyllene Oil	
Farnesene Oil	
Substitutes	Hallertau, Fuggle
Style Guide	Lager, American Ale, Porter

References
https://www.hopunion.com/mt-rainier/
http://www.brew-dudes.com/mount-rainier-hops/808

MultiHead

MultiHead is a neomexicanus breed native to New Mexico and is so named because of its tendency to produce dual cones. It is a unique hop in the industry and in brewing features a heady, floral aroma and some citrus elements.

Homebrewer's Comments

I get peach, apricot, cantaloup, and some citrus. They are incredible and unique. I really would love to grow them. As low AA% as they are they would make amazing pale ales IMHO! *(moorerm04 via homebrewtalk.com)*

Also Known As	
Characteristics	Heady, floral aroma, some sweet fruit and citrus
Purpose	Bittering & Aroma
Alpha Acid Composition	3.5%-5.5%
Beta Acid Composition	5.5%-8%
Cohumulone Composition	45%
Country	US
Cone Size	
Cone Density	
Seasonal Maturity	Early to mid
Yield Amount	
Growth Rate	
Resistant to	
Susceptible to	
Storability	
Ease of Harvest	
Total Oil	0.5-1.5 mL/100g
Myrcene Oil	48%
Humulene Oil	
Caryophyllene Oil	
Farnesene Oil	
Substitutes	
Style Guide	Pale Ale

References

http://www.rnventerprises.com/files/Variety_Descriptions_20134.pdf
http://www.greatlakeshops.com/multihead---neomexicana.html

Nadwislanska

Likely descended from Czech hops, Polish-grown Nadwislanska is a green-stem variety in stark contrast to Lubelska's red stem, despite their tandem emergence. It features pleasant, noble aroma characteristics. It was bred disease free but to the disappointment of its developers, its poor yield did not improve. It is no longer grown anywhere commercially.

Also Known As	Nadwislanski
Characteristics	Noble aroma characteristics
Purpose	Aroma
Alpha Acid Composition	3%-5%
Beta Acid Composition	2.5%-5%
Cohumulone Composition	23%
Country	Poland
Cone Size	
Cone Density	
Seasonal Maturity	Early
Yield Amount	220-450 kg/hectare (200-400 lbs/acre)
Growth Rate	Low
Resistant to	Moderately resistant to downy mildew
Susceptible to	
Storability	Retains 58% alpha acid after 6 months storage at 20ºC (68ºF)
Ease of Harvest	
Total Oil	0.5 mL/100g
Myrcene Oil	32%
Humulene Oil	27%
Caryophyllene Oil	8.2%
Farnesene Oil	13.5%
Substitutes	
Style Guide	

References

http://www.ars.usda.gov/SP2UserFiles/person/2450/hopcultivars/21114.html

https://books.google.com.au/books?id=W2oDHNDpmjkC&pg=PA73&lpg=PA73&dq=nad
wislanski+hops&source=bl&ots=Y8l-
1LfiLu&sig=OIkx5L2RmLA2HVQXbNjzjr6aYQw&hl=en&sa=X&ved=0CCYQ6AEwAmoV
ChMIi43Iqs_pyAIVonSmCh2SbggQ#v=onepage&q=nadwislanski&f=false

Nelson Sauvin

Nelson Sauvin's name is derived from the Sauvignon Blanc wine grape to which many agree has similar flavor and aroma characteristics. Developed in New Zealand and released in 2000, it is considered too wild for many major brewers. Despite this, Nelson Sauvin has found significant use among craft breweries and home brewers for its eccentric characteristics.

They variety has gained popularity in American-style Pale Ales but is definitely a hop that requires prudent and discerning application in brewing. Nelson Sauvin's oil profile is complex and fortunately works well as an aroma hop, flavor hop and also for bittering. Low cohumulone is responsible for its smooth bittering qualities. It is descended from Smoothcone.

Homebrewer's Comments

> I have been using these for a few years now. They really are still a hidden gem and it surprises me that they have not blown up more. I think half the problem is the bogus description that says they impart wine like characteristics that maybe turns people off. I never did much experimentation with them, After i got my first pound of pellets and got a smell of them my mind instantly told me that these are the hop to use with IPA's & Pale ales. They pack a lot of punch, you don't have to use a crap ton to get good results and in the flavor and aroma department, it always comes through really well in the finished beer. *(martymoat via homebrewtalk.com)*

Also Known As	
Characteristics	Smooth bittering, rich, fruity, gooseberry and white-wine flavors
Purpose	Bittering & Aroma
Alpha Acid Composition	12%-13%
Beta Acid Composition	6%-8%
Cohumulone Composition	24%
Country	New Zealand
Cone Size	
Cone Density	Compact
Seasonal Maturity	Mid to late
Yield Amount	
Growth Rate	High
Resistant to	
Susceptible to	
Storability	
Ease of Harvest	
Total Oil	1.1 mL/100g
Myrcene Oil	22.2%
Humulene Oil	36.4%
Caryophyllene Oil	10.7%
Farnesene Oil	0.4%
Substitutes	Pacific Jade, Pacifica
Style Guide	American Pale Ale, India Pale Ale, Pale Ale

References

http://hopunion.com/new-zealand-nelson-sauvin/
http://www.nzhops.co.nz/variety/nelson-sauvin
https://ychhops.com/varieties/nelson-sauvin
https://www.craftbrewer.com.au/shop/details.asp?PID=598

Neo1

Neo1 is another neomexicanus breed, this time with a potent lemon-citrus character. Native to New Mexico, it is a true sun-worshipping hop, with quite lively growth when exposed to maximum sunlight. It is also said that Neo1 is naturally pest resistant due to its abundance of limonene and linalool. Noe1 is a sister to Amallia.

Also Known As	
Characteristics	Significant lemon-citrus character
Purpose	Bittering & Aroma
Alpha Acid Composition	7%-9%
Beta Acid Composition	3%-3.3%
Cohumulone Composition	
Country	US
Cone Size	
Cone Density	
Seasonal Maturity	Very early
Yield Amount	
Growth Rate	
Resistant to	
Susceptible to	
Storability	
Ease of Harvest	
Total Oil	
Myrcene Oil	
Humulene Oil	
Caryophyllene Oil	
Farnesene Oil	
Substitutes	
Style Guide	

References

http://www.homebrewing.org/New-Mexican-Neo1-Hop-Rhizomes-_p_3511.html

Neoplanta

Slovenian hop Neoplanta hails from a combination between Northern Brewer, Savinsky Golding and a wild Slovenian male. First appearing in the late 1960's, the variety was bred alongside Vojvodina and Dunav in the hopes of replacing the land race variety Backa which was suffering from poor yields.

Also Known As	
Characteristics	
Purpose	Bittering & Aroma
Alpha Acid Composition	7%-12%
Beta Acid Composition	2.9%-5%
Cohumulone Composition	36%
Country	Slovenia
Cone Size	
Cone Density	
Seasonal Maturity	Late
Yield Amount	1435 kg/hectare (1280 lbs/acre)
Growth Rate	High to very high
Resistant to	Moderately resistant to resistant to downy mildew
Susceptible to	
Storability	Retains 63% alpha acid after 6 months storage at 20°C (68°F)
Ease of Harvest	
Total Oil	1.3 mL/100g
Myrcene Oil	49%
Humulene Oil	20%
Caryophyllene Oil	8.9%
Farnesene Oil	5%

References

http://www.ars.usda.gov/SP2UserFiles/person/2450/hopchem/21082.html

https://bsgcraftbrewing.com/Resources%5CCraftBrewing%5CPDFs%5CAgricultural_Reports_and_Papers/TheBreeding_Varieties.pdf

https://books.google.com.au/books?id=mROkAgAAQBAJ&pg=PA250&lpg=PA250&dq=neoplanta+hops&source=bl&ots=9Up8rX41DS&sig=duJi-JXanex7YMlvkuN9wVP38AQ&hl=en&sa=X&ved=0ahUKEwicoKjS9cnMAhVDKJQKHe5-DGYQ6AEINTAF#v=onepage&q=neoplanta%20hops&f=false

https://books.google.com.au/books?id=fctJLwKUzX4C&pg=PT596&lpg=PT596&dq=neoplanta+hops&source=bl&ots=DZvZYVXxrv&sig=HGdZMh1AOv7WeJy2VyzPALYUWfo&hl=en&sa=X&ved=0ahUKEwicoKjS9cnMAhVDKJQKHe5-DGYQ6AEIOjAG#v=onepage&q=neoplanta%20hops&f=false

http://freshops.com/usda-named-hop-variety-descriptions/#usda_id_21082

Newport

Newport is the offspring of Magnum and a USDA male variety. Oregon State University and the USDA successfully bred it in 2002 in an effort to address concerns over mildew resistance. It was said to have helped save Northwest US hops production around this time when mildew issues threatened multiple hops varieties.

Newport features flavors ranging from wine-like to balsamic but with its exceptionally high alpha content, it is mostly used early in the boil for clean bitterness.

Homebrewer's Comments

> I used them in my best beer yet, my American Winter Brown. So far as I can tell, they gave me a nice clean bitterness. *(Coastarine via homebrewtalk.com)*

Also Known As	New Port
Characteristics	Clean bitterness, flavors of wine and balsamic
Purpose	Bittering
Alpha Acid Composition	13.5%-17%

Beta Acid Composition	7.2%-9.1%
Cohumulone Composition	36%-38%
Country	
Cone Size	Medium to large
Cone Density	Loose to moderate
Seasonal Maturity	Mid to late
Yield Amount	1990-2250 kg/hectare (1775-2000 lbs/acre)
Growth Rate	Moderate
Resistant to	Resistant to powdery mildew and downy mildew
Susceptible to	
Storability	Retains 60% alpha acid after 6 months storage at 20ºC (68ºF)
Ease of Harvest	Difficult
Total Oil	1.6-3.6 mL/100g
Myrcene Oil	47%-54%
Humulene Oil	9%-1%
Caryophyllene Oil	1%-7%
Farnesene Oil	0%-1%
Substitutes	Galena, Nugget
Style Guide	Pale Ale, Amecan Lager

References
http://beerlegends.com/newport-hops
https://www.hopunion.com/newport/

Nordgaard

Nordgaard is an old Belgian or Danish land race that has been used for breeding, particularly in Solvenia in the 1970's. It's exact original is unclear. The result of Spalter crossed with an unknown variety, it is said to impart pleasant continental aroma characteristics and is high in humulene.

Also Known As	
Characteristics	Pleasing continental aroma
Purpose	Aroma
Alpha Acid Composition	7.5%
Beta Acid Composition	3.4%
Cohumulone Composition	29%
Country	Uncertain (Belgium or Denmark)
Cone Size	
Cone Density	
Seasonal Maturity	Early
Yield Amount	340-1230 kg/hectare (300-1100 lbs/acre)
Growth Rate	Low to moderate
Resistant to	Moderately resistant to tolerant to downy mildew
Susceptible to	
Storability	Retains 79% alpha acid after 6 months storage at 20°C (68°F)
Ease of Harvest	
Total Oil	0.94 mL/100g
Myrcene Oil	47%
Humulene Oil	27%
Caryophyllene Oil	11%
Farnesene Oil	1.7%
Substitutes	
Style Guide	

References

http://www.ars.usda.gov/sp2userfiles/person/2450/hopcultivars/21215.html

https://www.diva-portal.org/smash/get/diva2:736988/FULLTEXT01.pdf

Northdown

Northdown was developed at Wye College in England in the early 1970's and was initially bred primarily for its resistance to downy mildew. It is the offspring of Northern Brewer and Challenger and an aunt to Target.

It is a dual-purpose hop but is particularly good in the early to mid stages of the boil. It is considered slightly higher impacting in flavor than its parent, Challenger. This flavor is considered fresh, flowery and piney with notes of berry and spice.

Homebrewer's Comments

> I feel like Northdown and Target both allow the flavor and aroma hops to really shine. They play more supporting roles in a brew. *(Golddiggie via homebrewtalk.com)*

Also Known As	
Characteristics	Fresh, flowery, piney, berry and spice
Purpose	Bittering & Aroma
Alpha Acid Composition	7%-10%
Beta Acid Composition	4%-5.5%
Cohumulone Composition	24%-32%
Country	
Cone Size	Medium to large
Cone Density	Loose
Seasonal Maturity	Mid
Yield Amount	1320-1700 kg/hectare (1180-1520 lbs/acre)
Growth Rate	Moderate to high
Resistant to	
Susceptible to	
Storability	Retains 60%-70% alpha acid after 6 months storage at 20°C (68°F)
Ease of Harvest	Difficult
Total Oil	1.2-2.5 mL/100g
Myrcene Oil	23%-29%
Humulene Oil	37%-45%
Caryophyllene Oil	13%-17%

Farnesene Oil	0%-1%
Substitutes	Challenger, Admiral
Style Guide	Blonde Ale

References

http://beerlegends.com/northdown-hops

http://www.britishhops.org.uk/northdown/

https://www.craftbrewer.com.au/shop/details.asp?PID=624

https://ychhops.com/varieties/northdown

Northern Brewer

Northern Brewer is a well-known dual-use hop developed at Wye College in 1934. Currently, it is being grown in several countries around the world. The original was a cross between Canterbury Golding and a Brewer's Gold male. Today, it is grown mostly in Germany and the US.

Northern Brewer is used majorly in European beers and ales, from Lambics to Porters and everything in between. It is also popular in California Common-style beers with its woody, piney and minty essence.

Homebrewer's Comments

> NB is a pretty versatile hop. I've used it in stouts, porters, and pale ales all with enjoyable results. I've not used it as a late addition but I have seen several recipes that do and those that have brewed them report good results. I find NB to be minty flavored and the bitterness to be very resiny and unique. *(KraphtBier via homebrewtalk.com)*

Also Known As	
Characteristics	Minty and resinous
Purpose	Bittering & Aroma
Alpha Acid Composition	9.5%
Beta Acid Composition	4%
Cohumulone Composition	26%

Country	
Cone Size	
Cone Density	
Seasonal Maturity	Early
Yield Amount	900-1340 kg/hectare (800-1200 lbs/acre)
Growth Rate	Low to moderate
Resistant to	Moderately resistant to downy mildew and resistant to verticillium wilt
Susceptible to	
Storability	Retains 77% alpha acid after 6 months storage at 20°C (68°F)
Ease of Harvest	
Total Oil	1.61 mL/100g
Myrcene Oil	56%
Humulene Oil	21%
Caryophyllene Oil	7.6%
Farnesene Oil	0.1%
Substitutes	
Style Guide	Lambic, Porter, California Common, European Ales, Stout

References
https://en.wikipedia.org/wiki/List_of_hop_varieties#Northern_Brewer
https://ychhops.com/varieties/northern-brewer
http://freshops.com/usda-named-hop-variety-descriptions/#usda_id_64107

Northern Brewer (GR)

Northern Brewer was originally developed in England in 1934 but is now largely grown in Germany. German-grown Northern Brewer is considered identical to the original UK-bred variety though subtle differences attributable to the different growing region may be evident.

Northern Brewer is also grown in notable quantity in the US though this variety is now genetically distinct from the original. In brewing, it is useful as both a bittering and aroma hop but is used predominantly as an early addition by commercial brewers in Germany.

Also Known As	Hallertau Northern Brewer, Hallertauer Northern Brewer
Characteristics	
Purpose	Bittering
Alpha Acid Composition	7%-10%
Beta Acid Composition	3%-5%
Cohumulone Composition	27%-33%
Country	UK
Cone Size	
Cone Density	
Seasonal Maturity	
Yield Amount	1600 kg/hectare (1420 lbs/acre)
Growth Rate	
Resistant to	
Susceptible to	
Storability	
Ease of Harvest	
Total Oil	1-1.6 mL/100g
Myrcene Oil	25%-45%
Humulene Oil	35%-50%
Caryophyllene Oil	10%-20%
Farnesene Oil	< 1%
Substitutes	Perle, Northern Brewer (American)
Style Guide	Steam Beer, German Ale, German Lager

References

http://beerlegends.com/northern-brewer-us-hops
http://www.homebrewtalk.com/wiki/index.php/Hallertau_Northern_Brewer

Northern Brewer (US)

Genetically distinct from the original English variety, US Northern Brewer was created as a cross between Northern Brewer and a Native American variety. The result is much better suited to US growing conditions.

For a long time Northern Brewer was relegated solely to Europe, but is now enjoying a resurgence in US craft beers, particularly Steam and California Common-style brews. It's considered useful in a wide variety of other beer and ale types though.

Also Known As	
Characteristics	
Purpose	Bittering & Aroma
Alpha Acid Composition	8%-10%
Beta Acid Composition	3%-5%
Cohumulone Composition	20%-30%
Country	US
Cone Size	Medium
Cone Density	Moderate to compact
Seasonal Maturity	Early to mid
Yield Amount	1600-1800 kg/hectare (1420-1610 lbs/acre)
Growth Rate	Moderate
Resistant to	Resistant to downy mildew
Susceptible to	
Storability	Retains 70%-85% alpha acid after 6 months storage at 20ºC (68ºF)
Ease of Harvest	Difficult
Total Oil	1.5-2 mL/100g
Myrcene Oil	50%-60%
Humulene Oil	20%-30%
Caryophyllene Oil	5%-10%
Farnesene Oil	0%-1%

| Substitutes | Chinook |
| Style Guide | India Pale Ale |

References

http://beerlegends.com/northern-brewer-us-hops
https://ychhops.com/varieties/northern-brewer

Nugget

Nugget's super alpha acid content, low beta and low cohumulone percentages give it an excellent bittering kick popular in IPAs, Imperials and other super hoppy brews. It's high myrcene content also results in a green, herbal aroma.

Daughter of Brewer's Gold and mother of Millennium, Nugget's popularity has grown quickly. Released in 1983, by 1987 it was producing 14% of the Pacific Northwest's hops.

Brewmaster's Comments

Nugget and Bravo are my favourite for bittering. They provide very solid, repeatable bitterness and light flavour for most ales without adding astringency. *(Ryan Schmiege, Assistant Brewmaster at Deschutes Brewery)*

Homebrewer's Comments

I use it as my primary bittering hop for all styles, saving my other hops for flavoring and aroma. Never heard/or tried it as an aroma or flavor but curious myself what the results would be. *(PT Ray via homebrewtalk.com)*

Also Known As	
Characteristics	Solid bittering, light flavor, herbal aroma
Purpose	Bittering & Aroma
Alpha Acid Composition	9.5%-14%
Beta Acid Composition	4.2%-5.8%
Cohumulone Composition	22%-30%

Country	US
Cone Size	Medium to large
Cone Density	Compact
Seasonal Maturity	Mid
Yield Amount	1700-2200 kg/hectare (1520-1970 lbs/acre)
Growth Rate	Moderate
Resistant to	Resistant to prunus necrotic ring-spot virus, downy mildew and powdery mildew
Susceptible to	
Storability	Retains 70%-80% alpha acid after 6 months storage at 20ºC (68ºF)
Ease of Harvest	Difficult
Total Oil	1.5-3 mL/100g
Myrcene Oil	48%-59%
Humulene Oil	12%-22%
Caryophyllene Oil	7%-10%
Farnesene Oil	0%-1%
Substitutes	Galena
Style Guide	India Pale Ale, Imperial India Pale Ale

References
http://beerlegends.com/nugget-hops
http://freshops.com/shop/hop/bittering-hop/nugget-hop/
https://ychhops.com/varieties/nugget
http://brooklynbrewshop.com/themash/hop-of-the-month-nugget/

Olympic

Olympic has a complex lineage. Though its predominantly genetically derived from Brewer's Gold (3/4), it also owes its existence to Fuggle, East Kent Golding, Bavarian and fifth, unknown variety. As a result, Olympic is a spicy and citrus laden hop. It's grown primarily in Washington State and was released in the mid 1980s. It enjoyed solid growth upon its release reaching around one percent of total US hops production in 1986.

However by 1997 this figure had halved.

Homebrewer's Comments

> I brewed with Olympic last year...in a brown to get a feel for it. It certainly came out spicy. Had an oz for a couple years in the freezer, so needed to use it up. Haven't seen it since. Don't remember being particularily impressed...but don't think it was bad either. *(wxgod via tastybrew.com)*

Also Known As	
Characteristics	Notes of spice and citrus
Purpose	Bittering & Aroma
Alpha Acid Composition	10.6%-13.8%
Beta Acid Composition	3.8%-6.1%
Cohumulone Composition	31%
Country	US
Cone Size	
Cone Density	
Seasonal Maturity	Mid to late
Yield Amount	1790-2460 kg/hectare (1600-2200 lbs/acre)
Growth Rate	Very high
Resistant to	Moderately resistant to downy mildew and resistant to verticillium wilt
Susceptible to	Carries the Hop Mosaic and American Hop Latent Virus
Storability	Retains 60% alpha acid after 6 months storage at 20ºC (68ºF)
Ease of Harvest	
Total Oil	0.86-2.55 mL/100g
Myrcene Oil	40.8%
Humulene Oil	12.2%
Caryophyllene Oil	12%
Farnesene Oil	0.9%

| Substitutes | Chinook, Galena, Nugget |
| Style Guide | American Lager, American Ale, Pale Ale |

References
http://www.ars.usda.gov/SP2UserFiles/person/2450/hopcultivars/21225.html
https://www.hopunion.com/olympic/
http://www.brew-dudes.com/olympic-hops/4132

Omega

Omega, despite its pleasant European aroma, decent alpha, storage stability and wilt resistance, exhibited a yield far too low to gain any major foothold commercially. Omega was Dr. R. A. Neve's swansong before leaving his post in 1984 as head of the Hop Section at the esteemed English horticultural institution, Wye College.

Also Known As	
Characteristics	Pleasant European aroma
Purpose	Aroma
Alpha Acid Composition	9%-10%
Beta Acid Composition	3%-4%
Cohumulone Composition	29%
Country	UK
Cone Size	
Cone Density	
Seasonal Maturity	
Yield Amount	1040 kg/hectare (925 lbs/acre)
Growth Rate	Moderate to high
Resistant to	Moderately resistant to downy mildew
Susceptible to	
Storability	Retains 78% alpha acid after 6 months storage at 20ºC (68ºF)
Ease of Harvest	
Total Oil	1.72 mL/100g

Myrcene Oil	53%
Humulene Oil	17%
Caryophyllene Oil	5%
Farnesene Oil	Trace Amounts
Substitutes	
Style Guide	

References

http://www.ars.usda.gov/SP2UserFiles/person/2450/hopcultivars/21667.html

http://www.britishhops.org.uk/wp-content/uploads/2014/08/fact-sheet-press-day.-wye-hops.pdf

Opal

Developed by the Hull Hops Research Institute in Germany, Opal hops feature a clean aroma and flavor profile of spice and citrus with a hint of sweetness. It was released to the brewing world in 2004 and is considered useful for both aroma and bittering.

Homebrewer's Comments

I've been using opal hops a lot. Mostly late additions, some first wort hopping. They're actually very nice. You get a slightly lemon, bright, spice smell with some grassiness. There's a floral, grassy, spicy flavor that comes across. I tried them in a saison and a few tripels mostly in conjunction with Willamette or Saaz, both of which pair rather nicely. They would be outstanding in a kolsch, helles, wit, wheat anything, tripel, golden strong, belgian blonde. They mate well with estery and phenolic Belgian yeasts and I don't get much fruitiness from them at all. The lemon is not a fruit salad, it's just a light lemony thing that you can smell if you look for it. If you consider hallertau, tettnager, liberty, mt hood as an addition, you could easily swap it out for Opal to get a different flavor. Good hop. *(highgravitybacon via homebrewtalk.com)*

| Also Known As | |
| Characteristics | Flavors of spice and citrus, slight sweetness |

Purpose	Bittering & Aroma
Alpha Acid Composition	13%-14%
Beta Acid Composition	3.5%-5.5%
Cohumulone Composition	28%-34%
Country	Germany
Cone Size	
Cone Density	
Seasonal Maturity	Early to mid
Yield Amount	1600-1650 kg/hectare (1420-1470 lbs/acre)
Growth Rate	Moderate
Resistant to	Resistant to wilt, downy mildew and powdery mildew
Susceptible to	
Storability	Retains 60%-70% alpha acid after 6 months storage at 20ºC (68ºF)
Ease of Harvest	Difficult
Total Oil	0.8-1.3 mL/100g
Myrcene Oil	30%-45%
Humulene Oil	20%-25%
Caryophyllene Oil	9%-10%
Farnesene Oil	0%-1%
Substitutes	East Kent Golding, Styrian Golding
Style Guide	Pilsner, Hefeweizen, Helles, Lager, Brown Ale, Saison, Tripel, Wheat, Kolsch, Blonde Ale

References

http://beerlegends.com/opal-hops
https://ychhops.com/varieties/opal
http://brooklynbrewshop.com/themash/hop-of-the-month-opal/

Orbit

Orbit is a dynamic hop blend consisting of a constantly evolving selection of hops from New Zealand's 'Hops with a Difference' breeding program. The selected hops in Orbit change year to year based on an available crops quality and uniqueness. As such, no specific tasting notes are possible but usage in the past has resulted in flavors and aromas of tropical fruit.

Also Known As	
Characteristics	
Purpose	Bittering & Aroma
Alpha Acid Composition	4%-6%
Beta Acid Composition	4%-6%
Cohumulone Composition	25%
Country	New Zealand
Cone Size	
Cone Density	
Seasonal Maturity	
Yield Amount	
Growth Rate	
Resistant to	
Susceptible to	
Storability	
Ease of Harvest	
Total Oil	1.5 mL/100g
Myrcene Oil	33%
Humulene Oil	33%
Caryophyllene Oil	14%
Farnesene Oil	2%
Substitutes	
Style Guide	

References

http://www.craftbrewer.com.au/shop/details.asp?PID=4756
http://www.nzhops.co.nz/variety/orbit
http://www.hopsdirect.com/nz-orbit-t-90-hop-pellets/

Orion

The German Hop Research Institute in Huell, Germany developed Orion hops sometime during the 1980s. It is the result of a cross between Perle and a German male.

To date Orion is not widely produced and mostly relegated to Germany. Its pleasant European bittering and aroma qualities have made it popular for German Helles-type beers, which were originally brewed to compete with Czech Pils. It has a very low cohumulone content and high myrcene. The other oils are in fair balance. This variety is not easy to find commercially.

Also Known As	
Characteristics	
Purpose	Bittering & Aroma
Alpha Acid Composition	8%-9%
Beta Acid Composition	4.94%-5.73%
Cohumulone Composition	25%-29%
Country	Germany
Cone Size	
Cone Density	
Seasonal Maturity	Mid
Yield Amount	1500-1800 kg/hectare (1330-1610 lbs/acre)
Growth Rate	Moderate to high
Resistant to	Resistant to verticillium wilt and downy mildew
Susceptible to	
Storability	Retains 60%-70% alpha acid after 6 months storage at 20ºC (68ºF)
Ease of Harvest	Difficult
Total Oil	1.8-2.1 mL/100g
Myrcene Oil	41%-56%
Humulene Oil	17%-26%
Caryophyllene Oil	7%-13%

Farnesene Oil	0%-1%
Substitutes	Perle
Style Guide	Helles

References

http://beerlegends.com/orion-hops

http://www.brewerslair.com/index.php?p=brewhouse&d=hops&id=&v=&term=48

https://www.ars.usda.gov/SP2UserFiles/person/2450/hopcultivars/21675.html

Outeniqua

Mild, pleasant and slightly spicy, Outeniqua is an excellent, high alpha bittering hop from the land of milk and honey—a moniker of the South African region where it is grown. Primarily used only locally, Outeniqua features a well-balanced oil profile and a strong, punchy, hoppy aroma. Outeniqua is also the mother of high-alpha variety, Southern Star.

Also Known As	
Characteristics	
Purpose	Bittering
Alpha Acid Composition	12%-13.5%
Beta Acid Composition	4.1%-5.1%
Cohumulone Composition	25%-30%
Country	South Africa
Cone Size	Small to medium
Cone Density	Compact
Seasonal Maturity	Mid to Late
Yield Amount	1590-1940 kg/hectare (1420-1730 lbs/acre)
Growth Rate	Moderate
Resistant to	
Susceptible to	
Storability	Retains 60%-70% alpha acid after 6 months storage at 20ºC (68ºF)
Ease of Harvest	Difficult

Total Oil	1.6-1.6 mL/100g
Myrcene Oil	38%-43%
Humulene Oil	28%-33%
Caryophyllene Oil	9%-10%
Farnesene Oil	0%-1%
Substitutes	Southern Star
Style Guide	Pilsner

References
http://beerlegends.com/outeniqua-hops
http://www.breweryhistory.com/journal/archive/121/bh-121-094.htm

Pacific Gem

Pacific Gem is a New Zealand hops variety of interesting character. Bred at the New Zealand Horticultural Research Centre as a triploid cross between Smooth Cone, California Late Cluster and Fuggle, it is used around the world in various styles but most notably in European lagers. It was released in 1987.

Despite its high alpha acids its high cohumulone content makes its use as a bittering hop problematic. It can, and is, used as an early addition but is more well known for its aroma and flavor. When utilized as a late addition it can bring a delicate aroma character to the resulting beer that is smooth and oak-like with notes of blackberry.

Homebrewer's Comments

High bittering potential, but I like it for later additions. I prefer late/flameout additions over dry hopping for aroma. Its got a tangy blackberry flavor to me. *(m00ps via email)*

I can see it being used as an accent hop, maybe to increase the tannic character of Nelson Sauvin, but not as the feature or even sole hop in a beer. Containing up to 40% (!) cohumulone, I'd definitely not use it for bittering. *(ArcaneXor via homebrewtalk.com)*

Also Known As	
Characteristics	Notes of oak and blackberry
Purpose	Bittering & Aroma
Alpha Acid Composition	13%-16%
Beta Acid Composition	7%-9%
Cohumulone Composition	37%-40%
Country	New Zealand
Cone Size	Medium to large
Cone Density	Compact
Seasonal Maturity	Early to mid
Yield Amount	2380-2380 kg/hectare (2120-2120 lbs/acre)
Growth Rate	High
Resistant to	
Susceptible to	
Storability	Retains 70%-80% alpha acid after 6 months storage at 20°C (68°F)
Ease of Harvest	Difficult
Total Oil	1.2-1.4 mL/100g
Myrcene Oil	33%-55%
Humulene Oil	18%-30%
Caryophyllene Oil	7%-11%
Farnesene Oil	0%-1%
Substitutes	Fuggle
Style Guide	Strong Ale, European Lagers

References

http://beerlegends.com/pacific-gem-hops
http://www.nzhops.co.nz/variety/pacific-gem
https://www.craftbrewer.com.au/shop/details.asp?PID=594

Pacific Jade

Released from HortResearch's New Zealand Hop Research Program in

2004, Pacific Jade started its commercial existence predominately limited to the New Zealand domestic market. Now however, it is finding its way into inventories worldwide.

It exhibits an interesting flavor profile of lemon citrus and cracked pepper. As an early addition it imparts a soft, rounded bitterness. Ancestrally, Pacific Jade owes its existence to Saaz and fellow New Zealand-born variety, First Choice.

Homebrewer's Comments

> I used some with Centennial in a Wheat IPA. It's got a peppery/spicy aroma and flavor, with some citrus in the back. All I can say is it worked pretty well with the Centennial and it works as late addition/dry hop. *(Beehemel via homebrewtalk.com)*

Also Known As	
Characteristics	Flavors of lemon citrus and cracked pepper
Purpose	Aroma
Alpha Acid Composition	12%-14%
Beta Acid Composition	7%-8%
Cohumulone Composition	24%
Country	New Zealand
Cone Size	
Cone Density	Compact
Seasonal Maturity	Mid to late
Yield Amount	
Growth Rate	High
Resistant to	
Susceptible to	
Storability	
Ease of Harvest	
Total Oil	1.4 mL/100g
Myrcene Oil	33.3%

Humulene Oil	32.9%
Caryophyllene Oil	10.2%
Farnesene Oil	0.3%
Substitutes	Magnum
Style Guide	Pale Ale, India Pale Ale

References
http://www.nzhops.co.nz/varieties/pacific_jade.html
http://www.bear-flavored.com/2011/12/bear-flavoreds-ultimate-guide-to-hop.html
http://drinks.seriouseats.com/2012/07/new-hops-new-zealand-australia-nelson-sauvin-galaxy-southern-cross-sierra-nevada-southern-hemisphere.html
http://www.charlesfaram.co.uk/hop-varieties/pacific-jade/

Pacific Sunrise

Released in 2000 by HortResearch in New Zealand, Pacific Sunrise's take up by commercial breweries has been sluggish. Despite this, it features favorable bittering properties and a pleasant piney aroma. It is the result of a cross between the result of a European and New Zealand male on one side and a California Late Cluster and a Fuggle on the other.

Also Known As	
Characteristics	
Purpose	Bittering
Alpha Acid Composition	12.5%-14.5%
Beta Acid Composition	6%-6.5%
Cohumulone Composition	27%-30%
Country	New Zealand
Cone Size	
Cone Density	
Seasonal Maturity	
Yield Amount	
Growth Rate	High
Resistant to	
Susceptible to	

Storability	Retains 60%-70% alpha acid after 6 months storage at 20ºC (68ºF)
Ease of Harvest	
Total Oil	1.7-2 mL/100g
Myrcene Oil	45%-55%
Humulene Oil	19%-25%
Caryophyllene Oil	6%-9%
Farnesene Oil	0%-1%
Substitutes	Pacific Gem
Style Guide	Lager

References
http://beerlegends.com/pacific-sunrise-hops
http://www.johnihaas.com/wp-content/uploads/2015/01/Pacific-Sunrise.pdf

Pacifica

Bred in New Zealand, triploid aroma hop Pacifica, or Pacific Hallertau as it is sometimes known, is the result of open pollination breeding of German hop Hallertauer Mittelfrüher. The hop was released by HortResearch, New Zealand following promising brewing trials in 1994.

Like Hallertauer Mittelfrüher, Pacifica is mostly known for its aromatic properties. It features moderately low cohumulone and higher carophyllene, which gives it a spicy and decidedly floral aroma. Citrus notes are also evident and it is said to impart aromas of orange when used as a late in the boil.

Sierra Nevada brewery debuted Pacifica in their Southern Hemisphere Harvest fresh hops ale in April of 2014 featuring it as a bittering addition alongside Southern Cross and Motueka as its finishing hops.

Homebrewer's Comments

I used them in equal parts with Centennial in an amber a while back. Could definitely pick up waaaay more sweet orange in the aroma, but they just seemed to bulk up the normal Centennial flavor. Went very well with all the caramel malts I used in that beer. *(MrOH via homebrewtalk.com)*

Also Known As	Pacific Hallertau
Characteristics	Citrusy, spicy, orange and floral aromas
Purpose	Aroma
Alpha Acid Composition	5%-6%
Beta Acid Composition	6%
Cohumulone Composition	25%
Country	New Zealand
Cone Size	Medium
Cone Density	Loose
Seasonal Maturity	Early
Yield Amount	1700-1750 kg/hectare (1520-1560 lbs/acre)
Growth Rate	Moderate
Resistant to	
Susceptible to	
Storability	Retains 60%-70% alpha acid after 6 months storage at 20°C (68°F)
Ease of Harvest	Difficult
Total Oil	1.0 mL/100g
Myrcene Oil	12.5%
Humulene Oil	50.9%
Caryophyllene Oil	16.7%
Farnesene Oil	0.2%
Substitutes	Liberty
Style Guide	Porter

References
http://beerlegends.com/pacific-hallertau-hops
http://www.nzhops.co.nz/variety/pacifica

Palisade®

For brewers, Palisade® hops, bred by Yakima Chief Ranch feature complex floral, herbal and grassy aromas in addition to flavors of nectar fruits and citrus. For growers, it exhibits nothing short of incredible yield potential – at least in its native Yakima Valley, Washington environment. Palisade® is an open pollination cross from Swiss Tettnanger.

Homebrewer's Comments

I did an all-Palisade rye summer ale with Saison yeast at ale temps. It turned out good, but no one commented on the hop flavor. I detected some floral and very mild fruit flavors. I think Palisade would pair beautifully with an American wheat, Belgian wit, or fruit ale. *(Dr. Francois via homebrewtalk.com)*

Personally, I didn't find them anything like Willamette. I made a Palisade single-hop pale ale, and it had kind of perfumey aroma and a very mild flavor to them. The bitterness, even though it was calculated at 40 IBUs, was very very smooth to the point where I felt that the beer was underbittered. I would like to try them again, but haven't been able to find whole Palisade since getting that grab bag. *(just-cj via brewboard.com)*

Also Known As	
Characteristics	Flavors of nectar fruits and citrus, aromas that are floral, herbaceous and grassy
Purpose	Aroma
Alpha Acid Composition	5.5%-9.5%
Beta Acid Composition	6%-8%
Cohumulone Composition	24%-29%
Country	US
Cone Size	Medium
Cone Density	Moderate
Seasonal Maturity	Mid
Yield Amount	2400-3400 kg/hectare (2141-3033 lbs/acre)
Growth Rate	Moderate to high

Resistant to	Resistant to powdery mildew, downy mildew and podoshaera
Susceptible to	
Storability	Retains 60%-70% alpha acid after 6 months storage at 20°C (68°F)
Ease of Harvest	Difficult
Total Oil	1.4-1.6 mL/100g
Myrcene Oil	9%-10%
Humulene Oil	19%-22%
Caryophyllene Oil	16%-18%
Farnesene Oil	0%-1%
Substitutes	Styrian Golding, Willamette, Glacier, Chinook
Style Guide	Golden Ale, Pale Ale, English Ales, American Pale Ale

References

http://beerlegends.com/palisade-hops

https://www.hopunion.com/palisade-brand-ycr-14-cv/

http://www.usahops.org/graphics/File/HGA%20BCI%20Reports/Variety%20Manual%207-24-12.pdf

http://www.brew-dudes.com/palisade-hops/377

http://www.brewsupply.com/Newsletter/0906.html

Perle

The original Perle was created in Germany sometime during the 1960's or early-mid 1970's from Northern Brewer and a German male. It was released to the public in 1978.

Some European breweries have claimed that Perle is much like and a good substitute for Hallertau Mittelfrüher. Others in the US and Japan however have disagreed with that assessment. Perle is said to have a pleasant aroma, elements of mint and pine with a hint of spice.

Also Known As

Characteristics

Purpose	Bittering & Aroma
Alpha Acid Composition	8%-9%
Beta Acid Composition	8%
Cohumulone Composition	28%
Country	Germany
Cone Size	
Cone Density	
Seasonal Maturity	Mid (Germany), early (US)
Yield Amount	1680-2130 kg/hectare (1500-1900 lbs/acre)
Growth Rate	Very high
Resistant to	Resistant to verticillium wilt and downy mildew
Susceptible to	Moderately susceptible to powdery mildew
Storability	Retains 76% alpha acid after 6 months storage at 20°C (68°F)
Ease of Harvest	
Total Oil	0.6-1.2 mL/100g
Myrcene Oil	44%
Humulene Oil	29%
Caryophyllene Oil	10.2%
Farnesene Oil	0.2%
Substitutes	Perle (GR), Northern Brewer (GR)
Style Guide	Hefeweizen, Belgian Strong Ale, Lager, Pilsner, Kölsch

References

http://beerlegends.com/perle-us-hops

http://brooklynbrewshop.com/themash/hop-of-the-month-perle/

https://www.craftbrewer.com.au/shop/details.asp?PID=587

https://www.ars.usda.gov/SP2UserFiles/person/2450/hopcultivars/21227.html

Perle (US)

While genetically indistinct from the original Germany variety, US-grown Perle tends to exhibit higher alpha acids potential and a slightly different balance of oils. Specifically, it tends to be higher in myrcene with lower in humulene, which may make US-grown Perle marginally more useful for bittering.

Homebrewer's Comments

Perle is a true dual-purpose hop that will lend a pleasant spiciness to any beer. They lack some finesse compared to their Noble Euro counterparts, so they're maybe not the best choice for late editions but will do just fine in a pinch. I'd recommend using them sparingly towards the EOB with more mid-boil emphasis which is mostly how I use them. (*Beertracker via homebrewersassociation.org*)

Also Known As	
Characteristics	Faint spicy aroma
Purpose	Bittering & Aroma
Alpha Acid Composition	6%-10%
Beta Acid Composition	3%-5%
Cohumulone Composition	27%-32%
Country	US
Cone Size	Medium
Cone Density	Loose
Seasonal Maturity	Early
Yield Amount	1150-1600 kg/hectare (1020-1420 lbs/acre)
Growth Rate	Moderate
Resistant to	Resistant to prunus necrotic ring-spot virus, downy mildew and powdery mildew
Susceptible to	
Storability	Retains 80%-85% alpha acid after 6 months storage at 20ºC (68ºF)

Ease of Harvest	Difficult
Total Oil	0.7-1.2 mL/100g
Myrcene Oil	45%-55%
Humulene Oil	28%-33%
Caryophyllene Oil	10%-12%
Farnesene Oil	0%-1%
Substitutes	Perle (GR), Northern Brewer (GR)
Style Guide	Hefeweizen, Belgian Strong Ale, Lager, Pilsner, Kölsch

References
http://beerlegends.com/perle-us-hops
https://ychhops.com/varieties/perle
http://www.greatlakeshops.com/perle.html

Petham Golding

Hailing from Wye College in England, Petham Golding was one of the prevailing hop varieties grown in East Kent in the late 1800's. Descended from Canterbury Whitebine, much like other Golding varieties, the variety isn't around much anymore due to its lackluster yield, poor storage stability and infection with Hop Mosaic virus. In addition, it has an unusual upward-facing sidearm configuration that tends to break easily at the branching point. Little is known about its flavor and aroma profile but the variety is parent to popular US varietal, Chinook. Naturally one would assume these two varieties are likely to share some characteristics as a result.

Also Known As	
Characteristics	
Purpose	Aroma
Alpha Acid Composition	6.9%
Beta Acid Composition	2%
Cohumulone Composition	28%
Country	UK
Cone Size	

Cone Density	
Seasonal Maturity	Late
Yield Amount	1345 kg/hectare (1200 lbs/acre)
Growth Rate	
Resistant to	Moderately resistant to downy mildew and resistant to verticillium wilt
Susceptible to	Susceptible to Hop Mosaic virus
Storability	Retains 57% alpha acid after 6 months storage at 20°C (68°F)
Ease of Harvest	
Total Oil	1.15 mL/100g
Myrcene Oil	57%
Humulene Oil	16%
Caryophyllene Oil	9%
Farnesene Oil	Trace Amounts
Substitutes	
Style Guide	

References

http://www.ars.usda.gov/SP2UserFiles/person/2450/hopcultivars/68052.html

https://books.google.com.au/books?id=lXC8BQAAQBAJ&pg=PA10&lpg=PA10&dq=petham+golding+hops&source=bl&ots=3bExb4Stsi&sig=dMF8eBQhk4oyaZPqubnVH5awpd8&hl=en&sa=X&ved=0CEYQ6AEwCGoVChMI3srSy5f2yAIVheamCh3Awger#v=onepage&q=petham%20golding%20hops&f=false

http://zythophile.co.uk/2008/01/24/mr-goldings-descendants/

Phoenix

Despite its low yield, Phoenix has a lovely aroma and flavor and seems destined to become a favorite among craft brewers. It was first grown at Wye College in England in an effort to find a more disease resistant replacement for Challenger hops. Phoenix was selected as a seedling of Yeoman.

Though considered dual-purpose for brewing, Phoenix hops are usually employed early in the boil. Some brewers have claimed its use as a late addition often leads to flavors and aromas that are sometimes inconsistent and disappointingly mellow.

In general, the tasting notes for Phoenix tends to be complex, with an understated spicy aroma and floral notes of pine, chocolate and molasses. It was released to the public in 1996.

Homebrewer's Comments

> Used it in English styled brews- posters, stouts, browns, ESB, English IPA. I primarily used it as a bittering hop. Beers turned out fine. Then started using it for flavor and aroma in conjunction with my other English standards, kent goldings/ fuggles. I can't remember having any issues with any of the beers. I don't remember using more than 1 1/2-2 oz per 5 gallon batch though.

> It's been awhile, but if I recall it did have a fruity (berry) even sweet taste and aroma and was mildly spicy (maybe this is what people are calling "sharp"). Very complimentary of English styled ale. In fact when paired with EKG, I recall a candy like sweetness that was very good.

> My advice, use it. Stick with a darker English ale particularly a brown first. Low IBUs, and mix it with fuggle and/or EKG at different points so at least half hops are Phoenix. *(mhot55 via homebrewtalk.com)*

Also Known As	
Characteristics	Aromas of spice, pine, chocolate and molasses
Purpose	Bittering & Aroma
Alpha Acid Composition	8.5%-13.5%
Beta Acid Composition	3.3%-5.5%
Cohumulone Composition	24%-33%
Country	UK
Cone Size	Medium
Cone Density	Loose to moderate

Seasonal Maturity	Early
Yield Amount	980-1560 kg/hectare (870-1390 lbs/acre)
Growth Rate	Low to moderate
Resistant to	Resistant to verticillium wilt and powdery mildew
Susceptible to	Susceptible to downy mildew
Storability	Retains 80%-85% alpha acid after 6 months storage at 20°C (68°F)
Ease of Harvest	Difficult
Total Oil	1.2-3 mL/100g
Myrcene Oil	24%-32%
Humulene Oil	25%-32%
Caryophyllene Oil	8%-11%
Farnesene Oil	1%-1.4%
Substitutes	Northdown, Challenger, East Kent Golding
Style Guide	India Pale Ale, Bitter, Golden Ale, Triple India Pale Ale, English Ale, Extra Special Bitter, Stout, Brown Ale, Porter

References

http://beerlegends.com/phoenix-hops

http://www.britishhops.org.uk/phoenix/

http://www.rebelbrewer.com/shop/brewing-ingredients/hops/pellet-hops/phoenix-hops-1oz-pellets

http://www.charlesfaram.co.uk/hop-varieties/phoenix/

https://bellsbeer.com/store/products/Phoenix-(UK)-Hops-%252d-1-oz-Pellets.html

https://books.google.com.au/books?id=g1kWBQAAQBAJ&pg=PA76&lpg=PA76&dq=phoenix+hops+released&source=bl&ots=vA_Fb6EuXp&sig=Vks00rJgezytLtR9NIrW9qxqFb0&hl=en&sa=X&ved=0ahUKEwizju63nNHMAhWLE5QKHVGGAnoQ6AEITjAH#v=onepage&q=phoenix%20hops%20released&f=false

https://books.google.com.au/books?id=rR0lCgAAQBAJ&pg=PA161&lpg=PA161&dq=phoenix+hops+released&source=bl&ots=BVEFpCGNMF&sig=dwixwWQQv4qfXVB15iok2wjnIZ8&hl=en&sa=X&ved=0ahUKEwizju63nNHMAhWLE5QKHVGGAnoQ6AEIWDAJ#v=onepage&q=phoenix%20hops%20released&f=false

Pilgrim

Pilgrim's siblings, First Gold and Herald are both dwarf hop varieties, Pilgrim however is not. A cultivar of Wye College, England, Pilgram displays first-rate bittering qualities in addition to favorable aroma and flavor characteristics. It was released in the year 2000.

Considered round and full bodied with classic English-style bitterness, its complex flavor and aroma have been likened to grassy herbs, grapefruit citrus, berries and pears right through to spice, cedar and honey.

It has good storage stability, an excellent yield potential and resistance to wilt and mildew. Pilgrim is a true all-purpose hop, great in the boil from beginning to end.

Homebrewer's Comments

> I have used this hop quite often, although never in the final minutes. Tended to use it in darker beers where sweetness needed balancing. The beers tended to have a spicey bitterness, so maybe the flavour would be a bit spicy. Something like an agressive saaz. *(simple one via jimsbeerkit.co.uk)*

Also Known As	
Characteristics	Rounded bitterness, grassy herbs, pears, and spice
Purpose	Bittering & Aroma
Alpha Acid Composition	9%-13%
Beta Acid Composition	4.2%-5.2%
Cohumulone Composition	36%-38%
Country	UK
Cone Size	Medium to large
Cone Density	Moderate
Seasonal Maturity	Mid to Late
Yield Amount	2030 kg/hectare (1810 lbs/acre)
Growth Rate	High

Resistant to	Resistant to wilt, powdery mildew and downy mildew
Susceptible to	
Storability	Retains 60%-70% alpha acid after 6 months storage at 20°C (68°F)
Ease of Harvest	Difficult
Total Oil	1.8-1.8 mL/100g
Myrcene Oil	36%-36%
Humulene Oil	17%
Caryophyllene Oil	7%
Farnesene Oil	0.3%
Substitutes	Target, Pioneer, Challenger
Style Guide	English Pale Ale, India Pale Ale, Wheat Beer, Stout, Barley Wine, Imperial Stout

References

http://beerlegends.com/pilgrim-p38-hops
https://ychhops.com/varieties/pilgrim
http://www.britishhops.org.uk/pilgrim-2/
https://www.craftbrewer.com.au/shop/details.asp?PID=1072

Pilot

Pilot is a high-yielding hedgerow variety, well resistant to wilt, but not to mildew. Bred at Wye College and released in 2001, it's oil balance makes it distinct from most other English hops. It is said to have excellent, clean and refreshing bittering qualities with spicy aromatics of lemon and marmalade.

Also Known As	
Characteristics	
Purpose	Bittering
Alpha Acid Composition	8%-11.5%
Beta Acid Composition	3.3%-5%
Cohumulone Composition	28%-37%

Country	UK
Cone Size	
Cone Density	
Seasonal Maturity	
Yield Amount	
Growth Rate	
Resistant to	Resistant to wilt
Susceptible to	
Storability	
Ease of Harvest	
Total Oil	0.8-1.4 mL/100g
Myrcene Oil	30%-40%
Humulene Oil	3%-6%
Caryophyllene Oil	
Farnesene Oil	< 1%
Substitutes	
Style Guide	

References
http://www.britishhops.org.uk/pilot/
http://englishhops.co.uk/pdf/2014/04/Pilot-Variety-Sheet.pdf

Pioneer

Pioneer has a classic English aroma and mild-tempered bittering despite its very high cohumulone levels. It is considered more than suitable for use at any point in the brewing process.

It was bred at Wye College from Omega and is a sister to Herald. On the palate It features clean, refreshing bittering and an aroma profile of lemon and grapefruit citrus, herbaceous essences and trailing notes of cedar.

Homebrewer's Comments

I've brewed an IPA now with Pioneer hops in identical additions for all of bittering/flavour/aroma, and I have to say it's a very good hop. Pleasantly citrusy, but not like the American C-hops. Milder, less aggressive, with a pleasantly sweet lower note. Perhaps the aroma is a bit subdued compared to the flavour, so you may want to up the latest addition (or perhaps dry hop) for better balance, but overall very pleasant. *(Ølbart via homebrewtalk.com)*

Also Known As	
Characteristics	Clean bittering, aromas of citrus, lemon, grapefruit, herbs and cedar
Purpose	Bittering & Aroma
Alpha Acid Composition	8%-10%
Beta Acid Composition	3.5%-4%
Cohumulone Composition	36%-40%
Country	UK
Cone Size	Small to medium
Cone Density	Moderate to compact
Seasonal Maturity	Mid to Late
Yield Amount	1200-1500 kg/hectare (1070-1330 lbs/acre)
Growth Rate	Low to moderate
Resistant to	Resistant to verticillium wilt and downy mildew and powdery mildew
Susceptible to	
Storability	Retains 60%-70% alpha acid after 6 months storage at 20°C (68°F)
Ease of Harvest	Difficult
Total Oil	1-1.8 mL/100g
Myrcene Oil	31%-36%
Humulene Oil	22%-24%
Caryophyllene Oil	7%-8%
Farnesene Oil	0%-1%

| Substitutes | East Kent Golding |
| Style Guide | India Pale Ale, Red Ale, Specialty Ale, Strong Bitter |

References
http://beerlegends.com/pioneer-hops
http://www.britishhops.org.uk/pioneer/
http://www.charlesfaram.co.uk/hop-varieties/pioneer/

Pocket Talisman

Originating in Idaho, USA, Dwarf variety Pocket Talisman has proven difficult to establish with rhizomes often failing to produce bines. Originally selected from a field of regular Talisman hops in the 1970's, the initial test plot took three years to establish due to failed rhizome growth. Once established it produces well on a low trellis but is not currently grown commercially. Little is known of its exact aroma and flavor profile but it is said to share some similarities with Cluster.

Also Known As	
Characteristics	
Purpose	Aroma
Alpha Acid Composition	6%
Beta Acid Composition	3.2%
Cohumulone Composition	55%
Country	US
Cone Size	
Cone Density	
Seasonal Maturity	
Yield Amount	680 kg/hectare (600 lbs/acre)
Growth Rate	Moderate
Resistant to	Resistant to downy mildew
Susceptible to	
Storability	Retains 70% alpha acid after 6 months storage at 20°C (68°F)

Ease of Harvest	
Total Oil	0.63 mL/100g
Myrcene Oil	65%-70%
Humulene Oil	< 5%
Caryophyllene Oil	
Farnesene Oil	
Substitutes	Talisman, Cluster
Style Guide	

References

http://www.ars.usda.gov/SP2UserFiles/person/2450/hopcultivars/21115.html

http://www.newspapers.com/newspage/25113531/

Polaris

New to the scene, the Hop Research Institute in Hüll, Germany released Polaris in 2012. Commanding incredibly high alpha acids, Polaris features elements of spice, pine and intense mint alongside a strong but pleasant, fruity and floral aroma.

Homebrewer's Comments

> Polaris has about twice the oil content of Citra, so it literally drowns out every other hop it is combo'd with when used in normal amounts. When I used it, I just got intense, clingy, resin note from it. It basically seems like it would turn any beer into an IIPA from a flavor perspective. I've been gunshy to use it again, but I'm thinking that if you use maybe 1/3 to 1/4 your usual late-hop amounts you might get a different result. (*erockrph via homebrewersassociation.org*)

Also Known As	German Polaris
Characteristics	Floral and fruity aromas, spice, pine and mint
Purpose	Bittering & Aroma
Alpha Acid Composition	18%-23%
Beta Acid Composition	4.5%-6%

Cohumulone Composition	22%-28%
Country	Germany
Cone Size	
Cone Density	
Seasonal Maturity	
Yield Amount	
Growth Rate	
Resistant to	
Susceptible to	
Storability	
Ease of Harvest	
Total Oil	4.0-5.0 mL/100g
Myrcene Oil	50%
Humulene Oil	20%-35%
Caryophyllene Oil	8%-13%
Farnesene Oil	< 1%
Substitutes	
Style Guide	Ales, Pale Ales, India Pale Ale

References
http://hopunion.com/german-polaris/
https://ychhops.com/varieties/polaris
https://bsgcraftbrewing.com/german-polaris
http://beermebc.com/2015/11/01/craft-beer-hop-profile-polaris-hops/
http://www.brew-dudes.com/polaris-hops/4885

Precoce de Bourgogne

French in origin, Precoce de Burgnogne is likely a clone but it is unknown exactly from which variety. Established in 1977, translated its name means "Early Burgundy" and it is very closely related to the Tardif de Bourgogne (Late Burgundy) and Elsasser varietals. While it is listed as an aroma hop, little tasting information exists on Precoce de Bourgogne. It was at one time grown commercially in small quantities in its native Alsace but it is not clear if this is still the case.

Also Known As	Precoce de Burgnogne, Precoce d'Bourgogne
Characteristics	
Purpose	Aroma
Alpha Acid Composition	3.1%-3.7%
Beta Acid Composition	2.6%-3.5%
Cohumulone Composition	23%
Country	France
Cone Size	
Cone Density	
Seasonal Maturity	Early
Yield Amount	1345-1680 kg/hectare (1200-1500 lbs/acre)
Growth Rate	Low to moderate
Resistant to	
Susceptible to	
Storability	Retains 61% alpha acid after 6 months storage at 20°C (68°F)
Ease of Harvest	
Total Oil	0.34 mL/100g
Myrcene Oil	45%
Humulene Oil	20%
Caryophyllene Oil	5.9%
Farnesene Oil	10.6%
Substitutes	
Style Guide	

References

http://www.ars.usda.gov/SP2UserFiles/person/2450/hopcultivars/21168.html

https://translate.google.com.au/translate?hl=en&sl=nl&u=https://nl.wikipedia.org/wiki/Precoce_de_Bourgogne&prev=search

Pride of Kent

Developed in England at Wye College, Pride of Kent features a pleasant continental-type aroma. It was first developed sometime in the early to mid 20th century from open pollinated Brewer's. Pride of Kent is also the parent of the celebrated Australian variety, Pride of Ringwood.

Also Known As	
Characteristics	
Purpose	Bittering & Aroma
Alpha Acid Composition	8%-11%
Beta Acid Composition	6%-8%
Cohumulone Composition	35%
Country	
Cone Size	
Cone Density	
Seasonal Maturity	Early
Yield Amount	1010-1560 kg/hectare (900-1400 lbs/acre)
Growth Rate	High
Resistant to	Moderately resistant to downy mildew and verticillium wilt
Susceptible to	
Storability	Retains 42% alpha acid after 6 months storage at 20°C (68°F)
Ease of Harvest	
Total Oil	2.32 mL/100g
Myrcene Oil	70%
Humulene Oil	9%
Caryophyllene Oil	3%
Farnesene Oil	Trace Amounts
Substitutes	Galena Hops
Style Guide	

References

http://www.homebrewtalk.com/wiki/index.php/Pride_of_Kent
https://www.ars.usda.gov/SP2UserFiles/person/2450/hopcultivars/21280.html
http://beerlegends.com/pride-of-kent-hops

Pride of Ringwood

When Australian hop Pride of Ringwood was released in 1958 it had the distinction of being the hop with the highest alpha acid content in the world. Though that title has been long surpassed it is still an incredibly popular bittering hop. Best utilized fresh, Pride of Ringwood is primarily a bittering hop but also exhibits spicy, fruity aromas when used as a late addition.

The variety was developed by Bill Nash who then worked for the Carlton and United Brewery at the Ringwood Hop Research Station in Ringwood, Victoria. It was bred from English variety Pride of Kent through open pollination.

Pride of Ringwood once made up the vast majority of hops grown in Australia and at it's peak reached 90% of total crop acreage. Elsewhere Pride of Ringwood is considered too late harvest for the US but was at one stage also grown in Kashmir, India. While the Australian Pride of Ringwood crop is largely disease free, when grown in other locations it can be susceptible to downy mildew.

Though it is primarily used in Australian lagers, there are plenty of examples of its use in the US. Buffalo Bill Brewery uses it in their Tasmanian Devil brew. Australian's would be most familiar with its use in beers by Carlton and United Breweries, Fosters and Coopers.

Homebrewer's Comments

> As Aussie as they come - bitter, earthy, dry, tasteless?... Has no real aroma qualities… If you've tried any commercial Australian beer, you'll know what I mean. That said, PoR is brilliant as your bittering hop. If you like aroma, late add some aroma hops. Never late hop PoR it's a waste of time. Used in Aussie in lagers (Fosters, VB, XXXX) in dark ales (Tooheys Old, Carlton Black) and in Coopers (kits too). I love it, but use it wisely. It is often

maligned by people who don't use it properly. *(Fatgodzilla via homebrewtalk.com)*

Also Known As	
Characteristics	Spicy, fruity aroma
Purpose	Bittering
Alpha Acid Composition	7%-11%
Beta Acid Composition	4%-8%
Cohumulone Composition	33%-39%
Country	Australia
Cone Size	Medium to large
Cone Density	Compact
Seasonal Maturity	Mid-Late
Yield Amount	1010-1560 kg/hectare (900-1400 lbs/cre)
Growth Rate	High
Resistant to	Verticillium Wilt
Susceptible to	Downy mildew
Storability	Retains 45-55% alpha acid after 6 months storage at 20°C (68°F)
Ease of Harvest	
Total Oil	1-2 mL/100g
Myrcene Oil	25%-53%
Humulene Oil	2%-8%
Caryophyllene Oil	5%-10%
Farnesene Oil	< 1%
Substitutes	East Kent Goldings, Centennial, Galena, Cluster
Style Guide	Amber Ale, Lager, Fruit Lambic, Pale Ale, Australian Lager, Strong Ale, Golden Ale, American Pale Ale

References

http://www.homebrewtalk.com/wiki/index.php/Pride_of_Ringwood

https://books.google.com.au/books?id=jLabuEqJNNsC&pg=PA119&lpg=PA119&dq=Bill+Nash+hops+australia&source=bl&ots=J1gmCRdI8x&sig=15-N1rWTc9QOuj3yFnGEp_-9tTM&hl=en&sa=X&ved=0ahUKEwjdpZzVoL_MAhWGKZQKHezTCWkQ6AEIHjA

Progress

Progress was bred in the 1950's at Wye College in England and released in 1964 as a low-cost alternative for Fuggle hops. Slightly sweet with subtly bitter, it features pleasant and Fuggle-like floral aromas of grass, mint and earth.

It is the progeny of Whitbread Golding and an unnamed American male variety and is only grown commercially in England in limited amounts for a few specific breweries. Progress may also exhibit breeding potential on account of its exceptionally early seasonal maturity.

Homebrewer's Comments

> Personally I love Progress hops (and I've) used them alot in my brews. You can you use them as first addition hop, late addition hop or even in dry hopping so it's a very verstile hop...Progress works real well with East Kent Golding or any Goldings for that matter...works well in praticaly all ale types, stouts, porters, bitters and pales. I would describe the flavour as deep fruit flavours...I have even had a cherry flavour in my ale when I have used Progress late in the boil. It has sweet edge with a well balanced bitterness to follow. *(beer gut via jimsbeerkit.co.uk)*

Also Known As	
Characteristics	Sweet flavor, Fuggle-like aromas of grass, mint and earth. Subtle bitterness.
Purpose	Aroma
Alpha Acid Composition	6%-7.5%
Beta Acid Composition	2%-3.3%

Cohumulone Composition	25%-34%
Country	UK
Cone Size	
Cone Density	
Seasonal Maturity	Very early
Yield Amount	900-1120 kg/hectare (800-1000 lbs/acre)
Growth Rate	Low
Resistant to	Tolerant to downy mildew and verticillium wilt
Susceptible to	
Storability	Retains 74% alpha acid after 6 months storage at 20°C (68°F)
Ease of Harvest	Moderate to Easy
Total Oil	0.5-1.2 mL/100g
Myrcene Oil	24%-33.5%
Humulene Oil	36%-47%
Caryophyllene Oil	10.6%-14%
Farnesene Oil	< 1%
Substitutes	East Kent Golding, Fuggle
Style Guide	English Bitters, Pale Ale, Porter, Stout, Czech Pilsner, Bock, Cask Ale, Wheat

References

http://www.britishhops.org.uk/progress/
http://www.ars.usda.gov/SP2UserFiles/person/2450/hopcultivars/66051.html
http://englishhops.co.uk/wp-content/uploads/2014/04/Progress-Variety-Sheet.pdf
http://www.homebrewstuff.com/hop-profiles
http://www.willingham-nurseries.co.uk/hops/progress.html
https://www.hopunion.com/uk-progress/

Rakau

Rakau, or AlphaAroma as it was previously known, was developed in New Zealand. Languishing in its disease free habitat, Rakau features a high concentration of myrcene is said to pair it beautifully to dry-hopped American Pale Ales.

It was initially bred in the late 1970's from Smooth Cone through open pollination but it was not released to the market until 1983. It was re-released under the new name in 2007. According to New Zealand Hops Limited, 'AlphaAroma' no longer exists as a commercially named variety. Despite that, it is currently being grown and sold under its old name by Dutchess Hops of New York who planted it in the US in 2013.

Homebrewer's Comments

Using these in combo with cascade would make for a great Pale ale. They have a smooth apricot and pineapple flavor and should work for bittering too. *(wileaway via homebrewtalk.com)*

Also Known As	AlphaAroma
Characteristics	
Purpose	Bittering & Aroma
Alpha Acid Composition	5.8%-10.9%
Beta Acid Composition	2.6%-4.8%
Cohumulone Composition	27%
Country	New Zealand
Cone Size	
Cone Density	
Seasonal Maturity	Late to very late
Yield Amount	1230-3810 kg/hectare (1100-3400 lbs/acre)
Growth Rate	Very high
Resistant to	
Susceptible to	
Storability	Retains 72% alpha acid after 6 months storage at 20°C (68°F)
Ease of Harvest	
Total Oil	1.21 mL/100g
Myrcene Oil	44%-65%
Humulene Oil	15%

Caryophyllene Oil	3%-8%
Farnesene Oil	5%
Substitutes	
Style Guide	Pale Ale, Lager

References
http://beerlegends.com/alpharoma-hops
http://nzhl.info-prime.co.nz/variety/rakau
https://ychhops.com/varieties/rakau
http://dutchesshops.com/about/

Record

Originating in Belgium sometime prior to 1970, Record hops feature a pleasant European aroma. Bred from an open pollination Saaz and Northern Brewer, their aroma characteristics are said to closely resemble that of the later parent, Northern Brewer. Flavor-wise, they have been described as mild and somewhat fruity. Record has been grown in a commercial capacity in both Germany and Belgium.

Also Known As	
Characteristics	Pleasant European aroma, mildly fruity
Purpose	Aroma
Alpha Acid Composition	7%-12%
Beta Acid Composition	4%-8%
Cohumulone Composition	27%
Country	Belgium
Cone Size	Small
Cone Density	Compact
Seasonal Maturity	Early
Yield Amount	1345 kg/hectare (1200 lbs/acre)
Growth Rate	Moderate to high
Resistant to	Moderately resistant to downy mildew

Susceptible to	Infected with **Prunus Necrotic Ringspot, Hop Mosaic and Hop Latent** virus
Storability	Retains 58% alpha acid after 6 months storage at 20ºC (68ºF)
Ease of Harvest	
Total Oil	1.82 mL/100g
Myrcene Oil	< 50%
Humulene Oil	24%-28%
Caryophyllene Oil	8.2%
Farnesene Oil	0.16%
Substitutes	Northern Brewer
Style Guide	Ale, Lager, Pilsner, Wheat, Belgian Ale

References

http://www.ars.usda.gov/SP2UserFiles/person/2450/hopcultivars/21078.html

http://www.meadowplant.co.uk/recordhopsprofile.html

Red Earth

Red Earth hops bring with them an altogether "Australian" depth of character. They're a new Australian breed which carry a decidedly spicy, woody aroma and flavor with a citrusy under note. The name stems from the reddish hue cones exhibit as they emerge from the early, burr stage of development.

Developed by Rupert Ward in Western Australia, Red Earth is the culmination of a cross between Columbus and a Goldings-derived male variety. They were trialed recently over two seasons by Birbeck's Brewing Company but they don't appear to have been picked up in a commercial capacity by anyone else just yet. No analytical data appears to be available.

Also Known As	
Characteristics	Spicy, woody aroma and flavor with an undernote of citrus
Purpose	Aroma

Alpha Acid Composition

Beta Acid Composition

Cohumulone Composition

Country   Australia

Cone Size

Cone Density

Seasonal Maturity

Yield Amount

Growth Rate

Resistant to

Susceptible to

Storability

Ease of Harvest

Total Oil

Myrcene Oil

Humulene Oil

Caryophyllene Oil

Farnesene Oil

Substitutes

Style Guide   California Common, American Pale Ale

References

http://aussiehomebrewer.com/topic/65327-red-earth-hops/

http://aussiehomebrewer.com/topic/70658-red-earth/

http://westaussiebrewcrew.com/forum/index.php?topic=407.0

Riwaka

Considered to be one of the darling hops of the New Zealand craft beer scene, Riwaka's abundant oil content is nearly twice that of its parent variety Saaz. This unique oil balance alongside a near 1:1 ratio of alpha to beta acids gives it a strong sweet citrus note that, according to one brewer, makes it the "ultimate" for hoppy beers. Riwaka, formerly known as D Saaz, is a product of HortResearch's New Zealand Hops "hops with a difference" program and was officially released to the brewing world in

1997.

Homebrewer's Comments

I brewed AHS Riwaka Red and dry hopped with an additional ounce of Riwaka. There's no word for Riwaka other than kumquat. (*John Whipple / 944play via homebrewtalk.com*)

Also Known As	D Saaz
Characteristics	Notes of grapefruit and kumquat
Purpose	Aroma
Alpha Acid Composition	4.5%-6.5%
Beta Acid Composition	4%-5%
Cohumulone Composition	29%-36%
Country	New Zealand
Cone Size	
Cone Density	Loose
Seasonal Maturity	Early
Yield Amount	
Growth Rate	
Resistant to	
Susceptible to	
Storability	
Ease of Harvest	
Total Oil	0.8 mL/100g
Myrcene Oil	68%
Humulene Oil	9%
Caryophyllene Oil	4%
Farnesene Oil	1%
Substitutes	Saaz
Style Guide	India Pale Ale, Pilsner, American Pale Ale

References

http://nzhops.co.nz/varieties/riwaka.html
http://www.brew-dudes.com/riwaka-hops/1975

Saaz

Officially registered in 1952, the original Saaz, or Czech Saaz as it is sometimes known, has established itself as a staple variety for brewers and dates back more than 700 years. Originating in Zatec, Bohemia (now part of the Czech Republic) it is an esteemed red-bine variety that is now grown around the world. New Zealand in particular has embraced Saaz, breeding several descendants including the popular Motueka and Riwaka varieties (B & D Saaz, respectively).

Saaz is one of the four original Noble hops and has a distinctive and classic aroma. Known for its prominent use in Stella Artois and countless Bohemian Lagers and Pilsners. Its warm, herbal character stems from a high level of farnesene while its other oils are in fair balance.

With such a low alpha acid percentage, Saaz is inarguably an aroma hop, however, when used as an early addition it is thought to add a delicate bitterness. Additionally, its elevated content of polyphenols aids in abating oxidation, giving beer brewed with Saaz a notably longer shelf life.

Growing Saaz is not without its difficulties. Specifically, it endures a meager yield, has weak mildew resistance and light cones. The original Saaz variety has been successfully cloned 9 times between 1952 and 1993 in an effort to improve these factors. Originally, growers were hesitant to hybridize, fearing the loss of its signature and delicate aroma. This hybridization has become necessary though to breed resistance to wilt and mildew and make it a more viable crop. Despite these few shortcomings, breweries use it prolifically worldwide.

Brewmaster's Comments

I love Saaz, Hallertau and Tettnang when brewing pilsners or a traditional kolsch. The spicy, peppery, herbal qualities are unmatched for such styles. They can be used early, middle and/or late for these beers. *(Ryan Schmiege, Assistant Brewmaster at Deschutes Brewery)*

Homebrewer's Comments

I think the bittering properties are very similar, the US may be slightly more aggressive. The differences would probably stand out more in flavoring and aroma additions with the Czech variety being rounder and maybe a bit more defined that the American version. *(Steelers77 via homebrewtalk.com)*

Also Known As	Saaz, Czech Saaz, Saazer, Czech Saazer
Characteristics	Noble, herbal character
Purpose	Aroma
Alpha Acid Composition	2.5%-4.5%
Beta Acid Composition	4%-6%
Cohumulone Composition	23%-26%
Country	Czech Republic
Cone Size	Small to medium
Cone Density	Loose to moderate
Seasonal Maturity	Mid
Yield Amount	800-1200 kg/hectare (714-1071 lbs/acre)
Growth Rate	Moderate
Resistant to	
Susceptible to	Susceptible to downy mildew, powdery mildew and wilt
Storability	Retains 45%-55% alpha acid after 6 months storage at 20ºC (68ºF)
Ease of Harvest	Moderate
Total Oil	0.4-0.8 mL/100g
Myrcene Oil	25%-40%
Humulene Oil	15%-30%
Caryophyllene Oil	6%-9%
Farnesene Oil	14%-20%
Substitutes	Saaz (US), Sterling, Polish Lublin, Moteuka, Centennial, Amarillo®
Style Guide	Lager, Pilsner

References

https://en.wikipedia.org/wiki/Saaz_hops#cite_note-hopstats-1
http://www.chizatec.cz/download/page5038.pdf
http://www.chizatec.cz/en/czech-hop-varieties/?arc=36
http://beerlegends.com/saaz-hops
http://www.beertutor.com/articles/hops_guide.shtml

Saaz (US)

Despite exhibiting a low yield, Saaz (US) is a popular commercial aroma variety and is used in many US beers today. Bred from the original centuries-old Czech Saaz variety, it carries the same noble qualities but with some subtle differences. Its flavor and aroma profile is mild, earthen and spicy and its alpha is slightly higher than its Czech twin. Saaz (US) is primarily used in Lagers and Pilsners.

Homebrewer's Comments

> Its not the same as Czech saaz for aroma and flavor, similiar but not exactly alike. To me its a bit more herbal than the czech saaz. *(BargainFittings via homebrewtalk.com)*

Also Known As	US Saaz, American Saaz
Characteristics	Mild, earthy, spicy, herbal
Purpose	Aroma
Alpha Acid Composition	3%-4.5%
Beta Acid Composition	3%-4.5%
Cohumulone Composition	24%-28%
Country	US
Cone Size	Small to medium
Cone Density	Loose to Moderate
Seasonal Maturity	Early
Yield Amount	600-1000 kg/hectare (540-890 lbs/acre)
Growth Rate	Low
Resistant to	
Susceptible to	

Storability	Retains 45%-55% alpha acid after 6 months storage at 20°C (68°F)
Ease of Harvest	Moderate
Total Oil	0.5-1.0 mL/100g
Myrcene Oil	25%-37%
Humulene Oil	23%-40%
Caryophyllene Oil	7%-11%
Farnesene Oil	9%-13%
Substitutes	Saaz, Hallertau, Tettnanger, Lubelska, Sterling
Style Guide	Lager, Pilsner

References

http://beerlegends.com/saaz-us-hops
https://www.hopunion.com/saaz/
http://brooklynbrewshop.com/themash/hop-of-the-month-saaz/
http://www.midwestsupplies.com/us-saaz-pellet-hops.html

Santiam

Developed at the Agriculture Research Service in Corvallis, Oregon, Santiam hails from parent varietals Swiss Tettnanger, German Hallertauer Mittelfrüher and a slightly more distant Cascade (US)-derived cultivar. It was released to the brewing public in 1997 and features a well-balanced oil profile.

The resultant tasting notes are a pleasantly soft, herbal essence alongside floral and fruity aromas with hints of pepper and spice. Santiam is often used by brewers to embellish the aroma of India and American Pale Ales.

Homebrewer's Comments

I used them as the only hop in my Witbier and it turned out fantastic. I used .75 oz at 60 minutes and .25 oz at 30 minutes. It really added a nice spicy/citrus character to the beer, it'll be my go to hop for several styles moving forward! (*guitarist970 via homebrewtalk.com*)

Also Known As	
Characteristics	Soft, herbal, floral, fruity aromas with hints of pepper and spice
Purpose	Aroma
Alpha Acid Composition	5%-8%
Beta Acid Composition	5.3%-8.5%
Cohumulone Composition	18%-24%
Country	US
Cone Size	Small to medium
Cone Density	Loose
Seasonal Maturity	Mid
Yield Amount	1430-1780 kg/hectare (1280-1580 lbs/acre)
Growth Rate	Moderate to high
Resistant to	Resistant to downy mildew
Susceptible to	Susceptible to powdery mildew
Storability	Retains 40%-50% alpha acid after 6 months storage at 20°C (68°F)
Ease of Harvest	Difficult
Total Oil	1.3-1.7 mL/100g
Myrcene Oil	25%-36%
Humulene Oil	23%-26%
Caryophyllene Oil	4.8%-8.8%
Farnesene Oil	13%-16%
Substitutes	Tettnanger, Spalter, Spalter Select, Hallertau, Liberty
Style Guide	American Blonde Ale, American Lager, India Pale Ale, American Pale Ale, Wheat, Bock

References
http://beerlegends.com/santiam-hops
https://www.hopunion.com/santiam/
http://alestolagers.blogspot.com.au/2010/06/hop-of-week-santiam.html
http://www.greatlakeshops.com/santiam.html

Saphir

Released in 2002, Saphir features elements of spice and fruit amid refined citrus notes of tangerine. It is considered well suited to Belgian Whites as well as Pilsners and German Lagers.

Bred at the Hop Research Center in Hüll, the initial goal of its creators was to produce a more commercially viable alternative to German Hallertau Mittelfrüh through increased disease resistance and the retention of Hallertau's noble characteristics. In that capacity, Saphir would most certainly be considered a success.

Homebrewer's Comments

> Saphir is similar to Hallertauer...Saphir does have a bit of citrus, but nothing like the big 3 C's. *(david_42 via homebrewtalk.com)*

Also Known As	Sapphire
Characteristics	Sweet citrus aromas with hints of tangerine
Purpose	Aroma
Alpha Acid Composition	2%-4.5%
Beta Acid Composition	4%-7%
Cohumulone Composition	12%-17%
Country	Germany
Cone Size	
Cone Density	
Seasonal Maturity	Early
Yield Amount	1600-1900 kg/hectare (1427-1695 lbs/acre)
Growth Rate	
Resistant to	
Susceptible to	
Storability	
Ease of Harvest	
Total Oil	0.8-1.4 mL/100g

Myrcene Oil	25%-40%
Humulene Oil	20%-30%
Caryophyllene Oil	9%-14%
Farnesene Oil	< 1%
Substitutes	Hallertau Mittelfrüh, Hallertau Tradition, Spalter Select
Style Guide	Pilsner, Lager

References

https://www.hopsteiner.de/info/nc/en/pdf/hop-variety-finder/variety-information/sdb/saphir-1.html?filename=Saphir.pdf

https://www.hopunion.com/german-saphir/

http://www.brew-dudes.com/saphir-hops/502

https://en.wikipedia.org/wiki/List_of_hop_varieties#Saphir

Satus®

Satus® is a trademarked variety of Yakima Chief Ranches in Washington State. It is a high alpha dual-use hop considered great as a clean foundational hop when used at the beginning of a boil and when an extra punch of hops is desired. When used late, strong citrus notes come to the fore.

To date, Satus® has not enjoyed any significant commercial use and as of 2016 no reference to the variety exists on the YCH HOPS website. It's future appears uncertain.

Also Known As	
Characteristics	
Purpose	Bittering
Alpha Acid Composition	12.5%-14%
Beta Acid Composition	8.5%-9%
Cohumulone Composition	32%-35%
Country	US
Cone Size	Medium
Cone Density	Moderate

Seasonal Maturity	
Yield Amount	2450-2550 kg/hectare (2190-2275 lbs/acre)
Growth Rate	Moderate to high
Resistant to	Resistant to powdery mildew and sperotheca
Susceptible to	
Storability	Retains 60%-70% alpha acid after 6 months storage at 20ºC (68ºF)
Ease of Harvest	Moderate
Total Oil	1.5-2.8 mls/100 grams
Myrcene Oil	40%-45%
Humulene Oil	15%-20%
Caryophyllene Oil	7%-10%
Farnesene Oil	0%-1%
Substitutes	Nugget, Galena
Style Guide	India Pale Ale, Pale Ale, Stout, Barley Wine, Imperial Stout

References

http://beerlegends.com/satus-hops

https://trademarks.justia.com/757/09/satus-75709482.html

http://www.brewerslair.com/index.php?p=brewhouse&d=hops&id=&v=&term=57

Saxon

Saxon was developed in England at the esteemed Wye College. It was bred from Svaloef, an old Swedish variety that is no longer grown and an unnamed male varietal. Sister to Viking, Saxon does have a pleasant aroma when used in brewing but is not grown commercially. It is instead used predominantly for breeding. Its yield is poor in the US, but higher in England.

Also Known As	Wye Saxon
Characteristics	Pleasant aroma

Purpose	Aroma
Alpha Acid Composition	8%-10%
Beta Acid Composition	4%-5%
Cohumulone Composition	20%
Country	UK
Cone Size	
Cone Density	
Seasonal Maturity	Early
Yield Amount	500 kg/hectare (450 lbs/acre)
Growth Rate	Low to moderate
Resistant to	Resistant to verticillium wilt, moderately resistant to downy mildew
Susceptible to	
Storability	Retains 75% alpha acid after 6 months storage at 20°C (68°F)
Ease of Harvest	
Total Oil	0.95 mL/100g
Myrcene Oil	54%
Humulene Oil	11.8%
Caryophyllene Oil	5.6%
Farnesene Oil	6.7%
Substitutes	
Style Guide	

References
http://www.ars.usda.gov/SP2UserFiles/person/2450/hopcultivars/21282.html
http://www.brewerslair.com/index.php?p=brewhouse&d=hops&id=&v=&term=58

Serebrianka

Serebrianka, or Silver as it is sometimes called, is a Russian aroma hop and parent to Cascade. Its commercial viability was tested for a staggering 20 years in the US before it was discarded in 1991 for a number of faults, most notably, its incredibly low yield. It is however still available for homebrewing use.

Given its origin and flavor profile, Serebrianka is thought to possibly be related to Saaz and is said to impart some interestingly unique aroma characteristics that include hints of black tea, herbs and even tobacco. It has high humulene and farnesene, which no doubt contributes to its pleasant and largely continental aroma and taste.

Homebrewer's Comments

> I did a hop tea with them and I would agree that it has the floral and perfume character. I did not detect a C hop character at all. I liked them a lot and can't wait to use them in my next saison. Next saison will be a blend of serebrianka and french strisselspalt. *(smokinghole via homebrewtalk.com)*

Also Known As	Silver Hop, Silver
Characteristics	Continental aroma and taste with hints of black tea, herbs and tobacco
Purpose	Aroma
Alpha Acid Composition	3%-4%
Beta Acid Composition	3%
Cohumulone Composition	23%
Country	Russia
Cone Size	
Cone Density	
Seasonal Maturity	Early
Yield Amount	220 kg/hectare (200 lbs/acre)
Growth Rate	Low
Resistant to	Moderately resistant to downy mildew
Susceptible to	
Storability	Retains 53% alpha acid after 6 months storage at 20ºC (68ºF)
Ease of Harvest	
Total Oil	0.41 mL/100g
Myrcene Oil	30%

Humulene Oil	27%
Caryophyllene Oil	8%
Farnesene Oil	12%
Substitutes	
Style Guide	

References

http://www.ars.usda.gov/SP2UserFiles/person/2450/hopcultivars/21045.html

http://www.hopsdirect.com/serebrianka-pellet/

https://books.google.com.au/books?id=gYVLHMmplRcC&pg=PA726&lpg=PA726&dq=ser
ebrianka+hops&source=bl&ots=MHbfukShZ4&sig=dzF2fCZ9Gf-
KG0yRGUVBKB3WadM&hl=en&sa=X&ved=0CEAQ6AEwBjgKahUKEwjatYuX5PbIAhXj
46YKHS_CAkk#v=onepage&q=serebrianka%20hops&f=false

https://www.morebeer.com/articles/homebrew_beer_hops

Shinshuwase

Grown exclusively in Japan, Shinshuwase is a high yielding aroma hop. It dates back to the early 1900's, possibly earlier. While it still exists, it has largely been replaced by Kirin No. 2, Toyomidori, Kitamidori and Eastern Gold as a commercial crop.

A cross between Saaz and open pollinated White Vine, Shinshuwase was originally used as a bittering hop, but after the introduction of super alpha varieties, it is now considered far more useful as an aroma hop. Shiga Kogen Beer currently uses it in that capacity for their Draft Pale Ale and Miyama Blonde and describes its aroma as lemon-centric.

Also Known As	Shinshu-Wase, Shinshu Wase
Characteristics	Lemon aromas
Purpose	Aroma
Alpha Acid Composition	4.7%-8.3%
Beta Acid Composition	4%-6.1%
Cohumulone Composition	51%
Country	Japan
Cone Size	
Cone Density	Loose

Seasonal Maturity	Late
Yield Amount	1790-2470 kg/hectare) (1600-2200 lbs/acre)
Growth Rate	Very high
Resistant to	Resistant to verticillium wilt, moderately resistant to downy mildew
Susceptible to	Infected with the cherry and apple strains of the Prunus Necrotic Ringspot Virus, Hop Latent Virus and American Hop Latent Virus
Storability	Retains 61% alpha acid after 6 months storage at 20ºC (68ºF)
Ease of Harvest	
Total Oil	0.42-0.98 mL/100g
Myrcene Oil	57.5%
Humulene Oil	12%
Caryophyllene Oil	20.3%
Farnesene Oil	0.1%
Substitutes	Saaz, Hallertau, Santiam
Style Guide	

References

http://www.ars.usda.gov/SP2UserFiles/person/2450/hopcultivars/60042.html

http://japanbeertimes.com/2013/02/shiga-kogen-beer/

https://translate.google.com.au/translate?hl=en&sl=ja&u=http://www.tamamura-honten.co.jp/&prev=search

Simcoe®

Released to the world in 2000 by Yakima Chief Ranches, American variety Simcoe® has become wildly popular with craft brewers. With a high alpha percentage and low cohumulone, it makes a very nice foundational bittering hop. It is also noted though for its favorable aroma qualities. It has a pleasantly fruity, yet earthy herbal and piney aroma.

Flying Fish used it to create its 10-year anniversary Barley Wine – 5 additions of it alongside Magnum. Sierra Nevada also uses it in one of their High Altitude bold beers Hoptimum®. It has been referred to as "Cascade on steroids".

Brewmaster's Comments

Great for any hoppy beer, Simcoe has a bright citrus and grapefruit flavor, with earthy undertones. It's best used, in my opinion, for late kettle, whirlpool and dry hop additions. Additions from .5-1.0 lbs/bbl result in a nice flavor/aroma in the beer for whirlpool and dry hop additions. *(Mark Medlin, Brewmaster at SweetWater Brewing Company)*

Simcoe is definitely one of my favorites. Love the piney, grapefruit notes, great for flavor additions and especially dry hopping. Very unique and obvious. *(Jeremy S Kosmicki, Brewmaster at Founders Brewing Co.)*

Homebrewer's Comments

I've done a couple brews with Simcoe as aroma/flavor hops, and have found them to give some unique grapefruit or tangerine - like notes to pale ales. I haven't really used them in huge quantities, but with their relatively high AA%, they pose a real opportunity for different uses in beers (good aroma/flavor, good bittering). *(ericburnley via tastybrew.com)*

Also Known As	
Characteristics	Bright citrus flavors with earthy undertones, aromas of grapefruit, pine and herbs
Purpose	Bittering & Aroma
Alpha Acid Composition	12%-14%
Beta Acid Composition	4%-5%
Cohumulone Composition	15%-20%
Country	
Cone Size	Medium
Cone Density	
Seasonal Maturity	

Yield Amount	2300-2500 kg/hectare (2050-2230 lbs/acre)
Growth Rate	Moderate to high
Resistant to	Resistant to powdery mildew and sperotheca
Susceptible to	
Storability	Retains 70%-80% alpha acid after 6 months storage at 20ºC (68ºF)
Ease of Harvest	Difficult
Total Oil	2-2.5 mL/100g
Myrcene Oil	60%-65%
Humulene Oil	10%-15%
Caryophyllene Oil	5%-8%
Farnesene Oil	0%-1%
Substitutes	Summit™
Style Guide	Double India Pale Ale, India Pale Ale, Pale Ale

References

http://beerlegends.com/simcoe-hops
https://ychhops.com/varieties/simcoe-brand-ycr-14-cv
http://www.brew-dudes.com/simcoe-hops/215
https://www.craftbrewer.com.au/shop/details.asp?PID=615

Sladek

Sladek, meaning 'brewer', is a high yielding aroma variety and cross between Saaz and Northern Brewer. Originally registered as VUCH 71 In 1987, it was renamed to Sladek in 1994. Sladek features a classic hoppy aroma atop a fruity flavor profile with essences of peach, passionfruit and grapefruit.

Homebrewer's Comments

I used them (100%) in a high gravity, heavily hoped Pils and they worked well. In a Belgian they would be a good sub for a saaz type hop. *(Kaz via tastybrew.com)*

Also Known As	Czech Sladek, VUCH 71
Characteristics	Classic hoppy aroma, flavors of peach passionfruit and grapefruit
Purpose	Aroma
Alpha Acid Composition	4.5%-8%
Beta Acid Composition	4%-7%
Cohumulone Composition	23%-30%
Country	Czech Republic
Cone Size	
Cone Density	
Seasonal Maturity	
Yield Amount	
Growth Rate	
Resistant to	
Susceptible to	
Storability	
Ease of Harvest	
Total Oil	1.0-2.0 mL/100g
Myrcene Oil	35%-50%
Humulene Oil	20%-40%
Caryophyllene Oil	9%-14%
Farnesene Oil	< 1%
Substitutes	Saaz
Style Guide	Lager, Pilsner

References
http://hopunion.com/czech-sladek/
http://www.chizatec.cz/download/page5038.pdf
http://www.chizatec.cz/en/czech-hop-varieties/?arc=36
http://www.bohemiahop.cz/varieties/sladek

Smaragd

Smaragd is another interesting hop to come out of the Hop Research

Institute in Germany. Bred with the purpose of creating a more disease resistant alternative to Hallertauer Mittelfrüh, it was released for large-scale production in 2007.

Meaning 'emerald' in German, Smaragd is a low acid, low cohumulone aroma hop with an interesting oil balance. Myrcene and farnesene make up the majority of its oil composition. Its aroma is predominantly fruity but with some floral elements as well. Its flavor profile has been described as spicy. Daughter of Hallertau Gold, Smaragd is a wonderful dual-purpose hop.

Homebrewer's Comments

I used these as the main flavoring hop in an Amber ale a while back. I'd agree that they are more on the noble end of the flavor spectrum--earthy/spicy. Calling them a german attempt at amarillo is good marketing, but their attempt failed. Not unpleasant by any means. *(wileaway via homebrewtalk.com)*

I use these a lot in Exports. They give a delicate spicy aroma if used in late additions. *(aegir via tastybrew.com)*

Also Known As	Emerald, German Emerald
Characteristics	Predominantly fruity aroma with bold floral notes, flavors of earth and spice
Purpose	Bittering & Aroma
Alpha Acid Composition	4%-6%
Beta Acid Composition	3.5%-5.5%
Cohumulone Composition	13%-18%
Country	Germany
Cone Size	
Cone Density	
Seasonal Maturity	Mid to late
Yield Amount	1850 kg/hectare (1651 lbs/acre)
Growth Rate	
Resistant to	Wilt, downy mildew and powdery mildew
Susceptible to	

Storability	Retains 60%-70% alpha acid after 6 months storage at 20ºC (68ºF)
Ease of Harvest	
Total Oil	0.7-1.7 mL/100g
Myrcene Oil	20%-40%
Humulene Oil	30%-50%
Caryophyllene Oil	9%-14%
Farnesene Oil	1%
Substitutes	
Style Guide	Ale, Amber

References
http://hopunion.com/german-smaragd-emerald/
http://beerlegends.com/smaragd-hops
http://www.brew-dudes.com/smaragd-hops/4972
http://www.barthhaasgroup.com/en/varieties-and-products/hop-varieties?id=262
https://ychhops.com/varieties/smaragd
https://translate.google.com.au/translate?hl=en&sl=nl&u=https://nl.wikipedia.org/wiki/Smaragd_(hop)&prev=search
http://www.highgravitybrew.com/store/pc/Smaragd-Emerald-Hops-p4754.htm
http://nikobrewhops.blogspot.com.au/2014/12/smaragd-hops-and-you.html

Smooth Cone

Smooth Cone is a New Zealand hop variety. It is no longer grown commercially but can still be found. Developed in the 1960's, the variety was introduced alongside two other Black Root Rot resistant varieties, First Choice and Calicross after the disease savaged New Zealand's hops industry during the mid 20th century.

It is the offspring of an open pollination of a California Cluster and a sibling to First Choice. Although it has a moderate alpha acid content itself, it has been used to breed several high alpha New Zealand varieties, including SuperAlpha and Green Bullet.

Also Known As	SmoothCone
Characteristics	

Purpose	Bittering & Aroma
Alpha Acid Composition	7%-9.5%
Beta Acid Composition	3.4%-5.2%
Cohumulone Composition	31%-31%
Country	New Zealand
Cone Size	
Cone Density	
Seasonal Maturity	
Yield Amount	650-1520 kg/hectare (580-1360 lbs/acre)
Growth Rate	Moderate to high
Resistant to	
Susceptible to	
Storability	Retains 60%-70% alpha acid after 6 months storage at 20ºC (68ºF)
Ease of Harvest	
Total Oil	0.38-1.14 mL/100g
Myrcene Oil	55%
Humulene Oil	21%
Caryophyllene Oil	6%
Farnesene Oil	0%-1%
Substitutes	Cluster
Style Guide	Lager

References

http://beerlegends.com/smooth-cone-hops

https://www.ars.usda.gov/SP2UserFiles/person/2450/hopcultivars/66056.html

http://www.nzhops.co.nz/new-zealand-hop-industry-overview

https://books.google.com.au/books?id=oWQdjnVo2B0C&pg=PA407&lpg=PA407&dq=smooth+cone+hops&source=bl&ots=wmR2mT_iHT&sig=NgCn7KHdjWizIJB5ad3f5zOGFKY&hl=en&sa=X&ved=0ahUKEwiRqYScstHMAhVHrJQKHbILC_44ChDoAQg4MAU#v=onepage&q=smooth%20cone%20hops&f=false

Sonnet

Sonnet is a new, Oregon-grown hop said to have Saaz and Styrian

Golding characteristics. It has a low alpha acid content and makes a nice aroma hop, exhibiting deeply floral, grassy and earthy notes alongside a balanced, rounded bitterness. Flavor-wise it is said to demonstrate some fruitiness with hints of oak and honey.

Homebrewer's Comments

> I bought 1 lb last year and brewed a Best Bitter, ESB, Scotch Ale and Porter all 100% Sonnet. They taste similar to Goldings but a little more flowery with perhaps a dash of fruit. They are woodier like UK Goldings and seem to taste a bit more like them then they do US Goldings. So Sonnet to me is a woody and flowery British hop. *(alecoholic via homebrewtalk.com)*

Also Known As	Sonnet Golding
Characteristics	Deep floral aroma, grass, earth, flavors of oak and honey
Purpose	Aroma
Alpha Acid Composition	2.6%-6%
Beta Acid Composition	
Cohumulone Composition	
Country	US
Cone Size	
Cone Density	
Seasonal Maturity	
Yield Amount	
Growth Rate	
Resistant to	
Susceptible to	
Storability	
Ease of Harvest	
Total Oil	
Myrcene Oil	
Humulene Oil	
Caryophyllene Oil	
Farnesene Oil	

Substitutes	Saaz, East Kent Goldings, Crystal, Strisselspalt, Hersbrucker
Style Guide	English Ales, American Ales, German Ales, Belgian Ales, Lager

References

http://www.hopsdirect.com/sonnet-golding-c-v-pellet/

http://www.hifihomebrewandbbq.com/shop/sonnet-hop-pellets/

http://bsghandcraft.com/index.php/hops/hop-pellets-domestic/sonnet-us-pellets-1-oz.html

http://www.rebelbrewer.com/shop/brewing-ingredients/hops/pellet-hops/sonnet-hops-us-1oz-pellets

http://www.charlesfaram.co.uk/hop-varieties/sonnet/

Sorachi Ace

If you've ever enjoyed Sapporo, then you know what Sorachi Ace can do. Originally produced by the Sapporo Brewery in Hokkaido, Japan in the mid-1980s, it was resurrected in the US in 2006. It is a cross between Saaz, Brewer's Gold and BeiKei No. 2.

Sorachi Ace is considered excellent in several beer styles, particularly those desiring a distinct lemon citrus flavor. Some brewers have even reported flavors of orange, cilantro, dill and oak.

Brewmaster's Comment

Sorachi Ace has a very odd, lemony, almost dill-like aromatic. I find that it is rarely used successfully; it really clashes with any residual sugar. But it can work really well in super-dry beers like saisons. It can work well both in the kettle and in dry hopping, but as I said, it is not easy to use well. *(Garrett Oliver, Brewmaster at Brooklyn Brewery)*

Homebrewer's Comments

I've used them in about 5 beers and have loved them. I would pair them with something. Citra, Amarillo, and Centennial are good ones. But it depends on the style. Saisons can handle Sorachi Ace by itself, for example. An IPA is going to need a bit more complexity in the hop bill. *(kjjohns5 via*

Also Known As	
Characteristics	Flavors of lemon citrus, orange, dill, cilantro
Purpose	Bittering & Aroma
Alpha Acid Composition	11.5%-16%
Beta Acid Composition	6%-7.5%
Cohumulone Composition	23%-28%
Country	Japan
Cone Size	
Cone Density	
Seasonal Maturity	Mid
Yield Amount	
Growth Rate	High
Resistant to	Resistant to downy mildew and botrytis
Susceptible to	
Storability	
Ease of Harvest	
Total Oil	1.5-3 mL/100g
Myrcene Oil	44%-55%
Humulene Oil	20%-26%
Caryophyllene Oil	7%-11%
Farnesene Oil	2%-5%
Substitutes	
Style Guide	Saison

References

http://yakimachief.com/wp-content/uploads/2013/05/sorachiAce.pdf
https://ychhops.com/varieties/sorachi-ace
http://www.johnihaas.com/wp-content/uploads/2015/01/Sorachi-Ace.pdf
https://www.craftbrewer.com.au/shop/details.asp?PID=3988

Southern Brewer

Parent of Southern Promise, Southern Brewer was developed in the early 1970's after the primary South African hops variety at the time, Golden Cluster, was devastated by black root rot. It is the result of an open pollinated cross of Fuggle.

Southern Brewer is used primarily for bittering and is not considered to be particularly distinguished in either aroma or flavor.

Southern Brewer did not do well with relatively limited hours of sunlight and required supplemental grow lighting. This made the variety considerably more expensive to produce. The development and introduction of Southern Promise and Outeniqua solved much of that issue.

Also Known As	
Characteristics	
Purpose	Bittering
Alpha Acid Composition	5.6%-12%
Beta Acid Composition	2.8%-5%
Cohumulone Composition	33%-42%
Country	
Cone Size	Medium to large
Cone Density	Moderate to compact
Seasonal Maturity	Early to mid
Yield Amount	1320-2210 kg/hectare (1180-1980 lbs/acre)
Growth Rate	Moderate to high
Resistant to	Resistant to powdery mildew and verticillium wilt
Susceptible to	
Storability	Retains 60%-70% alpha acid after 6 months storage at 20ºC (68ºF)
Ease of Harvest	Difficult
Total Oil	0.4-1.5 mL/100g

Myrcene Oil	50%-62%
Humulene Oil	10%-26%
Caryophyllene Oil	4%-10%
Farnesene Oil	3%-11.2%
Substitutes	Southern Promise
Style Guide	

References
http://beerlegends.com/southern-brewer-hops
http://freshops.com/usda-named-hop-variety-descriptions/#usda_id_21187

Southern Cross

Southern Cross was created by New Zealand's HortResearch breeding program as a cross between Smooth Cone and the result of a Californian and English Fuggle. It was released in 1994.

In brewing, citrus and Spice and everything nice is how one might describe New Zealand's Southern Cross variety. A soft bitterness makes it a good early addition to the boil. As a later addition, it features a heady lemon zest and pine needle essence, which makes it a star among its kind.

There doesn't seem to be any substitute that can come close to the characteristics of Southern Cross. Sierra Nevada brewery released their Southern Hemisphere Harvest fresh hops ale in April of 2014 using Southern Cross, along with Pacifica and Motueka as its finishing hops.

Homebrewer's Comments

> Incredible aroma. I made an IIPA with them that came out amazing. A lot more pine flavor than I had read in any descriptions of the variety. *(drummerguysteve via homebrewtalk.com)*

Also Known As	
Characteristics	Soft bitterness, lemon zest and pine needles

Purpose	Bittering & Aroma
Alpha Acid Composition	13%-14%
Beta Acid Composition	6%-7%
Cohumulone Composition	28%
Country	New Zealand
Cone Size	
Cone Density	
Seasonal Maturity	Late
Yield Amount	850 kg/hectare (750 lbs/acre)
Growth Rate	Very high
Resistant to	
Susceptible to	
Storability	Retains 71% alpha acid after 6 months storage at 20ºC (68ºF)
Ease of Harvest	
Total Oil	1.59mL/100g
Myrcene Oil	58%
Humulene Oil	14%
Caryophyllene Oil	4%
Farnesene Oil	5%
Substitutes	
Style Guide	Pale Ale, India Pale Ale, Lager

References

http://beerlegends.com/southern-cross-hops
http://nzhl.info-prime.co.nz/variety/southern-cross
https://ychhops.com/varieties/southern-cross
https://www.craftbrewer.com.au/shop/details.asp?PID=596
https://bsgcraftbrewing.com/southern-cross-nz

Southern Promise

Southern Promise was bred specifically for the South African region. Created from Southern Brewer and a wild Slovenian male, it was developed in an effort to produce a variety that would grow well in areas with limited sunlight.

It has fairly high alpha acids and low cohumulone giving it bright and smooth bittering qualities. It is largely considered a nice dual-use hop with a pleasant and unobtrusive woody and earthy quality.

Homebrewer's Comments

> A bittering hop. I have used it as an aroma hop and it does not really give much even if used in large quantities. *(ChristianSA via thebrewingnetwork.com)*

Also Known As	
Characteristics	Smooth bitterness, woody, earthy
Purpose	Bittering & Aroma
Alpha Acid Composition	9.5%-11.5%
Beta Acid Composition	3.6%-5.4%
Cohumulone Composition	20%-22%
Country	Slovenia
Cone Size	Medium
Cone Density	Moderate to compact
Seasonal Maturity	Mid
Yield Amount	1760-2210 kg/hectare (1570-1980 lbs/acre)
Growth Rate	Moderate to high
Resistant to	
Susceptible to	
Storability	Retains 60%-70% alpha acid after 6 months storage at 20°C (68°F)
Ease of Harvest	Difficult
Total Oil	0.7-0.7 mL/100g
Myrcene Oil	22%
Humulene Oil	26%-26%
Caryophyllene Oil	9%
Farnesene Oil	0%-1%

| Substitutes | Southern Brewer |
| Style Guide | Lager, Pale Ale |

References

http://beerlegends.com/southern-promise-hops

http://www.hopsteiner.de/info/nc/en/pdf/hop-variety-finder/variety-information/sdb/southern-promise-1.html?filename=Southern%20Promise.pdf

http://www.johnihaas.com/wp-content/uploads/2015/01/Southern-Promise.pdf

http://www.barthhaasgroup.com/johbarth/images/pdfs/hop-varieties/en/Sortenblatt_Engl_SOUTH-AFRICA_SouthernPromise.pdf

Southern Star

Released in 2001, Southern Star was developed in South Africa around 10 years after Outeniqua and Southern Promise. Like it's two predecessors it is also considered a day neutral variety, meaning it can be grown in locations with reduced daylight. It is used primarily for bittering but also features a spicy, tangy flavor and some aroma.

Also Known As	
Characteristics	
Purpose	Bittering
Alpha Acid Composition	12%-14%
Beta Acid Composition	4.8%-5.2%
Cohumulone Composition	31%-31%
Country	South Africa
Cone Size	Medium
Cone Density	Moderate to compact
Seasonal Maturity	Mid
Yield Amount	1590-2470 kg/hectare (1420-2205 lbs/acre)
Growth Rate	High
Resistant to	
Susceptible to	
Storability	Retains 60%-70% alpha acid after 6 months storage at 20ºC (68ºF)

Ease of Harvest	Difficult
Total Oil	1.6-1.6 mL/100g
Myrcene Oil	39%
Humulene Oil	22%
Caryophyllene Oil	15%
Farnesene Oil	12%-12%
Substitutes	Outeniqua
Style Guide	

References
http://beerlegends.com/southern-star-hops

Sovereign

The granddaughter of Pioneer, Sovereign is an English variety bred at Wye College in the mid-1990s. Released in 2006, Sovereign is gaining respect for its complex and delicate aroma profile.

Floral, grassy and minty on the nose, its bittering qualities are classic and well rounded. It has also been reported to impart subtle green tea and vanilla aspects to a beer. Works well in conjunction with Goldings.

Homebrewer's Comments

Nice hops which seem to add a slight vanilla flavour, I used them alongside EKG and/or Fuggles. *(jeltz via jimsbeerkit.co.uk)*

Also Known As	
Characteristics	Complex aroma, subtle notes of green-tea and vanilla
Purpose	Bittering
Alpha Acid Composition	4.5%-6.5%
Beta Acid Composition	2.1%-3.1%
Cohumulone Composition	26%-30%
Country	UK

Cone Size	
Cone Density	
Seasonal Maturity	
Yield Amount	
Growth Rate	
Resistant to	
Susceptible to	
Storability	
Ease of Harvest	
Total Oil	0.6-1 mL/100g
Myrcene Oil	25%-30%
Humulene Oil	21%-26%
Caryophyllene Oil	7.9%-8.1%
Farnesene Oil	3.5%-3.7%
Substitutes	
Style Guide	American Lager, American Pale Ale

References

https://ychhops.com/varieties/sovereign

http://www.britishhops.org.uk/sovereign-2/

Spalt

Surely one of the world oldest hop varieties, Splat hops date back as far as the 8th century and in the 16th century they were the first variety to be granted the German hop seal – a historically significant certification system predating the current, German Hop Provenance Law. Grown primarily in the Spalt region of Germany, it is one of the original landrace hops.

Not to be confused with its offspring, Spalter Select, Spalt features notes of earth and spice alongside noble aroma qualities and has been likened to Tettnanger and Saaz. It's not grown commercially in the US due to its low yield, something that is problematic even in its native Germany. Despite this, the variety is in high demand by brewers and often outstrips supply.

Homebrewer's Comments

I have used Spalt in my Kolsch and Alts as a bitter/flavoring hop usually with several additions at the 30 and 45 minute marks of a 60 minute boil. I'd describe it as somewhat spicy and earthy, a little floral. I really like it but i went so far as to do a Double Alt with nothing but Spalt hops and was disappointed in the result. I do not think it has enough all-around properties to carry a beer. Mixed with Hallertau and or Saaz it is great. My two cents. *(jeffg via homebrewtalk.com)*

Also Known As	Spalter, Spalt Spalter, Spalter Spalt, German Spalt
Characteristics	Earth, spice
Purpose	Aroma
Alpha Acid Composition	2.5%-5.7%
Beta Acid Composition	3%-5%
Cohumulone Composition	22%-29%
Country	Germany
Cone Size	Small to medium
Cone Density	Compact
Seasonal Maturity	Early
Yield Amount	1120 kg/ hectare (1000 lbs/acre)
Growth Rate	Poor
Resistant to	Resistant to verticillium wilt and downy mildew
Susceptible to	
Storability	Retains 50%-60% alpha acid after 6 months storage at 20ºC (68ºF)
Ease of Harvest	Moderate
Total Oil	0.5-0.9 mL/100g
Myrcene Oil	20%-35%
Humulene Oil	20%-30%
Caryophyllene Oil	8%-13%
Farnesene Oil	12%-18%

Substitutes	Saaz, Tettnanger, Santiam, Liberty, Hallertau
Style Guide	German Ale, Lager, Pilsner, Bock, Kolsch

References

https://www.hopunion.com/german-spalt/

http://hvg-germany.de/en/quality-insurance/hops-origin-statute-certification-system-quality-appraisal

http://beerlegends.com/spalt-hops

http://brooklynbrewshop.com/themash/hop-of-the-month-spalt/

Spalter Select

Released in 1993, Spalter Select was bred in Hüll, Germany in an effort to increase yield potential and disease resistant and serve as a commercial replacement for Spalt. These efforts were quite successful.

The result of a cross of Spalt and Hallertau Mittelfrüher, Spalter Select retains some of the finer characteristics of both these varieties and is considered a slightly spicier version of Spalt. Brewing giant Anheuser-Busch replaced both Spalt and Tettnanger with Spalter Select.

Also Known As	Select Spalt, Spalt Select
Characteristics	
Purpose	Aroma
Alpha Acid Composition	3%-6.5%
Beta Acid Composition	2%-5%
Cohumulone Composition	20%-28%
Country	Germany
Cone Size	Small to medium
Cone Density	Compact
Seasonal Maturity	Mid to Late
Yield Amount	1750-2000 kg/hectare (1561-1784 lbs/acre)
Growth Rate	High

Resistant to	Resistant to verticillium wilt and downy mildew
Susceptible to	
Storability	Retains 60%-70% alpha acid after 6 months storage at 20ºC (68ºF)
Ease of Harvest	Difficult
Total Oil	0.5-1.2 mL/100g
Myrcene Oil	40%-50%
Humulene Oil	15%-20%
Caryophyllene Oil	6%-8%
Farnesene Oil	10%-22%
Substitutes	Saaz, Tettnanger, Spalt, Hersbrucker, Perle, Hallertau Tradition
Style Guide	Kölsch, Belgian Ale, French Ale, Lager, Bock, Helles, Alt, Pilsner, Marzen

References

http://beerlegends.com/spalter-select-hops

http://www.castlemalting.com/Publications/HopProducts/SelectSpalt_CMSpecA_organic.pdf

https://www.hopsteiner.de/info/nc/en/pdf/hop-variety-finder/variety-information/sdb/spalter-select-1.html?filename=Spalter%20Select.pdf

Star

Not to be confused with Southern Star, Star is an old Belgian land race variety, which is no longer grown commercially. It was largely discontinued due to poor vigor and yield but It is however still obtainable in small quantities for home brewing. It exhibits excellent storage stability and sports a lovely continental-type aroma.

Also Known As	
Characteristics	Pleasing continental-style aroma
Purpose	Aroma
Alpha Acid Composition	3.2%
Beta Acid Composition	1.7%

Cohumulone Composition	24%
Country	Belgium
Cone Size	
Cone Density	
Seasonal Maturity	Early
Yield Amount	560 kg/hectare (500 lbs/acre)
Growth Rate	Low
Resistant to	Tolerant to downy mildew
Susceptible to	
Storability	Retains 82% alpha acid after 6 months storage at 20ºC (68ºF)
Ease of Harvest	
Total Oil	0.47 mL/100g
Myrcene Oil	34.2%
Humulene Oil	33.9%
Caryophyllene Oil	11.7%
Farnesene Oil	3.7%
Substitutes	
Style Guide	

References
http://www.ars.usda.gov/SP2UserFiles/person/2450/hopcultivars/21217.html

Sterling

Sterling was successfully bred to overcome Saaz's susceptibility to mildew. Developed over 8 years in Corvallis, Oregon it was released in 1998.

Sterling's oil content is rather unusual with both very high farnesene and very low carophyllene. This creates a delicately spiced, citrusy aroma with both a floral and herbal punch. Sterling's heritage is complex too and is the result of a mix of Saaz, Cascade, Early Green, Brewer's Gold and another, unknown variety.

Homebrewer's Comments

Definitely similar to Saaz. Spicy, not floral, and neither Saaz or Sterling will give you the aroma wallop that many of the new American varieties do. Definitely a more subtle hop - but more than the traditional noble varieties. I find when I do a first wort hop addition with it I can get a faint citrus note as well. *(pjj2ba via homebrewtalk.com)*

Also Known As	
Characteristics	Spicy, citrus aroma, herbal notes
Purpose	Bittering & Aroma
Alpha Acid Composition	4.5%-9%
Beta Acid Composition	4%-6%
Cohumulone Composition	21%-28%
Country	US
Cone Size	Medium
Cone Density	Compact
Seasonal Maturity	Mid
Yield Amount	1800-2000 kg/hectare (1610-1785 lbs/acre)
Growth Rate	Moderate to high
Resistant to	Resistant to downy mildew and powdery mildew
Susceptible to	
Storability	Retains 60%-75% alpha acid after 6 months storage at 20°C (68°F)
Ease of Harvest	Difficult
Total Oil	0.6-1.9 mL/100g
Myrcene Oil	44%-48%
Humulene Oil	19%-23%
Caryophyllene Oil	5%-8%
Farnesene Oil	11%-17%
Substitutes	Saaz
Style Guide	India Pale Ale

References

http://beerlegends.com/sterling-hops
https://ychhops.com/varieties/sterling
http://www.usahops.org/index.cfm?fuseaction=hop_info&pageID=8
https://www.ars.usda.gov/SP2UserFiles/person/2450/hopcultivars/21689.html
https://bsgcraftbrewing.com/sterling-hop

Sticklebract

Sticklebract is a dual-use New Zealand variety and another variety bred to stem the issues from Black Root Rot that were present in the country during the mid 20th century. It was selected as a seedling in the 1970's from open pollinated First Choice.

Stickleback's dominant aroma comes from high selinene and high myrcene resulting in a somewhat English, piney-citrusy bouquet.

Also Known As	
Characteristics	Aromas of pine and citrus
Purpose	Bittering & Aroma
Alpha Acid Composition	13%-14.2%
Beta Acid Composition	7.5%-8.5%
Cohumulone Composition	40%-45%
Country	New Zealand
Cone Size	Medium to large
Cone Density	Moderate
Seasonal Maturity	Mid to Late
Yield Amount	1900-2560 kg/hectare (1695-2290 lbs/acre)
Growth Rate	High
Resistant to	
Susceptible to	
Storability	Retains 60%-70% alpha acid after 6 months storage at 20ºC (68ºF)
Ease of Harvest	Difficult

Total Oil	0.76-1.72 mL/100g
Myrcene Oil	51%-64%
Humulene Oil	8%-11%
Caryophyllene Oil	3%-6%
Farnesene Oil	4%-4.6%
Substitutes	Northern Brewer (GR)
Style Guide	Extra Special Bitter

References
http://beerlegends.com/sticklebract-hops
https://www.craftbrewer.com.au/shop/details.asp?PID=591
http://freshops.com/usda-named-hop-variety-descriptions/#usda_id_21403

Strisselspalt

Strisselspalt hails from the Alsace region of France around Strasbourg and is likely related to German Spalt and/or Hersbrucker hops. Thought to be an old land race, its acreage is dwindling due to its inherent low yield but it survives largely on the back of a strong domestic demand for the variety.

It is considered a pleasant continental-style aroma hop featuring subtle spicy notes, with herbal and floral aromas surrounding an undercurrent of citrus and fruit.

Homebrewer's Comments

IMO it is a soft noble hop with flavor more like Hallertau than Saaz, but I've never used it as single hop in a beer. *(Malticulous via homebrewtalk.com)*

Also Known As	French Strisselspalt, Strisselspalter
Characteristics	Pleasant continental-style aroma, herbal, floral, spicy, citrus, fruit
Purpose	Aroma
Alpha Acid Composition	1.8%-5.7%

Beta Acid Composition	2.5%-6%
Cohumulone Composition	20%-27%
Country	France
Cone Size	Medium
Cone Density	Moderate to compact
Seasonal Maturity	Mid
Yield Amount	900 kg/hectare (802 lbs/acre)
Growth Rate	High to Low
Resistant to	Resistant to verticillium wilt, moderately resistant to downy mildew
Susceptible to	
Storability	Retains 60%-70% alpha acid after 6 months storage at 20ºC (68ºF)
Ease of Harvest	Moderate
Total Oil	0.6-0.9 mL/100g
Myrcene Oil	35%-52%
Humulene Oil	12%-32%
Caryophyllene Oil	8%-10.3%
Farnesene Oil	< 1%
Substitutes	Liberty, Hallertau, Mt Hood, Crystal, Hersbrucker
Style Guide	Lager, Saison, Blonde Ale, Amber Ale, Belgian Ale, Bock, Maibock, Golden Ale, Belgian Pale Ale

References
http://www.ars.usda.gov/SP2UserFiles/person/2450/hopchem/21173.html
http://www.midwestsupplies.com/french-strisselspalt-pellet-hops.html
https://www.hopunion.com/french-strisselspalt/
http://beerlegends.com/strisselspalt-hops

Styrian Gold

Styrian Gold should not be confused with Styrian Golding (aka Savinjski

Golding, technically a Fuggle-type hop). Styrian Gold is a Slovenian hop, bred from a Savinjski Golding and a Slovenian wild male. It has a noble aroma and a balanced hoppiness, which stems from its 1:1 alpha/beta acid ratio. Styrian Gold also benefits from good storage stability. It was released in 2009.

Also Known As	
Characteristics	Balanced noble aroma
Purpose	Bittering & Aroma
Alpha Acid Composition	3.5%-6.5%
Beta Acid Composition	3.5%-5.9%
Cohumulone Composition	28%-35%
Country	Slovenia
Cone Size	
Cone Density	
Seasonal Maturity	Early
Yield Amount	1600-2400 kg/hectare (1430-1140 lbs/acre)
Growth Rate	
Resistant to	
Susceptible to	
Storability	
Ease of Harvest	
Total Oil	1.3-2.3 mL/100g
Myrcene Oil	38%-47%
Humulene Oil	19%-22%
Caryophyllene Oil	5%-10%
Farnesene Oil	6%-10%
Substitutes	Styrian Golding
Style Guide	

References

http://www.thehomebrewforum.co.uk/viewtopic.php?p=391466&sid=5f55afac4f1aef8f40eec6fa4e01746a#p391466

http://www.hopslist.com/katalog%20slovenskih%20sort.pdf

Styrian Golding

Styrian Golding or Savinjski Golding as it is commonly known, goes by a multitude of sometimes confusing aliases. Confusing still is the fact it actually doesn't come from a Golding at all, but is rather the result of the clonal selection of Fuggle and as such exhibits many Fuggle-like characteristics.

It was considered a major crop in the 1930's in both Styria, a state in Austria and across the Savinja river in Slovenia (former Yugoslavia). Its staying power has been attributed to its disease resistance, specifically, its resistance to mildew. It is now world-renowned hop and in high demand.

From a brewer's perspective, Styrian Golding is a lovely aroma hop and exhibits resinous, earthy flavors that are perhaps considered slightly more refined than Fuggle. It has also been described as imparting subtle aromas of white pepper to a brew.

Homebrewer's Comments

> Great for English and Belgian Ales mainly, although I've heard some say enough of them will come off sort or citrusy, although I can't speak to that. They are fantastic in NB's Inkeeper (Tim Taylor Landlord clone), that much I can say. *(duckmanco via homebrewtalk.com)*

Also Known As	Styrian, Savinja Golding, Savinjski Golding, Styrian Savinjski Golding, Yugoslavia Golding
Characteristics	Resinous and earthy with hints of white pepper
Purpose	Aroma
Alpha Acid Composition	2.8%-6%
Beta Acid Composition	2%-3%

Cohumulone Composition	25%-30%
Country	Austria and Slovenia
Cone Size	Medium
Cone Density	Compact
Seasonal Maturity	Early
Yield Amount	1150-1500 kg/hectare (1025-1330 lbs/acre)
Growth Rate	Moderate
Resistant to	
Susceptible to	
Storability	Retains 65%-80% alpha acid after 6 months storage at 20ºC (68ºF)
Ease of Harvest	Moderate
Total Oil	0.3-1 mL/100g
Myrcene Oil	27%-33%
Humulene Oil	34%-38%
Caryophyllene Oil	9%-11%
Farnesene Oil	2%-5%
Substitutes	Fuggle, Willamette, Bobek
Style Guide	Extra Special Bitter, Ale, Lager, Belgian Ale

References
http://beerlegends.com/styrian-golding-hops
http://www.ars.usda.gov/SP2UserFiles/person/2450/hopcultivars/21049.html
http://brooklynbrewshop.com/themash/hop-of-the-month-styrian-golding/
https://bsgcraftbrewing.com/slovenian-styrian-goldings

Summer

It's not difficult to see how the Australian hops variety, Summer, got its name after experiencing its sublime and delicate notes of apricot and melon. Others have even noted elements of grass, peach, passionfruit and citrus.

A descendant of Saaz, Summer was created by Hop Products Australia in 1997 and is a low alpha aroma hop that can be well-utilized late in the boil. It is however even better suited to dry hopping and it is in this capacity that its apricot and melon bouquet really shines. In any capacity, it is not as spicy as its Czech parent.

The Malt Shovel Brewery released their Mad Brewers Garden di Paradisi brew in February of 2014 with a mix of sweet, fruity hops that included Summer.

Homebrewer's Comments

> Ive used them a couple of times. I got apricot and grass off them. They are fairly mild and pleasant. Mild enough to use in an english style without it being off. I especially liked them paired with huell melon. *(Giraffe via homebrewtalk.com)*

> I use this in my house pale ale. Nice soft apricot/peach flavor and aroma. Pairs well with just about any fruit forward hop. *(m00ps via email)*

Also Known As	Australian Summer
Characteristics	Subtle flavors of apricot, melon, peach and grass
Purpose	Aroma
Alpha Acid Composition	5.6%-6.4%
Beta Acid Composition	4.8%-6.1%
Cohumulone Composition	20%-25%
Country	Australia
Cone Size	
Cone Density	
Seasonal Maturity	
Yield Amount	1800-2000 kg/hectare (1605-1784 lbs/acre)
Growth Rate	
Resistant to	
Susceptible to	

Storability	
Ease of Harvest	
Total Oil	1.4-2.0 mL/100g
Myrcene Oil	29%-38%
Humulene Oil	28%-50%
Caryophyllene Oil	8%-11%
Farnesene Oil	< 1%
Substitutes	Saaz
Style Guide	Ale, Wheat, Belgian Ale, American Ale, India Pale Pale

References

http://www.hops.com.au/products/summer-

https://www.hopunion.com/australian-summer/

https://bsgcraftbrewing.com/summer-hop

https://www.craftbrewer.com.au/shop/details.asp?PID=1164

http://www.brew-dudes.com/summer-hops/5273

Summit™

Summit™ has the distinction of being the first semi-dwarf variety hops to be bred in the US and the first dwarf grown in Washington's Yakima Valley. It has a complex pedigree, hailing from various combinations and pollinations of Nugget, Zeus and Lexus. It is currently the only low trellis variety in the Yakima Valley and is picked by hand.

Summit™ boasts citric aromas of tangerine, grapefruit and orange along with an impressive alpha content giving it a wide spectrum of potential use.

Homebrewer's Comments

Ninkasi Tricerahops is one of my favorite commercial IIPAs and it uses a decent amount of Summit. So does Green Flash Imperial IPA, another favorite of mine. I mainly detect dank resiny tangerine citrus from both of these beers, which use the majority of Summit early on and in the dryhop. For a replacement, Apollo or Columbus would probably be the most similar to Summit. Some people will tell you that the supposed oniony character only occurs when the grower leaves Summit on the bines for too long. But I believe there is a fallacy in this claim. My theory is that Summit will yield oniony traits if you overdo it in the 30-5 minute kettle boil range and don't balance it out with fruity hops like Amarillo or Citra. The effects might be magnified if you also incorporate this schedule with a substantial amount of Summit for a long, 10-14 day dryhop. *(bobbrews via homebrewtalk.com)*

Also Known As	
Characteristics	Citrus aromas
Purpose	Bittering
Alpha Acid Composition	16%-18%
Beta Acid Composition	3.3%-4.3%
Cohumulone Composition	26%-33%
Country	US
Cone Size	Medium
Cone Density	Moderate to compact
Seasonal Maturity	Mid
Yield Amount	2200-2700 kg/hectare (1965-2410 lbs/acre)
Growth Rate	High
Resistant to	Resistant to powdery mildew, verticillium wilt and phytophthora root rot
Susceptible to	Susceptible to downy mildew
Storability	Retains 85%-85% alpha acid after 6 months storage at 20ºC (68ºF)
Ease of Harvest	Difficult
Total Oil	1.5-3 mL/100g
Myrcene Oil	30%-50%
Humulene Oil	15%-25%
Caryophyllene Oil	10%-16%
Farnesene Oil	0%-1%

| Substitutes | Columbus, Simcoe®, Apollo |
| Style Guide | India Pale Ale, Barley Wine, Imperial Stout |

References
http://beerlegends.com/summit-hops

Sun

Currently considered as in-development at the S. S. Steiner Hop Farms in Washington State, Sun has not yet been registered or acquired USDA accession. Not much is known about its lineage yet but it is thought to be derived from Brewer's Gold and sister to Zeus. It has also been suggested that it possesses characteristic similarities to Galena.

What little we do know about the variety includes its classification as a high-alpha varietal, though not as high as Zues and that it exhibits very strong yield potential. When brewed, it is said to feature a pronounced herbaceous aroma and flavor.

Also Known As	
Characteristics	Pronounced herbaceous aroma and flavor
Purpose	Bittering
Alpha Acid Composition	12%-16%
Beta Acid Composition	4.5-7%
Cohumulone Composition	30%-40%
Country	US
Cone Size	
Cone Density	
Seasonal Maturity	Mid to late
Yield Amount	2250 kg/hectare (2000 lbs/acre)
Growth Rate	Very high
Resistant to	
Susceptible to	
Storability	
Ease of Harvest	

Total Oil	
Myrcene Oil	55%-70%
Humulene Oil	10%-15%
Caryophyllene Oil	5%-10%
Farnesene Oil	< 1%
Substitutes	Magnum, Galena, Zeus
Style Guide	Barley Wine, Imperial Stout

References

https://www.freshops.com/hops/usda-named-hop-variety-descriptions#usda_id_Sun

http://www.homebrewtalk.com/wiki/index.php/Sun

http://www.homebrewtalk.com/showthread.php?t=165510

Sunbeam

Not originally envisioned for use in brewing, Sunbeam is an ornamental hop that was discovered to be inadvertently useful as an aroma hop. Selected in 1992 in Corvallis, Oregon, it features characteristics similar to that of its parent variety, Saaz.

Homebrewer's Comments

> Similar to Saaz and good for pilsners. (*david_42 via homebrewtalk.com*)

Also Known As	
Characteristics	Saaz-style characteristics
Purpose	Aroma
Alpha Acid Composition	4%-5%
Beta Acid Composition	2.5%
Cohumulone Composition	36%
Country	US
Cone Size	
Cone Density	
Seasonal Maturity	Early

Yield Amount	
Growth Rate	Very high
Resistant to	Moderately resistant to downy mildew and verticillium wilt
Susceptible to	
Storability	
Ease of Harvest	
Total Oil	0.8-1.3 mL/100g
Myrcene Oil	56%
Humulene Oil	14%
Caryophyllene Oil	4%
Farnesene Oil	6%
Substitutes	Saaz
Style Guide	Pilsner, Ale

References
http://www.ars.usda.gov/SP2UserFiles/person/2450/hopcultivars/21697.html

Sunshine

Mother to Comet, Sunshine was developed via open pollination seedling selection at Wye College in England. It was selected by Professor E. R. Salmon in the early 1930's and exhibits a very similar oil profile to Comet.

While it is considered a brewing hop first and foremost, its lovely, lemon yellow colored leaves also give this variety ornamental potential. Like Sunbeam hops, it should to be grown in a shaded position or it risks sustaining necrotic burn when exposed to prolonged late summer sun. Its exact parentage is unknown.

Also Known As	
Characteristics	
Purpose	Aroma
Alpha Acid Composition	6.7%-8.2%
Beta Acid Composition	2.1%-3.1%

Cohumulone Composition	34%
Country	UK
Cone Size	
Cone Density	
Seasonal Maturity	Early to mid
Yield Amount	560-900 kg/hectare (500-800 lbs/acre)
Growth Rate	Moderate to high
Resistant to	Moderately resistant to downy mildew
Susceptible to	
Storability	Retains 50% alpha acid after 6 months storage at 20°C (68°F)
Ease of Harvest	
Total Oil	1.35 mL/100g
Myrcene Oil	55%
Humulene Oil	0.9%
Caryophyllene Oil	
Farnesene Oil	
Substitutes	
Style Guide	

References

http://www.ars.usda.gov/SP2UserFiles/person/2450/hopcultivars/21281.html

Super Pride

Super Pride is the offspring of Pride of Ringwood and a descendant of Yeoman. First bred at the Rostrevor Breeding Garden in Victoria in 1987 by Hop Products Australia, it was released in 1995 and since 2002 has become a mainstay bittering variety used in commercial beer production in Australia.

Though primarily used as a bittering hop, Super Pride does feature an understated bouquet with elements of resin, spice and citrus. It is most often used in Lagers and Imperial Pale Ales and is considered milder than Pride of Ringwood.

Homebrewer's Comments

Superpride goes very well in all Aussie style beers like standard lager, Hunter Old, Coopers Clones. I just use 20g boiled for 90 mins and the amount of hop character is amazing for such a seemingly small addition. It still turns out streets ahead of VB or XXXX in bitterness and hop flavour. *(Bribie G via aussiehomebrewer.com)*

Also Known As	
Characteristics	
Purpose	Bittering
Alpha Acid Composition	13.5%-15%
Beta Acid Composition	6.4%-6.9%
Cohumulone Composition	26.8%-28%
Country	Australia
Cone Size	
Cone Density	
Seasonal Maturity	
Yield Amount	2310-3200 kg/hectare (2060-2860 lbs/acre)
Growth Rate	
Resistant to	
Susceptible to	
Storability	
Ease of Harvest	
Total Oil	2.1-2.6 mL/100g
Myrcene Oil	19%-34%
Humulene Oil	1%-2%
Caryophyllene Oil	5%-8%
Farnesene Oil	0%-1%
Substitutes	Pride of Ringwood
Style Guide	Imperial Pale Ale, Lager

References

Sussex

Sussex hops are an award-winning dwarf variety discovered by Peter Cyster in Northiam, East Sussex in 2005. Its brewing use uncovers a powerful aroma alongside delicate tropical flavors and great flavor retention. It is considered to be forwardly fruity and its unique aroma afforded it third place in the hedgerow category of the Institute of Brewing and Distilling's British Hop Competition in 2012.

Analysis conducted by Wye Hops Ltd. concluded its oil profile is unlike that of any other hop variety. Brewing trials however have likened its delicate flavor to Fuggle. Though it is classified as being more useful as a flavor and aroma variety, when used as an early addition it imparts a well-rounded and classic bitterness.

Harvey's Brewery released its Sussex Wild Hop brew in July of 2013 with Sussex as its primary hop.

Homebrewer's Comments

> Nice hop, good bittering and quite a unique flavor, slightly citrus and also earthy notes. (*scuppeteer via jimsbeerkit.co.uk*)

Also Known As	
Characteristics	Delicate tropical flavors and a unique fruit-forward aroma
Purpose	Aroma
Alpha Acid Composition	4.3%-5.8%
Beta Acid Composition	2.4%-3.2%
Cohumulone Composition	29%-32%
Country	UK

Cone Size	
Cone Density	
Seasonal Maturity	
Yield Amount	
Growth Rate	High
Resistant to	Tolerant to verticillium wilt and moderately resistant to downy and powdery mildew
Susceptible to	
Storability	
Ease of Harvest	
Total Oil	0.4-0.6 mL/100g
Myrcene Oil	42%
Humulene Oil	23%
Caryophyllene Oil	8-7.2%
Farnesene Oil	< 1%
Substitutes	Progress, Whitbread Golding, Fuggle
Style Guide	English Ale, Pale Ale, Belgian Ale

References
http://www.britishhops.org.uk/sussex-hop/
http://englishhops.co.uk/our-varieties/#Sussex
http://brew-engine.com/ingredients/hops/sussex.html
https://www.morebeer.com/articles/homebrew_beer_hops

Sylva

Bred by Hop Products Australia in Tasmania in 1997, Sylva is an Australian aroma hop with a subtle and complex tasting profile. Progeny of Saaz, it is these roots that suit it well to light lagers and pilsners, imparting a bohemian-style hoppiness reminiscent of its Czech parent.

Some have described Sylva as decidedly earthen, with flavors akin to fresh-cut timber and the forest. It is perhaps apt then that its name be defined in English as "a descriptive flora of forest trees".

Also Known As	Australian Sylva, AU Sylva, Silva
Characteristics	Flavors of the forest and fresh-cut timber, subtle and hoppy bohemian-style aroma
Purpose	Aroma
Alpha Acid Composition	5.6%-7.3%
Beta Acid Composition	3%-4.6%
Cohumulone Composition	20%-25%
Country	Australia
Cone Size	
Cone Density	
Seasonal Maturity	
Yield Amount	
Growth Rate	
Resistant to	
Susceptible to	
Storability	
Ease of Harvest	
Total Oil	1.0-1.4 mL/100g
Myrcene Oil	26%-36%
Humulene Oil	18%-27%
Caryophyllene Oil	5%-8%
Farnesene Oil	22%-28%
Substitutes	Hallertau Mittlefrüh, Helga, Saaz
Style Guide	Pilsner, Lager, California Common, Pale Ale

References

https://www.hopunion.com/australian-sylvia/
http://www.brew-dudes.com/sylva-hops/5230
https://bellsbeer.com/store/products/Sylva-(AU)-Hops-%252d-1-oz-Pellets.html
https://www.craftbrewer.com.au/shop/details.asp?PID=4892
http://dictionary.reference.com/browse/sylva

Symphony

Despite Symphony's very high alpha content and excellent storage stability its extreme susceptibility to powdery mildew has largely deemed the variety untenable for commercial production.

So susceptible in fact, growers in the Pacific Northwestern United States agreed to stop growing it altogether in order to stem outbreaks of powdery mildew first discovered in the region in 1997.

Little is known about its proper utilization but with such an extremely high cohumulone content, those wishing to take advantage of its high alpha content by using as a sole early addition should proceed with caution. This is particularly true if 'smooth' bittering qualities are desired.

Also Known As	
Characteristics	
Purpose	Bittering
Alpha Acid Composition	16%-18%
Beta Acid Composition	5%-5.6%
Cohumulone Composition	44%
Country	
Cone Size	
Cone Density	
Seasonal Maturity	Late
Yield Amount	
Growth Rate	
Resistant to	
Susceptible to	
Storability	
Ease of Harvest	
Total Oil	2.6 mL/100g
Myrcene Oil	39%
Humulene Oil	
Caryophyllene Oil	9%

Farnesene Oil	8.8%
Substitutes	
Style Guide	India Pale Ale, Imperial India Pale Ale

References

http://apsjournals.apsnet.org/doi/abs/10.1094/PDIS-11-13-1127-PDN

http://www.homebrewtalk.com/showthread.php?t=145413

https://www.freshops.com/hops/usda-named-hop-variety-descriptions#usda_id_Symphony

Tahoma

Released in 2013 by the USDA and Washington State University, Tahoma is the daughter of Glacier. With alpha content higher than its parent, Tahoma features very low cohumulone giving it a subtle, yet lovely lemon citrus aroma and flavor with undertones of orange, woodiness and spice.

Homebrewer's Comments

There's some woody/earthiness with some faint citrus notes on the nose. I could see using them in a hoppier blonde ale or maybe an American wheat. They also probably would complement some of the more citrusy hops well too. *(iagainsti via homebrewtalk.com)*

Also Known As	
Characteristics	Subtle flavors and aromas of lemon citrus, orange, wood and spice
Purpose	Aroma
Alpha Acid Composition	7.2%-8.2%
Beta Acid Composition	8.5%-9.5%
Cohumulone Composition	15%-17%
Country	US
Cone Size	
Cone Density	
Seasonal Maturity	

Yield Amount	2000-2200 kg/hectare (1784-1962 lbs/acre)
Growth Rate	
Resistant to	
Susceptible to	
Storability	Retains 75% alpha acid after 6 months storage at 20°C (68°F)
Ease of Harvest	
Total Oil	1.0-2.0 mL/100g
Myrcene Oil	67%-72%
Humulene Oil	9%-11%
Caryophyllene Oil	2.9%-3.5%
Farnesene Oil	< 1%
Substitutes	
Style Guide	Blonde Ale, Wheat, Lager

References

https://www.hopunion.com/tahoma/

http://www.usahops.org/userfiles/image/1383233116_2013%20Hops%20Variety%20Manual.pdf

http://draftmag.com/3-new-hop-varieties-you-need-to-know/

http://www.yakimavalleyhops.com/TahomaLeaf16oz_p/hopsleaftahoma2-2014crop.htm

Talisman

Released in 1965, Talisman is an American Cluster variety descended from Late Cluster. Peaking at 4.6% of total US hop production in 1973, the popularity of Talisman has steadily declined ever since. Currently, it is no longer grown commercially. It has fairly low alpha acids, although up to 8% AAU was recorded in the Yakima Valley.

Also Known As	
Characteristics	
Purpose	Bittering & Aroma
Alpha Acid Composition	5.7%-6.7%

Beta Acid Composition	2.8%-3.6%
Cohumulone Composition	53%
Country	US
Cone Size	
Cone Density	
Seasonal Maturity	Very late
Yield Amount	2240-2700 kg/hectare (2000-2600 lbs/acre)
Growth Rate	Excellent
Resistant to	Moderately resistant to downy mildew and resistant to verticillium wilt
Susceptible to	
Storability	Retains 64% alpha acid after 6 months storage at 20ºC (68ºF)
Ease of Harvest	
Total Oil	0.72 mL/100g
Myrcene Oil	68%
Humulene Oil	4%
Caryophyllene Oil	5.9%
Farnesene Oil	0.2%
Substitutes	
Style Guide	

References

http://freshops.com/usda-named-hop-variety-descriptions/#usda_id_65101

https://books.google.com.au/books?id=_H1yBgAAQBAJ&pg=PA250&lpg=PA250&dq=talisman+hops&source=bl&ots=O9XD2K5Dmi&sig=7PiK_37Vi_D13Vz949SEO7OMeVs&hl=en&sa=X&ved=0ahUKEwiTmeicvNHMAhUI26YKHcyyAv0Q6AEINDAF#v=onepage&q=talisman&f=false

Tardif de Bourgogne

Translated into English, Tardif de Bourgogne means Late Burgundy. Similar to Precoce de Burgnogne (Early Burgundy), it is an aroma hop grown in small quantities in the Alsace region of France.

It is said to feature a mild European-style aroma and is thought to have come about via the clonal selection of an old French land race. Unfortunately, Tardif de Bourgogne is somewhat difficult to find on the open market.

Also Known As	
Characteristics	Mild, European-style aroma
Purpose	Aroma
Alpha Acid Composition	3.1%-5.5%
Beta Acid Composition	3.1%-5.5%
Cohumulone Composition	20%
Country	France
Cone Size	
Cone Density	
Seasonal Maturity	Late
Yield Amount	1345-1790 kg/hectare (1200-1600 lbs/acre)
Growth Rate	Moderate to high
Resistant to	Moderately resistant to downy mildew
Susceptible to	
Storability	Retains 66% alpha acid after 6 months storage at 20°C (68°F)
Ease of Harvest	
Total Oil	0.49-0.73 mL/100g
Myrcene Oil	44%
Humulene Oil	13%
Caryophyllene Oil	5.7%
Farnesene Oil	0.2%
Substitutes	Precoce de Burgnogne
Style Guide	Ale, Lager

References

http://beerlegends.com/tardif-de-bourgogne-hops
http://www.ars.usda.gov/SP2UserFiles/person/2450/hopcultivars/21169.html
https://translate.google.com.au/translate?hl=en&sl=nl&u=https://nl.wikipedia.org/wiki/Tar

Target

English dual-use variety Target was released in 1992 and features a lineage including Northern Brewer and Eastwell Golding. Though being somewhat closely related, Target's cousin, Challenger is considerably different.

Target's popularity has gone up and down over the years but it now seems to be popular with craft brewers, being used in Green Man Ale's IPA in Asheville, North Carolina and in many English craft brews. It yields well in England specifically but suffers poor storage stability.

Homebrewer's Comments

There's a Target right by me. I wish they sold hops there. *(mlanoue via homebrewtalk.com)*

Also Known As	Wye Target
Characteristics	
Purpose	Bittering & Aroma
Alpha Acid Composition	8%-12.5%
Beta Acid Composition	5%-5.5%
Cohumulone Composition	29%-35%
Country	UK
Cone Size	Small to medium
Cone Density	Compact
Seasonal Maturity	Late
Yield Amount	1350-1800 kg/hectare (1200-1610 lbs/acre)
Growth Rate	High
Resistant to	Resistant to powdery mildew, verticillium wilt
Susceptible to	Susceptible to downy mildew

Storability	Retains 45%-55% alpha acid after 6 months storage at 20°C (68°F)
Ease of Harvest	Difficult
Total Oil	1.6-2.6 mL/100g
Myrcene Oil	17%-22%
Humulene Oil	8%-10%
Caryophyllene Oil	0%-1%
Farnesene Oil	0%-1%
Substitutes	Fuggle, Willamette
Style Guide	Bitter, Pale Ale, Kentish Bitter, India Pale Ale, Brown Ale, American Lager

References
http://beerlegends.com/target-hops
https://ychhops.com/varieties/target
http://www.britishhops.org.uk/target/
http://brooklynbrewshop.com/themash/hop-of-the-month-target/
https://bsgcraftbrewing.com/uk-target

Teamaker

Developed over several decades by the USDA, Teamaker hops were officially released by the ARS Forage, Seed and Cereal Research Unit in Corvallis, Oregon in the late 2000's. They are a unique high beta, low alpha breed that have made their mark, not just in the brewing industry, but in the world of medicine and food as well.

Their strong antibiotic properties has seen them used in herbal teas, as an alternative antibiotic in livestock feed, right through to a bacterial inhibitor in the processing of sugar. As the name might suggest, they also make a tasty iced tea.

In beer brewing, Teamaker's flavor profile is somewhat similar to Crystal, except they don't seem to impart any bittering aspect at all. Expect floral aromas and use primarily as a late addition.

Also Known As	
Characteristics	No bitterness at all, floral aroma
Purpose	Aroma
Alpha Acid Composition	0.6%-1.8%
Beta Acid Composition	5.4%-13.2%
Cohumulone Composition	
Country	
Cone Size	
Cone Density	
Seasonal Maturity	Mid
Yield Amount	
Growth Rate	
Resistant to	
Susceptible to	
Storability	
Ease of Harvest	
Total Oil	
Myrcene Oil	
Humulene Oil	
Caryophyllene Oil	
Farnesene Oil	
Substitutes	
Style Guide	Pale Ale

References
http://www.greatlakeshops.com/teamaker.html
http://www.ars.usda.gov/is/pr/2008/080103.htm
http://imbibemagazine.com/new-hops-breeds/

Tettnanger

Selected from an old German land race, Tettnanger is grown the world over. Swiss, US and Australian varieties can be found on the market today though some foreign versions labeled "Tettnanger" are actually a hybridized mix with Fuggle and not considered a true Tettnanger hop. Tettnanger is grown around its native village of Tettnang in southwest Germany and in small quantities near lake Konstanz in Switzerland.

Though characteristically similar to Hallertau and genetically similar to Saaz, Tettnanger has notably more farnesene content giving it a soft spiciness and a subtle, balanced, floral and herbal aroma. It is also great as a dual-use hop, and considered by many as being particularly well suited to European lagers and pilsners.

Brewmaster's Comments

I love Saaz, Hallertau and Tettnang when brewing pilsners or a traditional kolsch. The spicy, peppery, herbal qualities are unmatched for such styles. They can be used early, middle and/or late for these beers. *(Ryan Schmiege, Assistant Brewmaster at Deschutes Brewery)*

Also Known As	Tettnang, Tettnang Tettnanger, German Tettnang, Tettnanger (GR), Schwetzinger, Deutscher Frühopfen
Characteristics	Balanced floral and herbal aromas with some spiciness
Purpose	Bittering & Aroma
Alpha Acid Composition	3%-5.8%
Beta Acid Composition	2.8%-5.3%
Cohumulone Composition	24%
Country	Germany
Cone Size	Medium
Cone Density	Moderate to compact
Seasonal Maturity	Early
Yield Amount	1120-1569 kg/hectare (1000-1400 lbs/acre)
Growth Rate	Moderate to high
Resistant to	Resitant to verticillium wilt, moderately resistant to downy mildew
Susceptible to	

Storability	Retains 61% alpha acid after 6 months storage at 20ºC (68ºF)
Ease of Harvest	
Total Oil	0.36-1.07 mL/100g
Myrcene Oil	40.6%
Humulene Oil	20.4%
Caryophyllene Oil	6.2%
Farnesene Oil	11.3%
Substitutes	Czech Saaz, Spalter, Santiam, Spalter Select, Saaz, Tettnanger (US)
Style Guide	Bitter, California Blonde Ale, Red Ale, Pilsner, Lager, American Amber Ale, Winter Ale, Pale Ale, Wheat Beer, Bavarian Hefeweizen, Cream Ale, American Lager

References

http://beerlegends.com/tettnanger-gr-hops

https://www.hopunion.com/german-tettnang/

http://www.ars.usda.gov/SP2UserFiles/person/2450/hopcultivars/21015.html

Tettnanger (Swiss)

While it was initially thought to be the same variety as the original German Tettnanger, the Swiss-grown version is now considered to be genetically unique. While the original variety is also known to be cultivated in Switzerland, much of the branded Tettnanger (Swiss) product is actually Fuggle-derived. Despite this, it is higher yielding than its German Tettnanger counterpart and features a similar, noble aroma.

Also Known As	
Characteristics	Noble aroma
Purpose	Aroma
Alpha Acid Composition	4.1%-6.3%
Beta Acid Composition	3.6%-5.7%
Cohumulone Composition	22%

Country	Switzerland
Cone Size	
Cone Density	
Seasonal Maturity	Early
Yield Amount	1120-1450 kg/hectare (1000-1300 lbs/acre)
Growth Rate	High
Resistant to	Moderately resistant to downy mildew
Susceptible to	
Storability	Retains 57% alpha acid after 6 months storage at 20ºC (68ºF)
Ease of Harvest	
Total Oil	0.42-1.13 mL/100g
Myrcene Oil	
Humulene Oil	
Caryophyllene Oil	
Farnesene Oil	
Substitutes	Tettnanger, Fuggle, Czech Saaz, Spalter, Ultra
Style Guide	Lager, Wheat Beer, Pilsner

References
http://www.homebrewtalk.com/wiki/index.php/Swiss_Tettnanger
http://www.ars.usda.gov/SP2UserFiles/person/2450/hopcultivars/61021.html

Tettnanger (US)

This variety has created so much industry confusion. In fact, you can still find sites online that describe American Tettnanger as a true Tettnanger. In reality, it is a clone of rhizomes imported as Swiss Tettnanger.

Recent tests have shown it to be genetically distinct from the original land race, Tettnang Tettnanger. Instead, the US varietal is more likely a Fuggle open pollinated with Tettnang Tettnanger. The original import was from a region in Switzerland directly across Lake Constance from Tettnang,

Germany.

American Tettnanger enjoyed some great popularity early on, being grown in Idaho, Washington and Oregon. It has noble hops aroma qualities with a bouquet of floral spice. However, in recent years, Anheuser Busch abandoned the variety.

It is said that US Tettnanger is a good hop for the boil as well as dry hopping whereas the original German variety is better used as a late addition.

Brewmaster's Comments

I love Saaz, Hallertau and Tettnang when brewing pilsners or a traditional kolsch. The spicy, peppery, herbal qualities are unmatched for such styles. They can be used early, middle and/or late for these beers. *(Ryan Schmiege, Assistant Brewmaster at Deschutes Brewery)*

Homebrewer's Comments

My fave hop.. They're a good all-purpose hop for lagers, especially german lagers. *(BryansBrew via tastybrew.com)*

Also Known As	US Tettnanger, American Tettnanger
Characteristics	
Purpose	Bittering & Aroma
Alpha Acid Composition	4%-5%
Beta Acid Composition	3%-4.5%
Cohumulone Composition	20%-25%
Country	US
Cone Size	Small to medium
Cone Density	Moderate
Seasonal Maturity	Early
Yield Amount	1000-1340 kg/hectare (890-1200 lbs/acre)
Growth Rate	Moderate
Resistant to	

Susceptible to	
Storability	Retains 55%-60% alpha acid after 6 months storage at 20ºC (68ºF)
Ease of Harvest	Moderate
Total Oil	0.4-0.8 mL/100g
Myrcene Oil	3%-45%
Humulene Oil	18%-23%
Caryophyllene Oil	6%-7%
Farnesene Oil	5%-8%
Substitutes	Spalter Select, Santiam, Czech Saaz, Spalter
Style Guide	Bitter, Blonde Ale, Red Ale, Pilsner, Lager, American Lager

References

http://beerlegends.com/tettnanger-gr-hops
http://beerlegends.com/tettnanger-us-hops
https://ychhops.com/varieties/tettnang
https://ychhops.com/varieties/tettnang-1
https://bsgcraftbrewing.com/tettnang-us-hop
http://brooklynbrewshop.com/themash/hop-of-the-month-tettnanger/

Tettnanger A

Tettnanger A was created in the 1970's at the University of Hohenheim in Germany via clonal selection from the original Tettnang Tettnanger hop. Sibling to Tettnanger B, Tettnanger A was originally thought to contain higher alpha percentages though testing in the US has brought this into question. It is said to have a pleasant, continental-style aroma and like its parent, is thought to be a descendant of Czech variety, Saaz.

Also Known As	
Characteristics	Pleasant continental-style aroma
Purpose	Aroma
Alpha Acid Composition	4.4%
Beta Acid Composition	5%

Cohumulone Composition	23%
Country	Germany
Cone Size	
Cone Density	
Seasonal Maturity	Early
Yield Amount	< 1120 kg/hectare (< 1000 lbs/acre)
Growth Rate	Moderate to high
Resistant to	Tolerant to downy mildew and verticillium wilt
Susceptible to	
Storability	Retains 60% alpha acid after 6 months storage at 20°C (68°F)
Ease of Harvest	
Total Oil	0.85 mL/100g
Myrcene Oil	47.2%
Humulene Oil	16.6%
Caryophyllene Oil	5.1%
Farnesene Oil	13.6%
Substitutes	Tettnanger, Saaz, Hallertau
Style Guide	Lager, Pilsner

References
http://cropandsoil.oregonstate.edu/hopcultivars/21496.html

Tettnanger B

Sister to Tettnanger A, Tettnanger B was also thought to be superior to its parent through heightened levels of alpha. Through US testing however, this is now in question. Bred in the 1970's through clonal selection from the original German Tettnang Tettnanger hop, it features pleasant, continental-style aroma characteristics. It is also very likely descended from Czech variety, Saaz, a variety to which it is genetically similar.

Also Known As	
Characteristics	Pleasant continental-style aroma
Purpose	Aroma
Alpha Acid Composition	5.3%
Beta Acid Composition	5.2%
Cohumulone Composition	23%
Country	Germany
Cone Size	
Cone Density	
Seasonal Maturity	Early
Yield Amount	< 1120 kg/hectare (< 1000 lbs/acre)
Growth Rate	Moderate to high
Resistant to	Moderately resistant to downy mildew and verticillium wilt
Susceptible to	
Storability	Retains 50% alpha acid after 6 months storage at 20ºC (68ºF)e
Ease of Harvest	
Total Oil	0.90 mL/100g
Myrcene Oil	53.8%
Humulene Oil	14%
Caryophyllene Oil	4.1%
Farnesene Oil	11.5%
Substitutes	Tettnanger, Saaz, Hallertau
Style Guide	Lager, Pilsner

References
http://www.ars.usda.gov/SP2UserFiles/person/2450/hopcultivars/21497.html

Tillicum®

Daughter of Galena and sibling to Chelan®, Tillicum® is a proprietary hop trademarked and grown only by J.I. Haas of Toppenish, Washington in the Yakima Valley. Developed in the late 1980's and released in 1995 it is an excellent yielding hop that keeps well and has high average alpha and beta acid content. It's said to share the stone fruit and citrus characteristics of its other family members.

Also Known As	
Characteristics	Elements of stone fruit and citrus
Purpose	Bittering
Alpha Acid Composition	13.5%-15.5.%
Beta Acid Composition	9.5%-11.5%
Cohumulone Composition	35%
Country	US
Cone Size	
Cone Density	
Seasonal Maturity	Early
Yield Amount	2240-2690 kg/hectare (2000-2400 lbs/acre)
Growth Rate	Very high
Resistant to	Moderately sisceptible to downy mildew
Susceptible to	
Storability	Retains 80% alpha acid after 6 months storage at 20ºC (68ºF)
Ease of Harvest	
Total Oil	1.5 mL/100g
Myrcene Oil	40%
Humulene Oil	14%
Caryophyllene Oil	7%
Farnesene Oil	None
Substitutes	Galena, Chelan
Style Guide	

References
http://www.usahops.org/index.cfm?fuseaction=hop_info&pageID=7
http://freshops.com/usda-named-hop-variety-descriptions/#usda_id_Tillicum

Tolhurst

Tolhurst hops were cultivated in the 1880's by James Tolhurst in Horsmonden, England and are thought to have originated from an old land race. They feature a pleasant, but subdued continental-style aroma and are no longer grown commercially due to their low yield and dreadful storage stability.

In the 1920's though, the variety was considered by some in the English brewing industry to be a perfect hop alternative for brewers using Fuggle or Golding varieties that "(do) not require a distinctive hop flavour" in their beers.

Also Known As	
Characteristics	Subdued but pleasant continental-style aroma
Purpose	Aroma
Alpha Acid Composition	2.2%
Beta Acid Composition	2.9%
Cohumulone Composition	31%
Country	UK
Cone Size	
Cone Density	
Seasonal Maturity	Early
Yield Amount	335-785 kg/hectares (300-700 lbs/acre)
Growth Rate	Low
Resistant to	Moderately resistant to downy mildew
Susceptible to	
Storability	Retains 49% alpha acid after 6 months storage at 20°C (68°F)
Ease of Harvest	
Total Oil	0.65 mL/100g
Myrcene Oil	42.5%
Humulene Oil	19.4%
Caryophyllene Oil	7.7%

Farnesene Oil   8.3%

Substitutes

Style Guide

References

http://cropandsoil.oregonstate.edu/hopcultivars/21396.html

http://onlinelibrary.wiley.com/store/10.1002/j.2050-0416.1923.tb02566.x/asset/j.2050-0416.1923.tb02566.x.pdf;jsessionid=5E5C13B8139410E3FC317D9B5954F50F.f03t01?v=1&t=igthuk26&s=692d294cd3888c541ee2923dd80da57a0649ff90

http://www.willingham-nurseries.co.uk/books/Hops/english%20hops.pdf

http://members.tripod.com/hatch_l/bbasehops.html

Topaz

Australian-born multi-purpose variety Topaz features elements of clove-like spice and a light, lychee-esque fruitiness. Samuel Adams uses it in their Tasman Red IPA. When used alongside a citrus-heavy hop (Samuel Adams used Galaxy®), it gives a surprising depth of flavor.

Created in 1985 by Hop Products Australia in the Rostrevor Breeding Garden in Victoria, Topaz was always intended to be a high-alpha hop. The result of a mix between an Australian high-alpha variety and a UK male sourced from Wye College in England, Topaz is a unique blend of Australian and European flavors and aromas.

Topaz was initially used as a bittering hop, but in the late 2000's increased experimentation with the variety uncovered its intense worth as a late addition. It features resinous and grassy notes when dry hopped and its fruity profile really shines when utilized in higher gravity recipes.

Homebrewer's Comments

Topaz and Galaxy are very solidly in the new world tropical fruit and berries part of the hop spectrum. My favorite IPA so far was a Rye IPA with Galaxy, Stella and Topaz. *(m00ps via homebrewtalk.com)*

I really ended up liking Topaz as a flavor addition. It has a lot of force to it. I found the flavor to be big citrus, though somewhat undefined. It's not clearly grapefruit, orange or lemon; rather some vague combination. It works great with a complimentary hop to give it a little more definition. *(bbrim via homebrewtalk.com)*

Also Known As	
Characteristics	Light, tropical fruit flavors of lychee, clove-like spice and resinous grassy tones when dry hopped
Purpose	Bittering & Aroma
Alpha Acid Composition	13.7%-17.7%
Beta Acid Composition	6.4%-7.9%
Cohumulone Composition	48%-51%
Country	Australia
Cone Size	
Cone Density	
Seasonal Maturity	
Yield Amount	3800-4200 kg/hectares (3390-3747 lbs/acre)
Growth Rate	
Resistant to	
Susceptible to	
Storability	
Ease of Harvest	
Total Oil	1.7-2.2 mL/100g
Myrcene Oil	34%-56%
Humulene Oil	8%-13%
Caryophyllene Oil	7%-13%
Farnesene Oil	< 1%
Substitutes	Galaxy, Citra®, Cascade, Riwaka, Rakau, Amarillo®
Style Guide	India Pale Ale, American Pale Ale, Bitter, Amber

References

http://www.hops.com.au/products/topaz-

Toyomidori

Produced in Japan for Kirin Brewery Co in 1981 and released in 1990, Toyomidori has since been largely discontinued due to problems with downy mildew. It was developed alongside Kitamidori and Eastern Gold as a high alpha variety but was the least successful of the three in this respect.

Toyomidori is a cross between Northern Brewer and a Wye male and is also the parent of Azacca.

Also Known As	
Characteristics	
Purpose	Bittering
Alpha Acid Composition	11%-13%
Beta Acid Composition	5%-6%
Cohumulone Composition	40%
Country	Japan
Cone Size	
Cone Density	
Seasonal Maturity	Mid
Yield Amount	1055 kg/hectare (940 lbs/acre)
Growth Rate	High
Resistant to	
Susceptible to	Moderately susceptible to downy mildew
Storability	Retains 63% alpha acid after 6 months storage at 20ºC (68ºF)
Ease of Harvest	
Total Oil	1.06 mL/100g

Myrcene Oil	59%
Humulene Oil	9%-12%
Caryophyllene Oil	4%-5%
Farnesene Oil	Trace Amounts
Substitutes	
Style Guide	

References
https://www.ars.usda.gov/SP2UserFiles/person/2450/hopcultivars/21676.html
http://www.charlesfaram.co.uk/hop-varieties/azacca/
http://www.agraria.com.br/extranet/arquivos/agromalte_arquivo/novas_variedades_japonesas_de_lupulo.pdf

Triskel

Developed in France in 2006, Triskel is a cultivar of the French hop, Strisselspalt and English varietal, Yeoman. With a more pronounced nose than its French parent, Triskel makes a unique first wort alternative and its notable aroma qualities make it well suited as a late addition or for dry hopping. Highly desired for Belgian-style or lighter ales, it features and elegant combination of both floral and subtle fruity notes with some citrus.

Triskel, Bouclier and Aramis are the first three officially registered varieties born of the Alsace hop sector's varietal research program. All three varieties were created in an ongoing effort to increase the alpha percentage of Strisselspalt while maintaining its prized aroma profile.

Homebrewer's Comments

> On opening the bag I was hit with an aroma that could probably best be described as fruitcake and citrus. The more I smelt them the more I could identify a similar arome to that of citra hops.
> *(boozy_shoes via thehomebrewforum.co.uk)*

Also Known As	French Triskel, FR Triskel
Characteristics	Floral aroma, subtly fruity, citrusy
Purpose	Aroma

Alpha Acid Composition	8%-9%
Beta Acid Composition	4%-4.7%
Cohumulone Composition	20%-23%
Country	France
Cone Size	
Cone Density	
Seasonal Maturity	
Yield Amount	
Growth Rate	
Resistant to	Tolerant to downy mildew
Susceptible to	
Storability	
Ease of Harvest	
Total Oil	1.5-2.0 mL/100g
Myrcene Oil	60%
Humulene Oil	13,5%
Caryophyllene Oil	6.1%
Farnesene Oil	< 1%
Substitutes	Strisselspalt, Ahtanum™, Centennial, Chinook, Simcoe®
Style Guide	Belgian Ale, Saison, Kolsch, Pilsner, Pale Ale, India Pale Ale, Lager, Wheat

References

https://www.hopunion.com/french-triskel/
http://www.hops-comptoir.com/25-hop-triskel-alsace
http://www.castlemalting.com/Publications/HopProducts/Triskel_CMSpecA.pdf
http://craftbrewer.com.au/shop/details.asp?PID=4895
http://www.hops-comptoir.com/content/18-varietal-rd
http://www.farmhousebrewingsupply.com/triskel-4-oz-fr-2013-sale/
http://www.probrewer.com/library/hops/hop-varieties/triskel/

Ultra

Ultra hops have traditionally only been grown only in the United States and even then in somewhat limited qualities. They were developed in Oregon in 1983, released commercially in 1995 and are a triploid variety rich in humulene, giving them a mildly spicy aroma and flavor.

A combination of four parts Hallertau one part Saaz and one part an as unnamed varietal, Ultra is well suited to lagers, pilsners, wheats and bocks both for finishing and aroma. Ultra also features an almost identical oil profile to Hallertau Mittelfrüh.

Also Known As	
Characteristics	Midly spicy aroma and flavor
Purpose	Aroma
Alpha Acid Composition	3%-5%
Beta Acid Composition	3.6%-5%
Cohumulone Composition	25%-35%
Country	US
Cone Size	Small
Cone Density	Moderate
Seasonal Maturity	Late
Yield Amount	2017-2241 kg/hectare (1800-2000 lbs/acre)
Growth Rate	Low to moderate
Resistant to	Moderately resistant to downy mildew and verticillium wilt
Susceptible to	
Storability	Retains 60%-65% alpha acid after 6 months storage at 20°C (68°F)
Ease of Harvest	Difficult
Total Oil	0.8-1.5 mL/100g
Myrcene Oil	25%-35%
Humulene Oil	30%-40%
Caryophyllene Oil	10%-15%
Farnesene Oil	0%-1%
Substitutes	Tettnanger (GR), Saaz, Hallertauer Tradition, Liberty

Style Guide	Oktoberfest, Blonde Ale, Harvest Ale, Lager, Pilsner, Pale Ale, American Lager, Bock

References
http://beerlegends.com/ultra-hops
https://www.hopunion.com/ultra/
http://www.ars.usda.gov/SP2UserFiles/person/2450/hopcultivars/21484.html

Universal

Universal was bred in the Czech Republic, but as of 1991 is no longer listed as a commercial variety. It is however still being produced in the US and has since become a darling of the craft brewing industry.

It has a pleasant noble aroma and a mild bitterness, good storage stability and due to its nearly identical oil profile, it is an excellent substitute for Hallertauer Mittelfrüher.

Also Known As	
Characteristics	Noble aromas and mild bitterness
Purpose	Bittering & Aroma
Alpha Acid Composition	5.2%
Beta Acid Composition	3.7%
Cohumulone Composition	23%
Country	Czech Republic
Cone Size	
Cone Density	
Seasonal Maturity	Early
Yield Amount	< 220 kg/hectare (< 200 lbs/acre)
Growth Rate	Low
Resistant to	
Susceptible to	Moderately susceptible to downy mildew
Storability	
Ease of Harvest	

Total Oil

Myrcene Oil

Humulene Oil

Caryophyllene Oil

Farnesene Oil

Substitutes   Hallertauer Mittelfrüher

Style Guide

References
http://cropandsoil.oregonstate.edu/hopcultivars/21531.html

Vanguard

Vanguard hops possess a unique acid profile. They feature a somewhat rare balance of low alpha acid and high beta acid and an oil profile dominated by high levels of humulene and yet very low levels of cohumulone.

Despite exhibiting some similarities to Hallertau Mittelfrüh, surely as a result of their close lineage, this unusual profile gives Vanguard a pronounced woody and herbal character atop a definitive spiciness. The spicy quality is suggested to be particularly evident when Vanguard is used as an early addition.

Vanguard was the final Hallertau-derived variety to come out of the USDA's hop breeding program and were released to the brewing world in 1997 after a long 15 years of development and testing. They are grown principally in the US and are considered great for adding a European-style aroma component to German-style beers.

Homebrewer's Comments

> I used them in some Munich Helles and Kolsches and they were good. Granted, all these beers were extra mild in hop character but Vanguard did just the trick to keep it that way. I'd compare them to Spalt and Hallertau. *(markg388 via homebrewtalk.com)*

Also Known As	
Characteristics	
Purpose	Aroma
Alpha Acid Composition	4.40%-6%
Beta Acid Composition	6%-7%
Cohumulone Composition	14%-16%
Country	US
Cone Size	Small to medium
Cone Density	Loose to Moderate
Seasonal Maturity	Early
Yield Amount	1300-1700 kg/hectare (1160-1520 lbs/acre)
Growth Rate	Moderate
Resistant to	Resistant to downy mildew
Susceptible to	
Storability	Retains 75%-80% alpha acid after 6 months storage at 20ºC (68ºF)
Ease of Harvest	Difficult
Total Oil	0.9-1.2 mL/100g
Myrcene Oil	20%-25%
Humulene Oil	45%-50%
Caryophyllene Oil	12%-14%
Farnesene Oil	0%-1%
Substitutes	Liberty, Mount Hood, Hallertauer Mittelfrüh, Saaz
Style Guide	Porter, Cream Ale, Lager, Rye Ale, Amber Ale, Belgian Ale, French Ale

References

http://beerlegends.com/vanguard-hops
https://www.freshops.com/hops/usda-named-hop-variety-descriptions#usda_id_Vanguard
https://www.hopunion.com/vanguard/
http://www.brew365.com/hops_vanguard.php
https://craftbrewer.com.au/shop/details.asp?PID=2967
http://www.usahops.org/userfiles/file/HGA%20BCI%20Reports/HGA%20Variety%20Manual%20-%20English%20(updated%20March%202011).pdf

Vic Secret

Vic Secret had her first commercial harvest in 2013. Developed in 2000 in Victoria, Australia alongside sister variety Topaz, Vic Secret features elements of tropical fruit, herbs and pine with clean notes of pineapple and passionfruit.

Tested abundantly by brewers, Vic Secret's is best utilized via whirlpool and dry hopping. It is also worth noting that late kettle additions impart a wonderful earthiness, but the fruitiness doesn't come through.

Homebrewer's Comments

I've been brewing with Vic a lot lately and it does well with fruity southern hemisphere varieties (galaxy/nelson) and some of the softer, citrusy US ones. (Amarillo, Centennial). However, in large amounts Vic can impart a strong herbal-grassy character (think basil) and it does lend higher polyphenols during dry hopping; so don't over do it. I'm finding I like it better as a part of a blend than a stand alone variety. *(bierhaus15 via homebrewtalk.com)*

Also Known As	Victoria, Victoria's Secret, Victoria Secret
Characteristics	Tropical fruit, pine, herbs
Purpose	Bittering & Aroma
Alpha Acid Composition	14%-17%
Beta Acid Composition	6.1%-7.8%
Cohumulone Composition	51%-56%
Country	Australia
Cone Size	
Cone Density	
Seasonal Maturity	
Yield Amount	2310-3290 kg/hectare (2060-2935 lbs/acre)
Growth Rate	
Resistant to	
Susceptible to	

Storability	
Ease of Harvest	
Total Oil	2.2-2.8 mL/100g
Myrcene Oil	38%-41%
Humulene Oil	12%-21%
Caryophyllene Oil	11%-15%
Farnesene Oil	0%-1%
Substitutes	Galaxy
Style Guide	Pale Ale, India Pale Ale, Stout, Porter

References

http://beerlegends.com/victoria-hops
http://www.hops.com.au/products/vic-secret
http://www.hops.com.au/media/W1siZiIsIjIwMTMvMDUvMjkvMTdfMzVfMTZfMjA3X0hQQV9WaWNfU2VjcmV0X1Byb2R1Y3RfU2hlZXQucGRmIl1d/HPA_Vic%20Secret_Product_Sheet.pdf
https://www.craftbrewer.com.au/shop/details.asp?PID=4893

Viking

Developed in 1968, Viking hops were first bred at Wye College in England as a cross between Svalof and an unnamed English male. They were released to the public in 1973. Sister to Saxon and grandchild of Bramling Cross and Northdown, this hybrid red-bine variety is considered part of a modern wave of British aroma hops with heightened alpha acids.

They were originally bred in an effort to stem the spread of Verticillium Wilt that plagued Kent in the 1950's and 1960's and in brewing trials, were compared heavily to great grandparent Northern Brewer – a highly wilt-tolerant variety. Unfortunately, Viking did not attain the desired wilt tolerance and they were deemed a failure in this regard. Despite this, they are described as being pleasantly hoppy and rated on par with Northern Brewer from a brewer's perspective in some commercial trials.

Also Known As	Wye Viking
Characteristics	Pleasantly hoppy

Purpose	Aroma
Alpha Acid Composition	8%-10%
Beta Acid Composition	4%-5%
Cohumulone Composition	21%-24%
Country	UK
Cone Size	
Cone Density	
Seasonal Maturity	Mid
Yield Amount	1120-1345 kg/hectare (1000-1200 lbs/acre)
Growth Rate	Low
Resistant to	Resistant to downy mildew
Susceptible to	Susceptible to verticillium wilt
Storability	Retains 70% alpha acid after 6 months storage at 20°C (68°F)
Ease of Harvest	
Total Oil	1.16 mL/100g
Myrcene Oil	47.3%
Humulene Oil	10.5%
Caryophyllene Oil	5.3%
Farnesene Oil	9.1%
Substitutes	Saxon
Style Guide	American Brown Ale

References

http://www.ars.usda.gov/SP2UserFiles/person/2450/hopcultivars/21283.html

https://books.google.com.au/books?id=gcJQAwAAQBAJ&pg=PA115&lpg=PA115&dq=wye+viking+hops&source=bl&ots=u-9ukBpmJt&sig=-MC4xvpWqjFZviq7gpg5HrONDwQ&hl=en&sa=X&ved=0ahUKEwikx42LzcHJAhUItpQKHQrSDKIQ6AEIUDAJ#v=onepage&q=wye%20viking%20hops&f=false

http://www.greatlakeshops.com/wye-viking.html

https://books.google.com.au/books?id=W2oDHNDpmjkC&pg=PA74&lpg=PA74&dq=wye+viking+hops&source=bl&ots=Y8l22E9jKw&sig=QO5jI4ohbHCVVAyok-Q20MQTanc&hl=en&sa=X&ved=0ahUKEwj35pb60MHJAhUHppQKHXCgCzw4ChDoAQgfMAE#v=onepage&q=wye%20viking%20hops&f=false

https://books.google.com.au/books?id=mROkAgAAQBAJ&pg=PA249&lpg=PA249&dq=wye+viking+hops&source=bl&ots=9UnfnP42CY&sig=AtOkzYoC5YtJnDIhW8EcJ4L6obU&hl=en&sa=X&ved=0ahUKEwikx42LzcHJAhUItpQKHQrSDKIQ6AEISzAI#v=onepage&q=

Vital

Vital is a new hop variety out of the Zatec breeding program in the Czech
Republic. Both high alpha and beta acid content gives it a spicy hop
aroma. To date, Vital has been used successfully in single-hopped pale
ales though it was originally bred for pharmaceutical and biomedical
purposes with its increased levels of xanthohumol – a potent antioxidant.

Also Known As	
Characteristics	Spicy hop aroma
Purpose	Bittering & Aroma
Alpha Acid Composition	14%-17%
Beta Acid Composition	8%-11%
Cohumulone Composition	
Country	Czech Republic
Cone Size	
Cone Density	
Seasonal Maturity	
Yield Amount	
Growth Rate	
Resistant to	
Susceptible to	
Storability	
Ease of Harvest	
Total Oil	
Myrcene Oil	
Humulene Oil	
Caryophyllene Oil	
Farnesene Oil	

References
http://www.bluebell.uk.eu.org/beer-cider-log-mainmenu-9/20-real-ales/1380-all-gates-vital
https://translate.google.com.au/translate?hl=en&sl=cs&u=http://www.kvasnyprumysl.cz/download.php%3Fclanek%3D663&prev=search
http://www.hobbybrauerversand.de/Vital-ca11-Alpha-Pellets-100-g_1

Vojvodina

The result of a cross between Northern Brewer and a Savinski Golding-derived male variety, Vojvodina is a hop with mild bittering properties, a woody aroma and notes of cedar and tobacco. It has some of the noble aroma characteristics of Northern Brewer, but is more intense and perhaps a little more rounded.

Vojvodina was initially created in the late 1960's at the Institute for Agricultural Research in Bački Petrovac in the former Yugoslavia in an attempt to replace Backa. Unsuccessful in that regard, commercial acreage remains scarce. It is the sibling of Dunav and Neoplanta and like Dunav, it features a reddish coloring on its main stem.

Also Known As	
Characteristics	Noble aroma characteristics
Purpose	Bittering & Aroma
Alpha Acid Composition	6.1%-10.5%
Beta Acid Composition	2.3%-4.7%
Cohumulone Composition	30%
Country	Yugoslavia
Cone Size	
Cone Density	
Seasonal Maturity	Late
Yield Amount	1720 kg/hectare (1540 lbs/acre)
Growth Rate	Very high
Resistant to	Resistant to downy mildew

Susceptible to	
Storability	Retains 76% alpha acid after 6 months storage at 20°C (68°F)
Ease of Harvest	
Total Oil	0.6-1.4 mL/100g
Myrcene Oil	67%
Humulene Oil	13%
Caryophyllene Oil	5%
Farnesene Oil	0.6%
Substitutes	Northern Brewer, Goldings
Style Guide	

References

http://www.ars.usda.gov/SP2UserFiles/person/2450/hopcultivars/21083.html

http://www.greatlakeshops.com/vojvodina.html

Wai-iti

A truly modern triploid hop, Wai-iti brings forth a fresh splash of lime and stone fruit. It was released to brewers in 2011 alongside Kohatu by New Zealand Plant & Food Research and features higher beta acids than alpha acids, low cohumulone and robust oil content.

Its heritage consists of notable varieties Hallertauer Mittelfrüh as a 1/3 parent and Liberty as its grandparent. Despite its low alpha content, low cohumulone and high farnesene would suggest a soft bitterness and potential suitability for single-hopped beers.

When brewed as a mid-late addition, Wai-iti's citrus aromas are said to take a back seat and make way for more of a stone-fruit presence. Wai-iti has been suggested by some as being similar to Riwaka yet more smooth and rounded.

Homebrewer's Comments

They are fantastic. I tried a single hop brew from a customer and they were as distinctive as the first time I tried Amarillo, tropical fruit. *(borischarlton via thehomebrewforum.co.uk)*

I have found them to be rather plain on their own. I would definitely use as a supporting hop along with more flavorful types. *(slickfish via homebrewtalk.com)*

Also Known As	
Characteristics	Lime citrus and stone fruit notes
Purpose	Aroma
Alpha Acid Composition	2.5%-3.5%
Beta Acid Composition	4.5%-5.5%
Cohumulone Composition	22%-24%
Country	New Zealand
Cone Size	
Cone Density	Compact
Seasonal Maturity	Early to mid
Yield Amount	
Growth Rate	
Resistant to	
Susceptible to	
Storability	
Ease of Harvest	
Total Oil	1.6 mL/100g
Myrcene Oil	30%
Humulene Oil	28%
Caryophyllene Oil	9%
Farnesene Oil	13%
Substitutes	Riwaka
Style Guide	Pale Ale, India Pale Ale, Wheat, Lager

References

http://www.brewshop.co.nz/hops/nz-hops/wai-iti-hops.html
https://www.craftbrewer.com.au/shop/details.asp?PID=4304
http://www.nzhops.co.nz/variety/wai-iti

Waimea

Waimea is a new New Zealand dual-use variety originally bred for high alpha and bittering qualities. Released in 2012, it's heritage stems from Californian Late Cluster, Fuggle and Saaz. Despite its incredibly high alphas, brewing characteristics of Waimea include some decidedly favorable flavor and aromas of fresh-crushed citrus and pine.

Homebrewer's Comments

> I have just opened my first bottle of a Session IPA brewed with 8oz total Waimea and Mosaic hops. It's really dank, in the best possible way, I am very familiar with Mosaic, Waimea reminds me a lot of Columbus hops, just fruitier and more intense. I have also brewed an IPA a few months back with equal amount of Waimea, Nelson and El Dorado. Waimea played the danky, sticky role. *(fab80 via homebrewtalk.com)*

Also Known As	
Characteristics	Citrus and pine
Purpose	Bittering & Aroma
Alpha Acid Composition	16%-19%
Beta Acid Composition	7%-9%
Cohumulone Composition	
Country	New Zealand
Cone Size	
Cone Density	Compact
Seasonal Maturity	Mid to late
Yield Amount	
Growth Rate	High
Resistant to	
Susceptible to	
Storability	
Ease of Harvest	
Total Oil	2.1 mL/100g
Myrcene Oil	60%

Humulene Oil	10%
Caryophyllene Oil	3%
Farnesene Oil	5%
Substitutes	Columbus
Style Guide	India Pale Ale, Pale Ale

References
https://ychhops.com/varieties/waimea
http://www.nzhops.co.nz/variety/waimea
https://bsgcraftbrewing.com/nz-waimea
https://www.craftbrewer.com.au/shop/details.asp?PID=4702

Wakatu

Wakatu, or Hallertau Aroma as it is sometimes know, is a New Zealand triploid hop with a lot going for it. 2/3 Hallertauer Mittelfrüher and 1/3 New Zealand male, it was released in 1988 from the Institute for Plant and Food Research's hop breeding program.

Its nicely balanced oil profile gives it an understated floral aroma atop pungent fresh lime. Considered largely dual-use, it can be added at any stage of the boil right and dry hopped with success. It has also been noted for its impressive flavor stability.

Homebrewer's Comments

I used them in conjunction with Galaxy in a Pale Ale. It has been among the better beers I've made. The flavoring additions at 15 and flameout were one ounce each Galaxy & Wakatu. No dirty diapers to speak of. The beer is full of the tropical flavor you'd expect from Galaxy. I haven't detected much lemon lime, but I there are herbal & floral notes as well, perhaps courtesy of Wakatu. *(wileaway via homebrewtalk.com)*

The hops in the bag smelled like fresh lime zest. I used 2oz in the boil from 20-0 and 2oz. in a 117F aroma steep for 20 minutes. I used some Willamette too. The wort smelled like limes with a little bit of floral. The Wakatu's juicy lime aroma didn't survive fermentation, but it made some lovely smells in my basement through the airlock. I dry hopped with 4oz. of Hallertau Hersbrucker and got a nice floral aroma, but not huge. The limey flavor of Wakatu was mild at 50ibu and with mostly late hopping. The bitterness was very smooth. Overall, it made a nice Belgian. It wasn't an aggressive hop, but it wasn't too mild either. (*Randy_Bugger via homebrewtalk.com*)

Also Known As	Hallertau Aroma, New Zealand Wakatu, Hal Aroma
Characteristics	Floral, lime aromas
Purpose	Bittering & Aroma
Alpha Acid Composition	6.5%-8.5%
Beta Acid Composition	8.5%
Cohumulone Composition	28%-30%
Country	New Zealand
Cone Size	
Cone Density	
Seasonal Maturity	
Yield Amount	
Growth Rate	
Resistant to	
Susceptible to	
Storability	
Ease of Harvest	
Total Oil	1.0 mL/100g
Myrcene Oil	36%
Humulene Oil	17%
Caryophyllene Oil	8%
Farnesene Oil	6.7%
Substitutes	
Style Guide	Lager, Pale Ale, Belgian Ale

References

http://www.craftbrewer.com.au/shop/details.asp?PID=595

https://ychhops.com/varieties/wakatu

https://en.wikipedia.org/wiki/Wakatu_Hops
https://bsgcraftbrewing.com/wakatu
https://www.craftbrewer.com.au/shop/details.asp?PID=595

Warrior®

Developed by Select Botanicals Group, proprietary American hop Warrior® is fast becoming a favorite, especially with US craft breweries. Among its desirable traits are its clean, smooth bittering and a somewhat inconspicuous citrusy and spicy aroma. Its pedigree is a unknown to the public. Dogfish Head Brewery employs Warrior® in many of its brews, most notably in its 60 Minute IPA.

Homebrewer's Comments

> I think Warrior is a good choice for an IPA bittering addition. With the high AA it doesn't take much to get the desired results. *(Chello via homebrewtalk.com)*

> I've used them as bittering in big American beers and they are great for that, I've found that if you use them in the same way for lesser beers around 1040 you will get some spicy notes, nothing unpleasant btw, and with high AA you don't need much. Also no reason to use them later. From the same crosses that produced Simcoe. DFH and Firestone Walker use them. *(good ed via craftbrewing.org.uk)*

Also Known As	
Characteristics	Aromas of citrus and spice
Purpose	Bittering
Alpha Acid Composition	14.5%-18%
Beta Acid Composition	4.3%-6%
Cohumulone Composition	22%-28%
Country	US
Cone Size	Medium
Cone Density	Moderate
Seasonal Maturity	Mid

Yield Amount	2400-2600 kg/hectare (2140-2320 lbs/acre)
Growth Rate	High
Resistant to	Resistant to powdery mildew and sphaerotheca
Susceptible to	
Storability	Retains 76%-76% alpha acid after 6 months storage at 20°C (68°F)
Ease of Harvest	Difficult
Total Oil	1-2.5 mL/100g
Myrcene Oil	40%-50%
Humulene Oil	15%-20%
Caryophyllene Oil	8%-11%
Farnesene Oil	0%-1%
Substitutes	Nugget, Columbus
Style Guide	India Pale Ale, American Ales

References

http://beerlegends.com/warrior-hops

https://ychhops.com/varieties/warrior-brand-ycr-5-cv

Whitbread Golding

Whitbread Golding enjoys a robust flavor and hoppiness particularly in comparison to other Golding varieties. With its pleasant, fruity, European-style aromatics, it has traditionally been very popular in England and is currently grown extensively for commercial, craft and home brewing use.

When used as an early addition, Whitbread Golding features a sharp and pronounced bitterness. Mid-boil it's flavor profile tends toward a sweet fruitiness and as an aroma addition, herbal, woody aromas spring to the fore.

First selected in 1911 by hop grower Edward Albert White, it is the result of open pollinated Bate's Brewer. Its current name however was not coined until after the Whitbread Brewing Company acquired the farm on which it was raised some years later. It also wasn't until 1953 that the variety was officially released for production.

Hailed as a savior variety by growers in Kent in the 1950's, Whitbread Golding's resistance to Verticillium Wilt helped cement it as an industry favorite after the disease devastated Golding and Fuggle crops in the region at that time.

Homebrewer's Comments

> I use them in almost all my bitters.. I perfer them mixed with First Gold or EKG for finishing and use them for bittering almost exclusively. Never tried them as a single hop. (*jlpred55 via beeradvocate.com*)

Also Known As	WGV, Whitbread, Whitbread Golding Variety
Characteristics	Pleasant, fruity, European style aroma
Purpose	Bittering & Aroma
Alpha Acid Composition	5%-7.5%
Beta Acid Composition	2.5%-3.5%
Cohumulone Composition	33%-37%
Country	UK
Cone Size	Medium
Cone Density	Loose
Seasonal Maturity	Early to mid
Yield Amount	1350-1450 kg/hectare (1190–1278 lbs/acre)
Growth Rate	Moderate to high
Resistant to	Tolerant to verticillium wilt
Susceptible to	Moderately susceptible to downy mildew
Storability	Retains 66% alpha acid after 6 months storage at 20°C (68°F)
Ease of Harvest	Hard
Total Oil	0.8-1.22 mL/100g

Myrcene Oil	24%-27%
Humulene Oil	38%-42%
Caryophyllene Oil	9%-13%
Farnesene Oil	<2.1%
Substitutes	Fuggle, East Kent Golding
Style Guide	Ale, Pale Ale, Bitter

References
http://hopsteiner.com/wp-content/uploads/2014/03/WGV.pdf
http://beerlegends.com/whitbread-golding-variety-hops
http://yaldinghistory.webplus.net/page237.html
https://books.google.com.au/books?id=K2gICotqYYoC&pg=PA67&lpg=PA67&dq=mr+%2
2e+a+white%22+kent+farm&source=bl&ots=c7Y_znbH6J&sig=s-
iX8R2Hi0W6iATUSB65Z2QpXec&hl=en&sa=X&ved=0ahUKEwi5xd3Z_cPJAhWj3KYKH
QWxCHAQ6AEIMTAE#v=onepage&q=mr%20%22e%20a%20white%22%20kent%20farm
&f=false
https://www.facebook.com/WillinghamNurseries/posts/283977065103298
http://www.ars.usda.gov/SP2UserFiles/person/2450/hopcultivars/21668.html
http://www.britishhops.org.uk/wgv/

Willamette

Considered a pillar of the US hops industry, Willamette is one of the most prolifically grown varieties in the US. First selected in Oregon in 1967, it received USDA accession in 1971 and was released the same year.

Willamette is a triploid aroma hop with its heritage being primarily derived from English variety Fuggle and Fuggle Tetraploid. It shares this same pedigree with its sister selection, Columbia. When brewed, Willamette features complex spiciness characterized by both herbal, floral and fruity notes.

Originally bred to replace Fuggle, it has excelled in popularity in recent times, particularly among craft brewers and accounts for approximately 20% of all commercially grown hops in the US today.

Homebrewer's Comments

> Willamette is a terrific aroma hop for any anglo-american style. I use it in my brown ale & my robust porter with nugget for

bittering. *(meatcleaver via homebrewtalk.com)*

Use it late boil or whirlpool but IMO do not dry hop with it as it is excessively grassy! Some people have told me that co dry hopping with a high oil variety will cover up the grassy taste. *(theheroguy via homebrewtalk.com)*

Also Known As	
Characteristics	Heraceous spiciness, floral, fruity
Purpose	Aroma
Alpha Acid Composition	4%-6%
Beta Acid Composition	3%-4%
Cohumulone Composition	30%-35%
Country	US
Cone Size	Small to medium
Cone Density	Loose to Moderate
Seasonal Maturity	Early to mid
Yield Amount	1340-1700 kg/hectare (1200-1520 lbs/acre)
Growth Rate	High
Resistant to	Resistant to prunus necrotic ring-spot virus and downy mildew
Susceptible to	
Storability	Retains 60%-65% alpha acid after 6 months storage at 20ºC (68ºF)
Ease of Harvest	Difficult
Total Oil	1-1.5 mL/100g
Myrcene Oil	30%-55%
Humulene Oil	20%-30%
Caryophyllene Oil	7%-8%
Farnesene Oil	5%-6%
Substitutes	Fuggle, Styrian Golding, Tettnanger (US), Glacier, Savinjski Golding
Style Guide	Ale, American Ales, Pale Ale, Brown Ale, English Ales, Porter

References

http://beerlegends.com/willamette-hops
http://www.ars.usda.gov/SP2UserFiles/person/2450/hopcultivars/21041.html
https://www.hopunion.com/willamette/
http://www.freshops.com/hops/variety_descriptions

Willamette (AUS)

Willamette (AUS) hops are a directly descended from US-grown Willamette and were introduced to Australia in 1988. Imported and primarily grown by Hop Products Australia, the Australian version of this iconic aroma hop features a mlld, spicy, resinous and floral character.

Sister of Columbia, Willamatte is a triploid variety directly descended from English variety Fuggle and Fuggle Tetraploid. Originally released in 1971 by the USDA, it is one of the most widespread crops in the US but does not share the same popularity in terms of acreage in Australia.

Also Known As	
Characteristics	Mildly resinous, spicy, floral character
Purpose	Bittering & Aroma
Alpha Acid Composition	5%-7.2%
Beta Acid Composition	3.9%-5.7%
Cohumulone Composition	30%-35%
Country	Australia
Cone Size	
Cone Density	
Seasonal Maturity	
Yield Amount	
Growth Rate	
Resistant to	
Susceptible to	
Storability	
Ease of Harvest	
Total Oil	1.4-2.0 mL/100g

Myrcene Oil	30%-40%
Humulene Oil	25%-35%
Caryophyllene Oil	7%-10%
Farnesene Oil	5%-7%
Substitutes	Fuggle, Styrian Golding, Tettnanger (US), Glacier, Savinjski Golding
Style Guide	Ale, American Ales, Pale Ale, Brown Ale, English Ales, Porter

References
http://www.hops.com.au/products/willamette

Willow Creek

Native to Colorado, neomexicanus variety Willow Creek is very new to the brewing scene. There is very little information about them available but they are reportedly considered to be similar to other available neomexicanus varieties Amallia, Neo 1, and Multihead.

Willow Creek is currently in the midst of production trials and hopefully some will be available soon for brewery trials.

Also Known As	
Characteristics	
Purpose	Bittering & Aroma
Alpha Acid Composition	
Beta Acid Composition	
Cohumulone Composition	
Country	
Cone Size	Large
Cone Density	
Seasonal Maturity	Early to mid
Yield Amount	
Growth Rate	

Resistant to

Susceptible to

Storability

Ease of Harvest

Total Oil

Myrcene Oil

Humulene Oil

Caryophyllene Oil

Farnesene Oil

Substitutes

Style Guide

References
http://www.homebrewtalk.com/f92/growing-hops-seed-397219/index6.html
https://www.fivebladesbrewing.com/neomexicanus-hops-whats-available/
http://www.greatlakeshops.com/willow-creek---neomexicana.html

Wuerttemberger

Wuerttemberger is an old, German, noble aroma hop which is no longer grown commercially. Thought to have come from a land race, its low vigor and poor yield made it untenable for commercial use.

If it can be found, it might be worth experimenting with for German-style lagers and pilsners and it is said to impart a pleasant European-style aroma on a beer. Some in the industry suspect it may actually be genetically identical to Tettnang Tettnanger but this is unproven.

Also Known As	Wurttemberger
Characteristics	Pleasant European-style noble aroma
Purpose	Aroma
Alpha Acid Composition	5%
Beta Acid Composition	4%
Cohumulone Composition	28%
Country	Germany

Cone Size	
Cone Density	
Seasonal Maturity	Early
Yield Amount	
Growth Rate	Moderate to high
Resistant to	Resistant to verticillium wilt, moderately resistant to downy mildew
Susceptible to	
Storability	Retains 72% alpha acid after 6 months storage at 20ºC (68ºF)
Ease of Harvest	
Total Oil	1.25 mL/100g
Myrcene Oil	59%
Humulene Oil	18%
Caryophyllene Oil	6%
Farnesene Oil	4%
Substitutes	
Style Guide	Lager, Pilsner

References

http://cropandsoil.oregonstate.edu/hopcultivars/21682.html
http://aussiehomebrewer.com/topic/15947-2007-hop-plantations/page-16#entry262016

Yakima Cluster

First grown in the late 1950's, Yakima Cluster is the daughter of Late Cluster and the granddaughter of Pacific Coast Cluster. It doesn't appear to be suited to either Idaho or Oregon growing regions in the US but seems to thrive in the drier Yakima Valley.

It is most often sold simply as a Cluster hop, with whom it shares near identical chemistry and traits. These traits include a moderate bittering, some earthy flavors and a flowery aroma with elements of sweet fruit.

Also Known As	Late Cluster L-8
Characteristics	
Purpose	Bittering
Alpha Acid Composition	4.4%-9.8%
Beta Acid Composition	3%-6.1%
Cohumulone Composition	42%
Country	US
Cone Size	
Cone Density	
Seasonal Maturity	Early
Yield Amount	2020-2250 kg/hectare (1800-2000 lbs/acre)
Growth Rate	High
Resistant to	
Susceptible to	Susceptible to downy mildew
Storability	Retains 85% alpha acid after 6 months storage at 20ºC (68ºF)
Ease of Harvest	
Total Oil	0.24-0.90 mL/100g
Myrcene Oil	45%-55%
Humulene Oil	18%
Caryophyllene Oil	6%-7%
Farnesene Oil	< 1%
Substitutes	Chinook
Style Guide	

References

http://www.homebrewtalk.com/wiki/index.php/Yakima_Cluster
https://www.ars.usda.gov/SP2UserFiles/person/2450/hopcultivars/65102.html
https://ychhops.com/varieties/cluster

Yakima Gold

Developed by Washington State University and released in 2013, Yakima

Gold has excellent mild bittering and aroma properties and makes for a great dual-use hop. It descends from Early Cluster and a wild Slovenian male, so it may display some Saaz-like qualities.

Also Known As	Yakima Goldings
Characteristics	
Purpose	Bittering & Aroma
Alpha Acid Composition	8.8%-10.5%
Beta Acid Composition	4.3%-5%
Cohumulone Composition	21%-23%
Country	US
Cone Size	
Cone Density	
Seasonal Maturity	
Yield Amount	
Growth Rate	
Resistant to	
Susceptible to	
Storability	
Ease of Harvest	
Total Oil	1.9-2.3 mL/100g
Myrcene Oil	45%-50%
Humulene Oil	21%-25%
Caryophyllene Oil	6%-8%
Farnesene Oil	9%-10%
Substitutes	
Style Guide	

References

http://hopunion.com/yakima-gold/
https://ychhops.com/varieties/yakima-gold
http://brooklynbrewshop.com/themash/hop-of-the-month-yakima-gold/
http://www.greatlakeshops.com/yakima-gold.html

Yeoman

Bred at Wye College in the 1970's, Yeoman is no longer available on the commercial brewing market, but instead has made its mark in breeding other notable varieties. It is responsible for Pioneer and also the Australian hop Super Pride, which has since superseded Pride of Ringwood.

Its alphas are very high for an English hop. It seems well equipped for disease resistance and sports a pleasant bitterness and a citrusy aroma.

Also Known As	Wye Yeoman
Characteristics	
Purpose	Bittering & Aroma
Alpha Acid Composition	12%-16%
Beta Acid Composition	4%-5%
Cohumulone Composition	25%
Country	UK
Cone Size	
Cone Density	
Seasonal Maturity	Early
Yield Amount	1610-1680 kg/hectare (800-1500 lbs/acre)
Growth Rate	Moderate to high
Resistant to	Resistant to verticillium wilt and downy mildew and powdery mildew
Susceptible to	
Storability	Retains 80% alpha acid after 6 months storage at 20ºC (68ºF)
Ease of Harvest	
Total Oil	1.7-2.4 mL/100g
Myrcene Oil	48%
Humulene Oil	20%
Caryophyllene Oil	10%
Farnesene Oil	Trace Amounts

Substitutes

Style Guide

References

http://beerlegends.com/yeoman-hops

http://www.greatlakeshops.com/yeoman.html

http://www.willingham-nurseries.co.uk/hops/yeoman.htm

https://www.ars.usda.gov/SP2UserFiles/person/2450/hopcultivars/21498.html

Zenith

Zenith is a hop of unknown pedigree but was grown as a high alpha hop with good resistance to disease. It has high alpha and high myrcene, low cohumulone and a myrcene/humulene ratio of about 2:1. Its rhizomes are usually available from November to February, which is also the best time to plant them.

Also Known As	
Characteristics	
Purpose	Bittering
Alpha Acid Composition	9%-11%
Beta Acid Composition	3%
Cohumulone Composition	25%
Country	
Cone Size	
Cone Density	
Seasonal Maturity	Early
Yield Amount	
Growth Rate	Moderate to high
Resistant to	Resistant to downy mildew and powdery mildew
Susceptible to	Susceptible to verticillium wilt
Storability	Retains 82% alpha acid after 6 months storage at 20ºC (68ºF)
Ease of Harvest	

Total Oil	1.76 mL/100g
Myrcene Oil	52%
Humulene Oil	18%
Caryophyllene Oil	7%
Farnesene Oil	Trace Amounts
Substitutes	
Style Guide	

References

http://www.ars.usda.gov/SP2UserFiles/person/2450/hopchem/21499.html

Zeus

Aptly named after the god of lightning and thunder, proprietary American hybrid variety Zeus is a high yielding hop with a pleasant aroma noted for its pungent hoppy "kick" and spicy, herbal flavor and aroma.

Though it is sometimes considered identical to Columbus and Tomahawk®, or CTZ as they are sometimes sold, it has been identified as being genetically distinct from these two varieties. It does share remarkable similarities to both however. Though the exact parentage of Zeus has not been identified it is suspected to have been derived from Brewers Gold.

Homebrewer's Comments

Just brewed and kegged a homegrown IPA featuring Zeus. I used a lot of late additions, and went for the flavoring. The bittering was fwh, so there isn't the crazy bite up front or on the back end. The nose is sweet citrus and herbal. The flavor I'm getting is fruity citrus, plum and apricot (could be a malt character from the special B and aromatic) peach (could be us05 at mid 60s ferment) , pine, lots of grapefruit without the sour. Malt backbone is bready, toasty, with dark fruit notes from the special B and aromatic. I'm greatly enjoying it, though I wish I gave it a little more of a late addition charge at 60 (maybe 0.5 oz.), as I think it may have balanced the flavor out with some more bitter bite. *(thaymond via homebrewtalk.com)*

Also Known As	CTZ
Characteristics	Sweet citrus, herbal aromas
Purpose	Bittering
Alpha Acid Composition	13%-17.5%
Beta Acid Composition	4%-6.5%
Cohumulone Composition	26%-40%
Country	US
Cone Size	
Cone Density	
Seasonal Maturity	Mid to late
Yield Amount	2690-3365 kg/hectares (2400-3000 lbs/acre)
Growth Rate	Very high
Resistant to	Resistant to powdery mildew
Susceptible to	
Storability	
Ease of Harvest	
Total Oil	2.4-4.5 mL/100g
Myrcene Oil	45%-55%
Humulene Oil	9%-14%
Caryophyllene Oil	5%-10%
Farnesene Oil	< 1%
Substitutes	Columbus
Style Guide	

References

http://beerlegends.com/zeus-hops
http://freshops.com/usda-named-hop-variety-descriptions/#usda_id_Zeus
https://ychhops.com/varieties/zeus
http://www.greatlakeshops.com/zeus.html

Zlatan

Released in 1976, Zlatan is native to the Czech Republic and is one of a great many clonal selections of Saaz. Created by the Hop Research Institute in Zatec, it, like many other Saaz clones were selected in an attempt to improve yields while retaining its parent's signature aroma profile.

In brewing it sports a mild bitterness and has been described as imparting a pleasant noble aroma upon a beer when used as a late addition.

Also Known As	
Characteristics	Mild bitterness, pleasant noble aroma
Purpose	Aroma
Alpha Acid Composition	5.2%
Beta Acid Composition	4.3%
Cohumulone Composition	21%
Country	Czech Republic
Cone Size	
Cone Density	
Seasonal Maturity	Early
Yield Amount	220 kg/gectare (200 lbs/acre)
Growth Rate	Low
Resistant to	
Susceptible to	Moderately susceptible to downy mildew
Storability	
Ease of Harvest	
Total Oil	
Myrcene Oil	
Humulene Oil	
Caryophyllene Oil	
Farnesene Oil	
Substitutes	
Style Guide	

References

http://www.zateckychmel.eu

https://www.freshops.com/hops/usda-named-hop-variety-descriptions#usda_id_21533

https://books.google.com.au/books?id=_H1yBgAAQBAJ&pg=PA201&lpg=PA201&dq=zlat
an+hops&source=bl&ots=O9VKYF6wqi&sig=OdomsEnyyFERVukKCThCz6yiKh0&hl=en
&sa=X&ved=0ahUKEwiSg42km8TJAhVmPKYKHSAsDUU4ChDoAQgmMAI#v=onepage
&q=zlatan%20hops&f=false

Zythos®

Created by Hopunion LLC, Zythos® is a proprietary hop blend created specifically with IPA's in mind. It features notes and aromas of tangerine, grapefruit, pine and even pineapple. Its high alpha acid content means it can be useful for bittering but is largely intended to shine as an aroma hop.

Homebrewer's Comments

Intensely grapefruity, and I get tons and tons of pineapple. My gf doesn't seem to get the pineapple anywhere near as much as I do. I don't get as much peachy, tangeriney, softly citrus from these as I do from Amarillo. Good hop for hoppy American ales though. *(Rundownhouse via homebrewtalk.com)*

I've been drinking my Pale Ale for about a week. I also get tons of tangerine/peach/apricot flavor as well as the grapefruit bitter citrus. I don't get very much of the pineapple but my brew wasn't all Zythos either. I used Columbus for bittering. I agree with the Amarillo comparison too though. Overall, the Columbus/Zythos combo worked well. Seems it will be a good APA/IPA hop. *(neovox via homebrewtalk.com)*

Also Known As	
Characteristics	Notes of tangerine, grapefruit, pine and pineapple
Purpose	Bittering & Aroma
Alpha Acid Composition	10%-12.5%
Beta Acid Composition	4.7%-6.2%
Cohumulone Composition	28%-31%

Country	US
Cone Size	
Cone Density	
Seasonal Maturity	
Yield Amount	
Growth Rate	
Resistant to	
Susceptible to	
Storability	Retains 70% alpha acid after 6 months storage at 20ºC (68ºF)
Ease of Harvest	
Total Oil	0.7-1.2 mL/100g
Myrcene Oil	
Humulene Oil	
Caryophyllene Oil	
Farnesene Oil	
Substitutes	Simcoe®, Amarillo®
Style Guide	American Ale

References
https://www.morebeer.com/products/zythos-pellet-hops.html
https://ychhops.com/varieties/zythos

Index

Lightning Source UK Ltd.
Milton Keynes UK
UKHW021315281120
374218UK00012B/962